Machos, Mistresses, Madonnas

Critical Studies in Latin American and Iberian Cultures

SERIES EDITORS:

James Dunkerley
John King

This major series – the first of its kind to appear in English – is designed to map the field of contemporary Latin American culture, which has enjoyed increasing popularity in Britain and the United States in recent years.

The series aims to broaden the scope of criticism of Latin American culture, which tends still to extol the virtues of a few established 'master' works and to examine cultural production within the context of twentieth-century history. These clear, accessible studies are aimed at those who wish to know more about some of the most important and influential cultural works and movements of our time.

A full list of series titles currently available can be found at the back of this book.

Machos, Mistresses, Madonnas

Contesting the Power of Latin American Gender Imagery

Edited by Marit Melhuus
and Kristi Anne Stølen

VERSO

London • New York

First published by Verso 1996
© this collection Verso 1996
© individual contributions the contributors 1996
All rights reserved

The rights of Marit Melhuus and Kristi Anne Stølen to be
identified as the editors of this work have been asserted
by them in accordance with the
Copyright, Designs and Patents Act 1988

Verso
UK: 6 Meard Street, London W1V 3HR
USA: 180 Varick Street, New York NY 10014–4606

Verso is the imprint of New Left Books

ISBN 1–85984–805–2
ISBN 1–85984–160–0 (pbk)

British Library Cataloguing in Publication Data
A catalogue record for this book is available from the British Library

Library of Congress Cataloging-in-Publication Data
A catalog record for this book is available from the Library of Congress

Typeset by Keystroke, Jacaranda Lodge, Wolverhampton
Printed by Biddles Ltd, Guildford and King's Lynn

Contents

Preface and

Acknowledgements

This book originated from a symposium on 'The Power of Latin American Gender Imagery' held at the 48th International Congress of Americanists in Stockholm/Uppsala in July 1994. The symposium was quickly overbooked – evidence that the proposed theme was enthusiastically received. Eighteen papers were presented in the course of two long days; nevertheless, few were daunted and the participants were active throughout, providing a good atmosphere for the lively and thought-provoking discussions that ensued. Although the context was interdisciplinary, most of the contributors were social anthropologists. This bias is also reflected in the book. The present volume contains a selection of the papers presented; in addition, it includes a contribution by Christian Krohn-Hansen.

In seeking to highlight the complexities and the ambiguities of Latin American gender imagery, the book's underlying premiss is that the meanings of gender in different sociocultural contexts in the region will vary. The intention has been to draw out the specific articulations of gender, emphasizing indigenous perceptions. More specifically, however, the aim has been to address the power of Latin American gender imagery. Nevertheless, it should be made clear that the idea of the book has not been to equate power with a simple notion of male dominance (and a concomitant female subjugation), which has so dominated discourses on gender in Latin America, nor to reverse the order by speaking of female power. Rather, the theme of gender imagery and power has been set with a view to elicit, at an empirical level, their mutual imbrication by exploring how gender relations are perceived and constructed; how gender is represented in discourse; and how representations of gender relate to other significant social phenomena. It has been our working hypothesis that gender differences in Latin America appear to take on commanding significance in the conceptualization of differences and the ordering of inequalities other than gender.

The essays reveal a multiplicity of representations of gender, in settings that range from effeminate transvestites in Mexico City and indigenous migrant women in the Highlands of Ecuador to narratives of football in Argentina. They are all grounded in empirical research as this has been developed within the discipline of social anthropology. The differences in empirical realities, combined with the shifting theoretical perspectives within the discipline as well as the continuing debates about the meanings of gender, are mirrored in the ways the authors have chosen to approach and interpret their ethnography. Thus what unites this book is its subject matter, the mutual imbrication of gender imagery and power, and its regional focus.

We are grateful to the Norwegian Research Council for granting financial support to organize the symposium, and to the Organizing Committee of the International Congress of Americanists for covering the costs of one of the Latin American participants. We also wish to thank the Department and Museum of Anthropology, University of Oslo, and Marius Lyngø for the necessary computer service to convert all the diskettes to a uniform standard.

Marit Melhuus
Kristi Anne Stølen

1

Introduction

Marit Melhuus and
Kristi Anne Stølen

This book seeks to highlight the complexities of Latin American gender imagery, simultaneously pointing to similarities and differences in the way gender is articulated and the meanings it seems to convey with respect to power. The emphasis is on the production, conjunctions and interfaces of gendered representations and the representations of gender. The notion of imagery, in this context, refers to more than just different forms of collective representations. It is used to conjure up a sense of the visual, the fixing of cultural images on social consciousness. Thus imagery can be seen to balance precariously between the imaginary and the naturalization – or essentialization – of the meanings of the imagined. It is the very fixation of an image as 'natural' which lends it its power. Yet this fixation occurs in fluid processes, and it is only by examining the processes whereby the images are evoked and crystallized that we can hope to grasp them and relate their meanings to social experiences. Narratives and discourses – as well as discursive practices – are all significant loci for the production of gender imagery, and thus represent an important access to these social phenomena.

More specifically, the unifying theme of the essays collected here is the power of Latin American gender imagery. This perspective has a double thrust, alluding on the one hand to power – *el poder* – as a notion intrinsic to Latin American cultures, one which has specific connotations when it is understood in terms of gender. In fact, it may be surmised that the notions of power are inherently gendered in so far as power, in many contexts, is understood as a male prerogative. On the other hand, in stressing the power of gender imagery the aim has been to draw attention to the significance of gender and the representations of gender differences as a vehicle for the construction of differences more generally. In other words, contrary to what Strathern claims for Melanesia – that 'inequalities between men and women seem to be "about" themselves',[1] it has been our working hypothesis that gender differences in Latin America appear to take on a commanding significance in the conceptualization of differences and the ordering of inequalities other than gender. Thus it seems that in the Latin American context the differences that obtain between men and women can be made to stand for other forms of differences, or that 'differences invoked in one context can be used to reformulate differences relevant to another'.[2] If that is so, an understanding of local notions of gender differences, and even perceptions of the very essences of gender itself, may be prerequisites for grasping the way other forms of social inequalities are conceived. Central to such an understanding are not only the values on which perceptions of gender relations rest but also the differing forms of evaluation of men and women as separate categories.

To conjoin the notions of gender and power may seem like doing the obvious, in so far as any consideration of gender relations invariably evokes a notion of power. Moreover, the relationship between notions of gender and notions of power is a potent one, fraught as it is with political tensions and scholarly disagreements. Hence, analytically as well as empirically, the concepts of gender and power are contested ones and no unifying theory of either, taken separately or together, underpins this book. Suffice it to say that at an analytical level both concepts are relational and relative, whereas their applications in indigenous discourse may be precisely the contrary: essentialist and objectifying.

This twofold approach has revealed not only that discourses on gender are multivocal, but also that the notions of gender and power may be conflated, as mutually constituted elements of a symbolic system. Moreover, we suggest, this very conflation creates cultural confusion or ambiguities in the perceptions of both gender and power, which can best be drawn out by focusing on the meanings – both implicit and explicit – embedded in the various discursive practices. If imagery is to be gleaned from different levels and forms of discourse, the discursive practices must be seen as on a par with any other forms of social practices and, ideally, related to them. Hence the force of these symbolic representations lies in the way they are produced and reproduced through the daily activities of men and women (by the work they do – or do not do – in all spheres of society) and the transcendent meanings implied in their very reproduction.

The essays in this book vary with respect to both regional localizations and thematic thrust. They also vary in the ways each contributor has chosen to approach the subject of gender imagery and power. These are diverse, and that is as it should be. Indeed, many of the contributors base their findings not only on a single long-term period of fieldwork in a specific locality, but on several periods of fieldwork within the same or adjacent communities. Some have returned several times over the years in order to follow the developments of a community or a people. Thus the reflections which have been brought to bear on the issues at hand emerge from detailed knowledge of the socio-cultural context from which they have been gleaned. Furthermore, the ethnography on which the various contributors base their analysis is also very diverse. Not only is there a span in terms of locality, there is also a spread in terms of the types of ethnographic sources drawn on. While some base their findings on fieldwork in local communities, be they urban or rural, others have focused on particular groups (e.g. homosexuals or ritual dance groups), yet others draw mainly on literary sources, and a few combine various sources. It follows from this that the subjects addressed will necessarily vary.

In this Introduction, we will discuss the material presented in the light of three themes. These themes serve as points of convergence for the somewhat disparate empirical and theoretical approaches. The first of these is the dismantling of the Latin American *macho*. Several of the contributors (e.g. Archetti, Krohn-Hansen, Nencel, Prieur) are concerned with the pinpointing and elaboration of variant masculinities, demonstrating the multiplicity of masculinities and their inherent ambiguities.

Thus they not only challenge but also undermine a unitary notion of a hegemonic Latin American male. Moreover, the focus on masculinities, and hence on relations between men, raises interesting questions about the relative importance of – as well as the differences between – same-sex and cross-sex relations for the construction of gendered identities.

The second theme revolves around the notions of power as articulated through dominant discourses and labelling processes (e.g. Prieur, Nencel, Villarreal, Stølen). Although the arguments related to this theme partially feed into the discourses on variant masculinities, they also raise – albeit in a different vein – the question of whether there is, nevertheless, reason to postulate a more all-encompassing understanding of gender. In other words, the application in analytical terms of a notion of dominant discourse implies a general recognition of the existence of such a discourse. It does not, of course, imply an agreement, at an empirical level, with what the discourse espouses. Hence it is only by examining concrete discursive practices that it is possible to extract evidence which can support claims of dominant discourses and concomitant subordinate, alternative, or even subversive discourses. The empirical cases put before us, read in the context of male dominance, raise important questions about the meanings of subordination, complicity and resistance (e.g. Stølen, Crain, Melhuus and Nencel). They also direct attention towards the relationship between dominant and subordinate discourses, and to a renewed discussion of the meaning of 'hegemonic male'.

The third theme revolves around the power of gender to speak to other issues than those referring back to gender as such. As we have already mentioned, discourses on gender in Latin America are multivocal. This, we suggest, has to do with the values with which gender is imbued, that is, the moralities which both encompass and ground the representations of gender. They embody meanings which go beyond their original reference of male–female differences, and hence become potent signifiers of more overarching moral issues. In fact, it appears that in some cases (e.g. Stølen, Melhuus, Villarreal) gender may be the vehicle through which morality speaks. The grounding of morality in gender implies that discourses on gender and gender inequalities contain a certain potential to order other discourses – not only of difference, but also of inequalities and even ambiguities. Thus gender becomes a way of structuring discourses on ethnicity (e.g. Crain, Stølen, Rostas) or a language through which discourses on nationalism or politics are constructed (e.g. Archetti, Melhuus, Krohn-Hansen).

However, before we go on to elaborate these themes further, two other issues must be addressed. We consider it necessary briefly to discuss the notion of Latin America and, moreover, to place this book in the context of ongoing research on gender in Latin America.

Latin America: a Meaningful Universe?

The title of this book suggests that it is legitimate to consider Latin America as a coherent entity for cross-cultural comparisons. We hope that we can do justice to that claim. Nevertheless, since we are well aware that such assumptions are no longer self-evident, and that such a shared premiss cannot be taken for granted a priori, it seems pertinent to offer some reflections on the status of the concept of region and its implications for Latin America. It is also pertinent to make explicit the salient factors which delineate Latin America as a significant entity for our purposes. However, we would like to clarify one point immediately: the fact that there are reasonable grounds for considering Latin America as a coherent unit for cross-cultural comparisons does not imply a notion of regional consistency. On the contrary, one of the aims of this book is precisely to address, within a regional context, the similarities and differences with respect to the issues we have set out to explore: the mutual imbrication of the representations of gender and power.

The notion of a region carries implicit and explicit ideas of a certain boundedness. Such boundedness articulates both the idea of a border, delimiting the region from other bordering regions, and the notion of an internal integrative bonding. In other words, it is precisely that which binds the region together which also sets it apart. However, as with many concepts that are grounded in the idea of an entity which is whole or bounded – for example, individual, society, culture, nation – and which have carried a certain analytical validity, the notion of a region, as an analytical concept, can also be questioned. In the face of globalization processes and Latin American diasporas, and the concomitant notions of disembedded or dislocated identities, one is led to argue for the use of the region as a relevant encompassing entity which permits meaningful comparisons and generalizations. One is also led to argue for a regional approach in lieu of discussions of the legitimacy of regional constructions where questions of colonial imposition and ethnocentric bias versus self-ascription and self-identification are central.[3]

Obviously, at one level, a regional delimitation – such as Latin America – is merely conventional, and can perhaps claim no unifying principle save that of a territorial connectedness expressed through a generally accepted geographical classification, corresponding to a certain number of nation-states, coupled with a transmitted historical legacy which has categorized and labelled Latin America (once the New World). And perhaps that is reason enough. The *Concise Oxford Dictionary* defines Latin America as 'the parts of Central and S. America where Spanish or Portuguese is the main language', while *El pequeño ESPASA* defines 'América Latina' as 'nombre con que se conoce al conjunto de Mexico, Centroamérica y América del Sur' (the name by which Mexico, Central America and South America is jointly known). Whereas the English definition combines geographical and cultural criteria (land plus language), and thus restricts what can be denoted as Latin America, the Spanish is content to minimize the criteria of identification to that of established territories. In the present context we have, unwittingly, followed the latter definition, with one difference: we have included the Caribbean, albeit the Spanish-speaking part.[4] Nevertheless, as a more all-encompassing notion, the term Latin America, in addition to territorial distinctions, evokes a series of associated images (not quite mythical, not quite stereotypical): Indian heritage and European dominance; *macho* men and stoical women; violent revolutions and ruthless dictatorships; agrarian reforms and urban congestion; dire poverty and sumptuous luxury; remote hinterlands and advanced industrial enterprises; *la casa* (the house) and *la calle* (the street); liberation theology and dependency theory. It evokes the magic realism of their literature; the flair of their fiestas; the rhythms of tango and salsa; the flavours of their food; the temperament of their athletes; the *caudillo* of politics; the triumph of *mañana*.

Most importantly, however, the term Latin America glosses those aspects of Latin American cultures which are perceived to be the products of the particular processes of transculturation which ensued as a result of a singular historical event: Columbus's arrival on the shores of America. The conquest of America has come to symbolize the destiny of the entire continent, notwithstanding the vast regional variations and an explicit recognition of these variations.[5] Three important processes which have jointly fed into the construction of this symbolism are the zeal with which the Catholic missionaries attacked their task of conversion, the subjugation or elimination of the native peoples by the *conquistadores*, and the wars for independence from Spain and Portugal.

The conquest not only established the invaders as rulers, but also inculcated a perception of these rulers as racially superior to their subject peoples. This attitude of different and unequal was nourished initially by the *conquistadores* and the Catholic Church. Despite syncretization, *mestisaje* and creolization, and the subsequent contested national identities, this initial creation of 'the other' has contributed to the constructions of pervasive dichotomies which permeate perceptions of Latin American societies. Although the roots of these dichotomies are lodged in the original opposition between 'Indian' and 'European', this polarization has, over the centuries, been transposed and yielded to a series of related oppositions: traditional/modern; backward/civilized; rural/urban; underdeveloped/developed. These oppositions operate both internally, in the perceptions structuring relationships between groups, and externally, positioning Latin America simultaneously, and hence ambiguously, at the core and periphery of the occidental world.

It is, perhaps, important to remember that Latin America has been integrated into the world market since the time of colonization, albeit on very unequal terms. The conditions for this integration laid the basis for its agrarian structures, which in turn have provoked many subsequent struggles for land tenure reforms, right down to our times. Moreover, Latin America was incorporated into the dominating cultural institutions of Europe. The Catholic Church has played a pivotal role since the time of colonization, leaving its definite mark on the educational system.[6] The forms of rule imposed by the colonizers established centralized bureaucratic systems and set the scene for urban developments; finally, political processes in Europe (and the USA) inspired the founding of the new independent states.

Although many overarching features contribute to notions of a shared cultural heritage in Latin Americans, the local conditions at the time of the conquest were extremely varied, implying very different forms of articulation and hence different socioeconomic and political trajectories.[7] Any understanding of the complexities and heterogeneity of modern Latin America must take these differences into account. It is therefore interesting to note the coexisting discourses of distinction and unity within Latin America, and it would perhaps also be interesting to trace these discourses and the varying terms and contexts which influence the formation of each. The notion of Latin America – implying a shared cultural heritage – is one that the political rhetoric of the continent's own politicians evokes (and is most clearly expressed through the existence of the Organization of American States), while at the same time internal differences and strife are rampant (e.g. the recent war between Ecuador and Peru; the continuing rivalry between Brazil and Argentina; Mexico's orientation towards North America through the North Atlantic Free Trade Agreement, and so on).

Taking all this into account, it seems that there are many different arguments that would justify a regional focus, from both an internal and an external point of view. In our opinion a regional focus is important – not just because it concurs with indigenous views, but also because it sets an agenda: the similarities and differences evoked by the essays in this book may permit comparisons and tentative generalizations; they may also, along with other and further studies, be used to reassess the value of the notion of Latin America as a region, with respect to the significance of gender as well as other social phenomena. The following pages, then, in addition to being read within their specific local contexts, should also be read in the context of a regional backdrop.

Gender Research in Latin America

Research on gender relations in Latin America gained momentum after the United Nations Women's Conference in Mexico in 1975, even though important initiatives had been taken before that.[8] Apart from a few anthropological studies of peasants and the urban poor, where families and households constituted the units of analysis, women had been notably absent from social science research in Latin America.[9] In the 1960s and 1970s the dominant perspective in the social sciences was that of dependency theory with the aim of formulating strategies for social transformation. The levels of extreme poverty and the fact that many Latin American states were run by military dictatorships were important factors influencing the subject matter and analytical thrust of social science research. The overall paradigm was Marxist; the main analytical category was perceived to be that of class: workers, peasants and capitalists; and the main social relation was that of exploitation, be it local or global. Within this framework, attention was directed to rural problems and agrarian reforms, with an increasing interest in urbanization and migration, as well as population studies. With the emphasis on production, labour was necessarily pivotal, and labour market studies, with a focus on differentiation (e.g. formal and informal labour markets), became central. Research on women was inscribed in these predominant trends; their subordinate position was assumed as a given and seen as a product of a capitalist, patriarchal society.

In contrast to the USA and Europe, where gender research developed in the wake of – and closely linked to – a militant and expansive feminist movement criticizing male dominance in academic institutions and male bias in social theory and research, Latin American research on women was the forerunner of the women's liberation movement, placed in the mainstream of the social sciences, closely linked to the political leftist movement and clearly non-feminist.[10] In fact, most feminist perspectives were considered not only inadequate but also politically suspect, as they tended to give gender inequality primacy over other kinds of inequalities, such as class and ethnicity. Such a position – which aligns women against men – subverted the basis for class struggle, which was perceived as the prime force for achieving social equality.[11]

As Alison MacEwen Scott suggests, the concept of class carried a special connotation: 'Class was the favoured concept for analysing the urban poor because of its explicit connection between economic structure and political action.'[12] In other words class, as a concept, represented the necessary link to possible action (notwithstanding the problem of determining the empirical reference of class). And it was this particular perception of social change which dictated the pre-eminence of class inequalities over gender inequalities, coupled with a view that a more equitable distribution of wealth and income, and a recognition of the need for gender equality, would lead to the liberation of all women, not only the more privileged ones. This overall concern for social inequities and social change (underpinning much social science research in Latin America at this time) also frames the initial studies on women. As elsewhere in the world, the thrust of the research was to make women visible: to document their lives and work, with the aim of disclosing their significance in productive and reproductive activities. This in turn would contribute to a political agenda which would include women, not least in the planning and implementing of social development programmes and projects. The predominance of a formalist class perspective, with its economic bias, reduced the problem of gender to one of women, and the problem of women to one of class. Although this perspective included an awareness of the class differences between women, issues such as subjectivity and identity were all but ignored, as was an appreciation of cultural values and meanings as a way of grasping the dynamics of social systems of inequality. Hence gender relations were not seen as articulating a specific system of inequality – or difference – which merited another methodological and analytical approach besides that of class. The question of gender remained confined to one of ideology, with the family as the main site of its ideological reproduction. Nevertheless, the importance of gender ideology was recognized, and questions about its continual persistence would come to represent an alternative to that of class.

Two anthologies, in addition to the series edited by Magdalena León,[13] can be said to represent two trends that have underpinned the further study of gender inequality in Latin America: *Female and Male in Latin America* (1973); and *Sex and Class in Latin America* (1980).[14] Whereas the former can be seen as representing a more culturalist interpretation of gender inequalities, the latter articulates the dominant perspectives outlined above. With its economic bias, *Sex and Class* is more representative of gender research in the region, focusing on the interrelationship between exploitation by sex and class and the impact of modernization and change on women's roles and status within different sectors of society. The emphasis is on women's productive roles, and the links between the sexual division of labour and women's participation in economic, social and political life. Attention is drawn to what is referred to as the 'ideological reinforcement of sexual subordination', but the contributions on ideologies and values are poor and stereotyped compared to the rich empirical substantiation of the other topics.

It is, perhaps, Evelyn Stevens's article in *Female and Male* which came to represent the challenge to the more economically orientated analysis.[15] Stevens is explicitly concerned with gender imagery, and more specifically with the image of the passive female and its implications for the understanding of male–female relationships. Her focus is on values and beliefs, and the meanings of myths for self-perception and self-identity – in particular the excessive veneration of the mother, through the figure of the Virgin. She explicitly contrasts *mestizo* culture with traditional Indian cultures. Contrary to the accepted views of the time, she suggests that Latin American *mestizo* women were content with their lot, and even benefited from their own submissiveness. To substantiate her argument, Stevens introduces the concept of 'marianismo' – 'the cult of feminine spiritual superiority, which teaches that women are semi-divine, morally superior to and spiritually stronger than men'.[16] Tracing the roots of *marianismo* to the Old World, she argues that it is the other face of *machismo* – the cult of male virility – in Latin America. Although the concept of *marianismo* is a contested one – not least because it is not indigenous – it has also inspired some Latin American scholars.[17]

Retrospectively, it is easy to understand why this essay was almost passed over in silence. Placing the burden of their situation on women themselves was not politically correct at the time! Moreover, the article was flawed. Not only did Stevens make generalizations about Latin American gender relations based on limited empirical material from middle-class Mexico, she also neglected the importance of economic and political conditions for the constitution of gender relations. Yet in some ways it is possible to say that she was ahead of her time in that she set another agenda – focusing on the role of the individual in the shaping of their own life situation, and emphasizing aspects of ambiguity and complexity in gender relations. Most importantly, however, her perspective made it possible to raise the awkward questions: are women merely passive victims of oppressive forces, or are they social agents who actively maintain the relations in which they are seemingly subordinate? If the latter, then how – or why – would women contribute to something that is detrimental to them? Moreover, her attempt to outline the workings of a symbolic system for the constitution of gendered identities, and her questioning of the ethnocentric biases in perceptions and analyses of gender relations in Latin America, were important elements for future discussions.

Studies grounded within the economic perspective, strongly emphasizing women's productive roles, detected a gross under-estimation of women's work, and emphasized the importance of this work for the economic welfare of families as well as for national economies.[18] They showed that women were far from unproductive and economically marginal. On the contrary, they were portrayed as highly integrated into the economy and society, but their integration was characterized by exploitation in terms both of class and gender. Moreover, the processes of integration had taken place without major changes in the sexual division of labour in the home. Concepts like 'la doble' or 'la triple jornada' entered the research vocabulary. These findings not only provoked a revision of the concept of labour and the categorization of economic activity, they also inspired a critical revision of the analysis and understanding of internal processes in households and families – of marriage, sexuality, and ideas and ideologies which contribute to the maintenance of particular gender relations. A number of studies addressed the links between production and social and biological reproduction, as well as those between family, household and the labour market.[19]

The collection of essays entitled *Women and Change in Latin America* (1986), which aims to sum up ten years of research on women, documents the persistence of a strong economic bias in gender research.[20] In the introduction to the book, June Nash states: 'we have not yet moved far enough beyond the structural definition of gender roles to encompass the cultural transformations that are symbols of and continue to affect women's subordination in many societies'.[21] She advocates a future research agenda which would stress the interplay between cultural and structural factors as a means of advancing theory and method in gender studies. She envisions a perspective that 'embraces values, beliefs, and expectations conditioning behaviour and attitudes about society at the same time that it relates to the structural constraints of a given mode of production and level of capital accumulation'. Nash also argues for the importance of introducing self-perception into the analysis. Future studies on gender should comprise consciousness, culture and material conditions, she concludes.[22] Recent years have seen a burgeoning of theoretical and empirical work on gender in Latin America, with a significant increase in the 'women and development' literature. Most of the studies continue to focus on different aspects of women's working life, in the agricultural sector or in the formal or informal urban sectors. A number have assessed the impact of processes of change – such as internal and international migration, urbanization, industrialization, economic restructuring and planned development – on women's lives.[23] The interrelationships between gender, class and ethnicity have also been addressed, particularly with reference to employment and political mobilization.[24]

There has, no doubt, been a gradual shift in perspective over the last years, and cultural factors are more frequently stressed, if only as a backdrop or a set of constraints which influence economic or political practices and opportunities. Cultural representations and the significance of symbolic systems have not been sufficiently problematized and analysed in their own right, except in the body of research on sexuality and sexual practices that started to appear in the wake of the expansion of AIDS and studies which deal with violence and the expansion of civil society and legal systems, as well as more recent studies which deal with moral–evaluative aspects of gender.[25]

With its emphasis on gender imagery and representations, this book is concerned with symbolic systems of inequality and difference. Thus it seeks, among other things, to counterbalance the strong economic bias that has underpinned gender research in Latin America. By focusing specifically on how gender differences are perceived, talked about, categorized and symbolized in a variety of contexts, and how they express and are expressions of power relations, the essays in this volume may throw new light on our understanding of class inequalities, and lead thereby to a better general comprehension of systems of inequality. Moreover, the book subtly demasks the stereotypical Latin American gender dichotomy – the image of the strong and dominant male and the meek and subservient woman – indicating that masculine and feminine images and identities are characterized by ambivalence and contradictions.

The Unsettling of the *macho*

If there is one term which is unambiguously associated with Latin America, it is the term *macho*, and its derivatives *machismo* and *machista*. Nevertheless, the term *macho* has travelled far and gained new meanings in new contexts.[26] Interestingly enough, despite its pervasiveness and obvious indigenous grounding, the term *macho* – or even *machismo* – has never gained the status of a gatekeeping concept. Rather, it has been used (and here we are referring to the literature) in a more offhand, self-evident way. This may be accounted for in part by the fact that *macho* is such an ordinary concept, used by every – or any – man and woman to characterize a true man, and in part by a more general assumption that everyone knows what a *macho* is, so there is little need for an explanation. Most importantly, however, we suggest that an earlier lack of interest in the status of the concept of *macho* reflects first and foremost the lack of interest in what constitutes the masculine make-up, and more generally in meanings of the social constructions of gender.[27] It is therefore significant that there is now a focus on the constitutive processes of masculinity, the various meanings of masculinity; and, morever, that reflections on masculinity are not necessarily grounded in the term *macho* itself. So although the *macho* is now being detailed in his own context – returned to his point of origin, as it were – he seems to have lost his gloss along the way.

Several of the contributors to this volume are explicitly concerned with masculinity, although their concerns have very different origins. Whereas Eduardo Archetti discusses masculinities through specific narratives of Argentinian football, Lorraine Nencel uses prostitution in Lima as her point of departure. Annick Prieur's focus is on the meanings of homosexuality in Mexico City, and Christian Krohn-Hansen works through the notion of 'tíguere' in Santo Domingo in order to elaborate on the meaning of masculinity for Dominican political rhetoric. Common to them all is a grounding of the notions of masculinity in an empirical reality and a nuanced analysis of the meanings of being male, and what constitutes maleness. Each presentation serves to unsettle any univocal notion of a Latin American male, yet at another level they also confirm the importance of masculinity as a constitutive element of significant cultural representations.

Basing his analysis on a careful and systematic reading of a men's sports magazine published in Buenos Aires between 1919 and 1940, Archetti focuses on the discourses about football and playing styles as reflecting a significant social arena where contrasting notions of masculinity are articulated. Not only is football an arena which is eminently masculine, it is also historically associated with the construction of an Argentinian national identity. Placing himself squarely in the debate on variant masculinities, Archetti shows how images of masculinities are variously produced and reproduced in contradistinction to each other. His argument is twofold: not

only does he demonstrate how the specific masculine imagery
of the football player evolves around 'el pibe' (the boy) – who
is carefree, irresponsible, and everything that 'the father' is not
– he also shows how the development of a particular Argentinian football – the *criollo* style – is produced as the negation
of the English playing style. Thus the emergent Argentinian foot-
ball-player-cum-style condenses an image of masculinity with
particular national symbolism – one which is not coincidental
with authority, responsibility and discipline, but is nevertheless
grounded in notions of 'conquest' over significant 'others', be
they near or far.

Nencel takes prostitution in urban Lima as her point of
departure in order to unravel the construction of male sexuality.
Her aim is explicitly to dismantle an assumed homogeneous
category of men. Her concern is the theoretical representations
of male sexuality and their implications for the notion of power,
as these are articulated in understandings of *machismo* and, more
specifically, in the image of the client in prostitution studies –
that is, of essentialist notions of male sexuality which perceive
prostitution as a necessary evil. In order to grasp the complexity
involved in the construction of men's sexual selves, Nencel insists
not only on the analytical split between sexuality and gender but
also on the fluidity of these concepts as distinct, plural, unfixed
and hence changing. The construction of the male sexual self,
she argues, can be approached by analysing sexual meanings
as these are expressed through their subjective experiences, in
conjunction with particular discourses on the feminine. Thus she
is able to draw out the various subjectivities which influence the
use and view of prostitutes. Moreover, she demonstrates how
discourses about the feminine are articulated through an ongoing
labelling process of women (by men). This labelling process tran-
scends the usual dual categorization of women (the decent
woman and the whore) into a tripartite classification (potential
partner, those who provide pleasure, and the prostitute). Nencel
argues that the labels used to categorize women are symbols for
men's projections of their sexual desires. Thus she shows how
the notion of men's sexual selves informs power relations
between men and women, and is therefore instructive for our
understanding of (their understanding of) female subordination.

Focusing on male homosexuals in Mexico City, Prieur explores the social competition between men. She is particularly interested in eliciting the local meanings attached to what in English would be called bisexual men – that is, men who have sexual relations with both men and women. Through a careful examination of local categorizations, she shows how these meanings feed into a discourse on masculinity, as this pertains to the relationships between homosexuals and their partners, and, perhaps more importantly, how such meanings are derived from the dominant perceptions of masculinity. Central to her argument is the symbolic meaning of penetration. Value is given to the man who penetrates women or other men, but never lets himself be penetrated. In her view, a man's defence of his body's boundaries, as well as his attack on other men's bodies, both mirror and symbolize the social competition among men. Like Nencel, she is also concerned with men's sexual pleasure, but she places her discussion within the world of homosexuals, demonstrating the complexity of social and sexual interactions.

In his article from the Dominican Republic, Krohn-Hansen focuses on masculinity as a dominant political discourse. He argues that notions of masculinity among Dominicans have played, and continue to play, a central part in the everyday production of political legitimacy. He shows how the prevailing notions of masculinity construct differences between men, and how these very differences feed into notions of the political. The main tension between men is that of the responsible father/ husband – the settled man whose life is limited to work and home – and the *mujeriego* – the womanizer, the irresponsible man, the nomad. According to Krohn-Hansen, the image of the nomadic seducer is concurrent with an image of politics – it implies being visible, which in turn implies being generous, having friends, and hence networks which can be put to political advantage. The thrust of his argument is to demonstrate how the masculine condenses a whole political vision, and how this vision is reproduced and enacted in daily life. The summarizing metaphor for this ambiguous masculinity is the *tíguere* – the image of the Dominican man which glosses the multiple meanings of masculinity. And it is Krohn-Hansen's contention that this metaphor makes it possible to express the paradoxes and ambiguities associated with power relations.

These essays share an explicit focus on variant masculinities and, more specifically, on the constitution of masculinity within same-sex relations. Departing from any notion of a fixed or singular male (and, by implication, female) form, their detailed expositions show how, in various contexts, alternative imagery is produced and reproduced. Nevertheless, although it is not explicitly addressed, there seems to be a background against which these multiple images rebound. In the case of Archetti, it is the authority figure, the one who represents discipline, responsibility and order – in other words, the father – who symbolizes the contrast to the 'pibe' who plays freely in his 'potrero'. And it is perhaps precisely the force of authority which makes the *pibe* such a powerful metaphor for masculine identity. The *pibe* is not only the counter-symbol of order and discipline, thus expressing intergenerational conflicts between men (for power and authority); he is also the potential father, the one who will at some point assume his role as a responsible citizen. Moreover, it is possible to imagine that the *pibe* – representing lost youth and freedom – comes to represent that which once was possible, but can never really be. In that sense, football, as the dominant arena of the 'boys' to whom the 'men' attach themselves, is no more – and no less – than a fantasy of an imaginary community of men which takes on exaggerated proportions. The reality of football comes to represent the reality of Argentina, albeit only partially – excluding, as it does, the seats of power – political, military and judicial – and, perhaps more importantly, the women. In fact, it is interesting that the notion of the streetwise, irresponsible but still innocent *pibe* does not evoke the sentiments of a concerned mother. This eminently male arena points to the relative importance of same-sex and cross-sex relations for the constitution not only of gendered identities but also – perhaps more significantly – of national identities.[28]

Prieur, too, evokes the meanings of same-sex and cross-sex relations for the construction of male identities, but in this Mexican case the emphasis is somewhat different. Prieur shows that the meanings attached to homosexuality are drawn from the dominant gender imagery. This is the background against which homosexuality is set. To be a homosexual is to be like a woman. Not only are homosexual men those who are penetrated by other men, they are also those who accentuate their very femininity to the extent of mutilating their bodies. In this case, then, the construction of the homosexual relation – which is a same-sex relation *par excellence* – is grounded in dominant notions of cross-sex relations. Attributes of femininity are the main markers distinguishing the true man from the homosexual. Thus any understanding of the constitution of the same-sex relations in this Mexican case necessarily entails an understanding of cross-sex relations. This would also hold true for Nencel's case. Although she is mainly concerned with men's subjectivities and their sexual selves, these are clearly related to their percep-tions of women. What we lack, however, is knowledge of how women categorize themselves, and in the case of Prieur, how women categorize homosexuals. Are women's views of them-selves concurrent with men's views of them, and do women accept the femininity of homosexual men as like their own? Or do women, as Marit Melhuus illustrates, ground their self-esteem in alternative representations, articulated in discourses which are concomitant to yet also contradict the discourses of male dominance?

In the same direction, Krohn-Hansen makes an interesting point, the implications of which he does not pursue. He states that the model of masculinity-cum-politics-cum-power is a confining one, with respect both to what constitutes political reality and to what is represented as politically imaginable. The fact that politics is framed in a masculine idiom raises important questions in the light of the prevailing presence of women in politics in the Dominican Republic. Are women evaluated according to the same criteria as men? Do women see their own role in politics as grounded on the same values as those of men? Is there a female *tíguere*? In other words, the fact that this model of power and politics simultaneously allows for actual female presence, while at the same time excluding women from the dominant imagery, suggests that there are other ambiguities besides those embedded in masculinity, which must also be accounted for if the full force of gender is to be understood. It may well be that this ambiguity has to be sought in the very configuration of gender, where the coincidence of the constitution of both same-sex and cross-sex relations must be explored if we are to grasp the construction of gendered identities and its implications for the political imagination. It seems that once the differences in the workings of same-sex and cross-sex relations are taken into account, the complexities of gender as a field of social relations become more apparent.

The Power of Discourse and Labelling

Recent discussions on gender and power have been particularly concerned with the importance of autonomy and choice for the understanding of power.[29] Neither the fact that women often comply with practices that subordinate them nor the fact that they resist the exercise of such practices can be understood in terms of the exclusively repressive view of power common in women's studies.[30]

Several of the essays in this volume deal directly or indirectly with a notion of dominance based on complicity. Complicity is what characterizes male–female relations among the farmers in Kristi Anne Stølen's study from Argentina. According to Stølen, this complicity is achieved through hegemony, understood as dominance based on common values or shared meaning, rather than on the use of coercion. Stølen demonstrates how the dominant local discourses on gender 'naturalize' the sexual division of roles in the family and the community. This discourse depicts men and women as different sorts of individuals, embodying different and mutually exclusive abilities and vocations, and thereby contributes to maintaining men's control over material and organizational resources and, through that, their control over women. The dominant gender discourses in Stølen's case are particularly influential, since they are rooted in Catholic beliefs and practices in a context where the Catholic Church is the most important producer and transmitter of gender ideology – not only through the Church itself, but also through other institutions of civil society. This implies that gender values and practices at the level of face-to-face interaction reflect and find support in a wider ordering of notions of femininity and masculinity.

Dominance based on complicity is also what characterizes the relationship between masculine men and homosexual transvestites in Prieur's study from Mexico City. The complicity in this case refers to the shared categorization and appreciation of what homosexuality is, and who the homosexual is. If only those men who are penetrated by another man are categorized as homosexuals, the penetrating partner remains 'normal' in the sense of being manly; his sexual activity is invisible, while that of his sexual companion is not: he is humiliated and stigmatized. As long as they play the penetrator's part, men may have sexual intercourse with other men without being categorized as homosexual. This way of categorizing homosexuality and homosexuals is shared by the effeminate homosexuals and their partners. Prieur argues that this 'labelling power' of heterosexual men gives them licence to pleasure. She neatly illustrates the power of gender imagery by demonstrating how representations of masculinity – where penetration is the key distinguishing factor – contribute to create fundamental distinctions between men. She also demonstrates how the partners in a homosexual relationship co-operate to maintain these distinctions.

Magdalena Villarreal is also concerned with the power involved in labelling processes, and her analytical aim is to challenge the very notion of a dominant discourse. She has followed the establishment of a beekeeping group among women in a rural Mexican community. Basing her analysis on interface situations, she seeks to demonstrate how women attempt to subvert the very categorizations to which they are subjected. Her argument is grounded in a dynamic notion of power which allows for a certain negotiation of the very premises on which power is constructed. The women in the beekeeping group are sensitive readers of their own culture, and well aware of the accepted limits on female behaviour. Villarreal shows how these women, in order to legitimize their activity, put their own knowledge of their cultural context to use. Through irony and a reconceptualization of the dominant imagery, they attempt to escape the moral stigma which works to sanction their movements. Yet it seems that in the last instance they are caught in the local web that gendered notions spin.

The contributions of Stølen and Prieur show that power

grounded in dominant discourses does not imply an imposition of ideas and categorizations on passive victims, as Villarreal seems to suggest. The farmer women of Santa Fé, as well as the effeminate homosexuals in Mexico City, are far from passive victims of circumstance. Like the women Villarreal describes, they actively shape their lives according to their own values. The issue is that they adhere to values that are embedded in notions of inequality, and thus help to reproduce them – and their own position. They are also exposed to alternative discourses, but these discourses are associated with groups that are seen to hold a subordinate position in society, and defined as abnormal, immoral or undesirable. The case Villarreal describes is interesting because it depicts a situation where there are competing rather than hierarchical gender discourses.[31] The government officials wishing to implement a development programme for women are transmitters of a particular gender discourse, representing alternative role models and values for women. This discourse, which is associated with the state and with access to resources, offers legitimate options for women which they, through their own agency and negotiating capacities, know how to exploit. This draws attention to the importance of the contextualization of gender discourses – a point raised by R. Connell,[32] who argues that gender discourses must be analysed with attention to context, institutionalization and group formation.

Where there is power, there is often also resistance. The effeminate homosexuals portrayed by Prieur struggle to over-come the contempt with which they are surrounded. On the one hand they advocate an essentialist view of homosexuality, describing it as innate and hence immutable; on the other, they try to turn the tables by cheating their sexual partners, stealing their money or their masculinity by penetrating them. As in Stølen's case, where women do negotiate and manipulate in order to have things their way, these acts of resistance are realized without threatening the dominant gender notions, which establish a hierarchy between men and women, and masculine men and homosexuals, respectively. The question remains whether this also holds true in Villarreal's case.

The Power of Gender Differences

As we said at the beginning, one of the assumptions that stimulated this book was the observation that gender differences in Latin America appear to assume a commanding significance in the ordering of differences other than gender. In other words, gender is a potent signifier, whether in terms of masculinity, or femininity, or both. We have already indicated the thrust of both Archetti's and Krohn-Hansen's arguments. Their concern is not the relationship between men as such but, rather, the differences upon which this relationship is perceived to be constituted. These differences are vital because they come to represent significant distinctions, while at the same time they create the space – or opening – through which discourses on nationalism and politics are constructed. Gender is also inscribed in discourses on ethnicity (e.g. Crain, Rostas and Stølen). In two of these instances (Crain and Stølen) the relation between gender and ethnicity is articulated through female imagery, as bearers of a cultural or a moral purity. Finally, gender appears to be a vehicle through which morality speaks (e.g. Melhuus, Villarreal, Stølen). Notions of morality are expressed in terms of gender and articulated through discourses on gender relations.

Both Mary Crain and Stølen situate the discourses on gender (in Ecuador and Argentina respectively) in the context of local perceptions of ethnic relations, indicating the mutual interdependence of the ordering of these two sets of relationships. Whereas Crain takes as her point of departure the conflation of ethnic categories and gender in highland Ecuador, Stølen is concerned with the discourses on moral righteousness and superiority among the *gringo* (northern Italian immigrant) settlers of Santa Fé, Argentina. She shows how the dominant discourse, grounded in gender, class and ethnicity, which distinguishes the *gringos* from the *criollos* (the local term for those of Indian/Spanish descent) is expressed in terms of sexuality.

Stølen explores the articulations of the relations between *gringos* and *criollos*, indicating how they have been historically constituted as unequal. The *gringos* control the land, the means of production and the local institutions (such as school, church and neighbourhood committees). They employ the *criollos* as seasonal labour. Stølen also explores the gender relation as it is articulated within the two ethnic groups, showing a marked difference in the sexual division of labour and in perceptions of sexuality. The *gringos* value female domesticity and chastity, and put women in two categories: those who are decent and those who are not. Whereas *gringas* are, by definition, decent, the opposite holds true for the *criollas* – they are considered loose and unable to control their sexual urges because of their hot blood. Stølen argues that the distinction between *gringos* and *criollos* hinges on moral perceptions of sexuality, and that these perceptions serve to uphold both gender and ethnic inequalities. Thus the *gringas*'s sexual behaviour becomes a symbol of the moral superiority of the *gringos per se*. However, the relations between *gringo* men and women, and *gringos* and *criollos*, are different: whereas the gender relation is based on shared values and complicity, the ethnic relation is one of resistance.

Crain argues that the conflation of gender and ethnic categories works in such a way that indigenous women of the Andes serve as visual icons of 'Indianness'. There is a certain essentialization of Indianness whereby the female Indian comes to represent the purity and continuity of an authentic cultural heritage. This essentialization responds both to processes internal to the ethnic group and to external ones. The thrust of Crain's essay is not only to demonstrate how 'identities are shifting, situational, and negotiated within fields of power relations' by focusing on the displacement of traditional icons to urban communities. She is also concerned with the way dominant elites 'tailored aspects of native women's gender and ethnic identities to dovetail with colonialist-inspired images of "Indianness" which would appeal to cosmopolitan audiences in metropolitan Quito'. Thus she discloses how specific historical processes, in conjunction with actual state policies, impinge on concepts of ethnic identities in a modern, urban context. She explores the process by which indigenous women from Quimsa are incorporated into the urban workforce in Quito, as they are fed into the tourist trade in new positions at a major international hotel.

Susanna Rostas, in a somewhat different vein, looks at the

meaning of gendered images in the context of indigenous revival in urban Mexico, expressed through the ritual dance of the Concheros, and links this to notions of *mexicanidad*, or Mexicanness. She is concerned not so much with situational identities as with the meanings of 'Indianity' – that is, the dancers' ideas about Indianness, and how these ideas contribute to the production of a specific gendered imagery within the dance. Most importantly, she links the Aztec imagery so central to the dances to historical processes, the way these processes have come to be interpreted, and what the representations displayed in the dance 'have to do with how the dancers "imagine" Mexico'. Combining literary and popular sources, she shows how ethnicity, summarized in the Aztec symbolism, and gender are invoked in order to assert a certain form of authentic 'Mexicanness'. The dances are thus inscribed as a ritual expression in the ongoing discourse of Mexican identity. The thrust of her argument is to place popular expressions of what constitutes national sentiments – a return to Bonfil's 'Mexico profundo' – within the turbulent processes of Mexican contemporary politics. In contradistinction to the Concheros, who seek balance and harmony between the sexes, Rostas shows how another group of dancers – the Mexica – privilege the masculine over the feminine, and thus equate the masculine with the struggle for dignity and power. An important observation that Rostas points out is the difference in the imagery related to maleness and femaleness. Whereas the male mythology is rooted in 'traits that are located in types or historical characters or stereotypical heroes', the female imagery is portrayed through two contrasting mythologies: the Virgin of Guadalupe and La Malinche.

Melhuus addresses tangential issues, basing some of her arguments on the same sources as Rostas. However, her reflections are centred around what she denotes as the enigma of Mexican *mestizo* gender imagery: a male-dominant society that nevertheless places its highest value on the feminine, indicating a split between perceptions of power and value. Her main argument is that there is an inherent ambiguity in the very configurations of gender, and that this quality of the gender relation imbues gender with a certain elusiveness. Moreover, it is this very elusiveness, she suggests, which contributes to make

gender a rich discursive field. Her discussion is grounded in three
different fields of Mexican reality: the literature on 'lo mexicano',
i.e. the Mexican's own exegesis of what it means to be Mexican;
the myths of the Virgin of Guadalupe and Malinche; and local
perceptions of gender and the gender relation as these have been
gleaned from her own fieldwork among villagers of a Spanish-
speaking Catholic community. Melhuus demonstrates that the
gender configuration rests on a double structuring, or two symbolic orders permitting both dominance and complementarity
for both men and women, where the female seems to escape the
male while the male cannot escape the female. This structuring
is founded on different forms of evaluation of men and women.
It is precisely these varying forms of evaluation which link gender
and morality ambiguously and inform the way discourses on
gender – and female imagery in particular – are used to evoke a
sense of the nation.

Although Villarreal's essay deals primarily with various
discursive practices, and their effects on the categorization
of women, her analysis also throws light on the significance of
gender as a language through which values are relayed. Again,
women are the focus for strategic investment, but in contrast to
the Indian women of Quimsa, who are seen to represent some
authentic past, the *mestizo* women in Ayaquila are to be the
vanguard of a future development. However, in order to be
incorporated into the mainstream of events, these women need
first to overcome certain traditional beliefs. This is the double
message conveyed by the extension workers from the Mexican
government. Hence, in this case, women are seen simultaneously
as both backward and the potential sites of radical change.
However, it is in the more detailed presentation of the reactions
by fellow villagers to the women's beekeeping project that the
multivocality of gender discourses becomes evident. Echoing
similar findings to those of Melhuus, Villarreal shows how on
the one hand women were concerned about their reputations as
decent and, on the other, how this very concern was reiterated
by the men in their attempts to defend their own access to land,
and thereby subvert the authorities and, by implication, the
women.

Conclusion

Although they draw on very different empirical material, each contribution in this volume, in its separate way, points to the centrality of gendered representations for the ordering of other significant distinctions. This occurs at different levels of discourse and within different processes of sociocultural expressions. On the one hand we find a conflation, or mutual constitution, of issues of gender and issues of morality, where the former are used to articulate the latter (as in the case Villarreal illustrates, where disputes over land rights are conducted in terms of gender). Thus, discourses about gender may simultaneously transmit messages about morality. However, as Melhuus indicates, if the gender relation itself is ambiguously constituted, the moral messages will be equivocal too. On the other hand, we find that perceptions of gender inequalities (between men and women) and differences (between men and between women) serve as points of articulation or representations of ethnic relations, national identities or political rhetoric.

One aspect which seems to emerge from the material in this book, whose implications have yet to be fully explored, is the differing yet mutual constitution of same-sex and cross-sex relations. It appears that there are different schemes of evaluation for men and for women. Men are classified according to degrees of masculinity; women are discretely classified according to their moral character. Whereas masculinity appears to be continuous – you are more or less of a man – women are dichotomized: a woman is either good (decent) or bad (indecent). These differing grounds of valuation for men and for women are perhaps at the core of the gender relation, making gender categorizations both complex and ambiguous. While same-sex relations have characteristics which are exclusive to each category, cross-sex relations appear to transcend this very exclusivity in their joint articulations. This is reflected, among other things, in the fertile field of imagery which can be evoked.

The relationships between discourses, representations and imagery are not easy to tease out. Moreover, with the focus on gender imagery the problem is compounded by the fact that the gender relation itself may be ambiguously constituted and multivocal. Hence the fact that gender differences are not merely self-referential but invoked in order to formulate other sets of differences may create some cultural confusion. Yet this confusion is subverted by the clear-cut fixation of the images. Thus it may be that the very processes which serve to fix an image simultaneously obscure the ambiguities which underpin it. In other words, the effect of visualization is to evoke unequivocal, easily recognizable images: images that are seemingly out of time and out of place – dislocated, disembedded, fetishized – and herein lies their power. The force of the images, then, can be understood only once the glue that makes them stick dissolves. The purpose of this book is in part to be a contributing solvent.

The fact that the meanings of gender, and hence the imagery evoked, will vary according to context does not detract from the overall thrust of the significance of gender. Rather, it appears that gender is central to an understanding of Latin American reality, past or present, whether we are concerned with economic, political or cultural processes. In many ways gender seems to bridge these different spheres of society, representing a nexus around which various experiences can be grafted and represented. Thus gender can be seen as a significant carrier through which meaning is constructed. Gender is not only reflected in the division of labour and at the different levels of political expression and organization, but it also underpins cultural representations. Nevertheless, only additional research will disclose whether gender and discourses on gender represent the subtext linking moralities and identities, and only more research will be able to reveal to what extent gender relations represent the nexus through which differences are constructed and perceived. There is thus a renewed challenge in linking the conceptualization of social inequalities and power based on class to those of gender.

Notes

We wish to thank Tordis Borchgrevink and Eduardo Archetti for their instructive comments on this Introduction.

1. Marilyn Strathern, 'Introduction', in Marilyn Strathern, ed., *Dealing with Inequality: Analysing Gender Relations in Melanesia and Beyond*, Cambridge 1987.

2. Henrietta Moore, *A Passion for Difference*, Cambridge 1994, p. 61.

3. The problematics of regional constructions and the ethnocentric bias they might represent was sparked by Edward Said's book *Orientalism*, New York 1978. For a further discussion, see Lila Abu-Lughod, 'Zones of Theory in the Anthropology of the Arab World', *Annual Review of Anthropology*, vol. 18, 1989. For a discussion of the meaning of place and gatekeeping concepts, see Arjun Appadurai, 'Theory in Anthropology: Center and Periphery', *Comparative Studies in Society and History*, vol. 28, no. 2, 1986; Marilyn Strathern, 'Concrete Topographies', *Cultural Anthropology*, vol. 3, no. 1, 1988. See also Richard Fardon, *Localizing Strategies: Regional Traditions of Ethnographic Writing*, Edinburgh 1990; Joao Piña-Cabral, 'The Mediterranean as a Category of Regional Comparison: A Critical View', *Current Anthropology*, vol. 30, no. 3, 1989; Nicolas Thomas, 'The Force of Ethnology: Origins and Significance of the Melanesia/Polynesia Division', *Current Anthropology*, vol. 30, no. 1, 1989; Strathern (ed.) 1987; Signe Howell and Marit Melhuus, eds, *Fjern og Nær. Sosialantropologiske perspektiver på verdens samfunn og kulturer*, Oslo 1994.

4. To limit Latin America to those parts where Spanish and Portuguese are the dominant languages implies excluding the native, pre-Columbian cultures. Within anthropology, research in Latin America has had a tendency to fall into two main categories: those dealing with native American indigenous cultures, and those more concerned with the articulation of social processes that have come in the wake of modernization and industrialization. Whereas the former studies focus primarily on the internal structurings of indigenous communities and have a specific regional embeddedness (e.g. the Andes or the Amazon), the latter, often called 'peasant studies', have been more concerned with the relations between local communities and the wider society, focusing on different forms of socioeconomic and cultural integration. In the present context, however, this differentiation has not been made relevant. Nevertheless, most of the contributions (with one exception) are based on fieldwork among Spanish-speaking peoples.

5. See, for example, for Mexico, Tzevetan Todorov, *La Conquête de l'Amérique*, Paris 1982; for Peru, N. Wachtel, *The Vision of the Vanquished: The Spanish Conquest of Peru Through Indian Eyes*, New York 1977; for the Dominican Republic, F. Moya Pons, *El pasado dominicano*, Santo Domingo 1986.

6. The first university, Universidad de San Marcos, was founded in Lima, Peru, as early as the sixteenth century.

7. See Eric Wolf and C. Hansen, *The Human Condition in Latin America*, New York 1972.

8. See Magdalena León, 'Presentación', in Magdalena León, ed., *La realidad columbiana. Debate sobre la mujer en America Latina y el Caribe*, Bogotá 1982. This book is the first volume in a series of three, all edited by León. The other two volumes are (II) *Las trabajadoras del agro* and (III) *Sociedad, subordinación y feminismo*. This series represented a timely and important contribution not only with respect to the information about women relayed, but also with respect to the debates it sought to raise.

9. One exceptional researcher is Oscar Lewis who, with his family and life history studies, explicitly focused on women's life trajectories (in addition to men's) and implicitly on gender relations. See, for example, Oscar Lewis, *Five Families*, New York 1961; and Oscar Lewis, *The Children of Sánchez*, New York 1961.

10. M. Navarro, 'Research on Latin American Women', *Signs*, vol. 5, no. 1, 1979.

11. These were perspectives that Latin American researchers shared to some extent with socialist feminists in Europe and the USA, who also emphasized the significance of capitalist reproduction for the inequalities between men and women. In their view, the subordination of women was associated with capitalism's drive for profit and its intrinsic need to reproduce itself. This in turn was seen to create a sex-divided workforce, the isolation of the family and the oppression of the housewife. See, for example, A. Kuhn and A.M. Wolpe, eds, *Feminism and Materialism*, London, Boston, MA and Henley 1978; L. Sargent, ed., *Women and Revolution*, London 1981; see also Michèle Barrett, *Women's Oppression Today: Problems in Marxist–Feminist Analysis*, London 1980; and Kate Young, Carol Wolkowitz and Rosalyn McCullagh, eds, *Of Marriage and the Market: Women's Subordination in International Perspective*, London 1981. Radical feminists, however, tended to focus narrowly on male–female relations, and often conceptualized women and men as social blocs linked by a direct power relation, with women in a subordinate and men in a dominant position. The implication of this view for strategies of social change was a direct mobilization of women, stressing their common interests as against those of men. See Susan Brownmiller, *Against Our Will: Men, Women and Rape*, New York 1975; Mary Daly, *Gyn/Ecology: The Metaethics of Radical Feminism*, Boston, MA 1978; Shulamith Firestone, *The Dialectics of Sex*, London 1979; Andrea Dworkin, *Pornography: Men Possessing Women*, London 1981. Other perspectives were more complex, treating the power of men and the subordination of women as effects of imperatives outside the direct relationship between the two. The 'need of social reproduction', the reproduction from generation to generation of social structures as well as bodies, was the perspective in Juliet Mitchell's *Psychoanalysis and Feminism*, New York 1975. A similar argument was put forward by Dorothy Dinnerstein, who deduced both the power of men and the submission of women from women's monopoly of early

childrearing – D. Dinnerstein *The Mermaid and the Minotaur*, New York 1976.

12. Alison MacEwen Scott, *Divisions and Solidarities: Gender, Class and Employment in Latin America*, London and New York 1994, p. 3.

13. See Note 8 above.

14. A. Pescatello, ed., *Female and Male in Latin America: Essays*, Pittsburgh, PA 1973; June Nash and Helen Safa, *Sex and Class in Latin America*, Massachusetts 1980.

15. Evelyn Stevens, 'Marianismo: The Other Face of Machismo in Latin America', in Pescatello (ed.) 1973.

16. Ibid. p. 91.

17. See, for example, Tracy Ehlers, 'Debunking Marianismo: Economic Vulnerability and Survival Strategies Among Guatemalan Wives', *Ethnology*, vol. 30, no. 1, 1991; and for a critical review, Marit Melhuus, 'Some Comments on Machismo and Marianismo', in *'Todos tenemos madre. Dios también.' Morality, Meaning and Change in a Mexican Context*, PhD thesis, University of Oslo, 1992. Some Latin American scholars inspired by the perspectives of Stevens in their analyses of female symbolism and identity are Rodriguez Sehk, 'La vírgen-madre: Símbolo de la feminidad latinoamericana', in *Texto y Contexto*, no. 7, Bogotá 1986; S. Montecino, M. Dussuel and A. Wilson, 'Identidad feminina y modelo mariano en Chile', in *Mundo de Mujer: Continuidad y Cambio*, Santiago 1988; Milagros Palma, ed., *Simbolica de la feminidad. La mujer en el imaginario mítico-religioso de las sociedades indias y mestizas*, Quito 1990; Sonia Montecino, *Madres y Huachos. Alegorias del mestizaje chileno*, Santiago 1993.

18. For example, Carmen Diana Deere, 'Changing Social Relations of Production and Peruvian Peasant Women's Work', *Latin American Perspectives*, no. 4, 1977; M. León, 1982, vol. II.

19. For example, June Nash, Helen Safa *et al.*, *Women and Change in Latin America*, South Hadley, MA 1986; M. León, 1982, vol. III; Brígida García, Humberto Muñoz and Orlandina de Oliveira, *Hogares y Trabajadores en la Ciudad de México*, Mexico 1982; Orlandina de Oliveira, Marille Pepin Lehalleur and Vania Salles, *Grupos domesticos y reproducción cotidiana*, Mexico 1989; Programa Interdisciplinario de Estudios de la Mujer, *Trabajo, poder y sexualidad*, Mexico 1989; Catalina Waineman, Elizabeth Jelin and María del Carmen Feijoó, *Del deber ser y el hacer de las mujeres. Dos estudios de caso en argentina*, Mexico 1983.

20. Nash and Safa, 1986.

21. June Nash, 'A Decade of Research on Gender in Latin America', in Nash and Safa, 1986, p. 14.

22. Some of the studies on gender in Latin America presented in K.A. Stølen's article 'Gender, Culture and Social Change in Latin America:

A Nordic Perspective', *Ibero Americana, Nordic Journal of Latin American Studies*, vol. XXIV: 1, Stockholm 1994, have been carried out within a perspective similar to that suggested by Nash.

23. See, for example, Carmen Diana Deere and Magdalena León, *Rural Women and State Policy: Feminist Perspectives on Latin American Agricultural Development*, Boulder, CO and London 1987; Fiona Wilson, *De la casa al taller: Mujeres, trabajo y clase social en la industría textil y del vestido*, Santiago Tangamanapio, Zamora 1990; Elizabeth Jelin, ed., *Family, Household and Gender Relations in Latin America*, London and Paris 1991; *Latin American Perspectives*, Special issue on 'Women in Latin America', vol. 2, no. 2, 1995.

24. MacEwen Scott, 1994.

25. See, for example, Silvia Chejter, *La voz tutelada, violación y voyeurismo*, Montevideo 1990; Olivia Harris, 'Condor and Bull: The Ambiguities of Masculinity in Northern Potosí', in Penelope Harvey and Peter Gow, eds, *Sex and Violence: Issues in Representation and Experience*, London 1994; Penelope Harvey, 'Domestic Violence in the Peruvian Andes', in Penelope Harvey and Peter Gow (eds) 1994; Roger Lancaster, 'Subject Honor and Object Shame: The Construction of Male Homosexuality and Stigma in Nicaragua', *Ethnology*, vol. 27, 1988; Roger Lancaster, *Life is Hard: Machismo, Danger, and the Intimacy of Power in Nicaragua*, Berkeley, CA 1992; Eduardo P. Archetti, 'Argentinian Tango: Male Sexual Ideology and Morality', in R. Grønhaug *et al.*, eds, *The Ecology of Choice and Symbol*, Bergen 1991; Kristi Anne Stølen, *Gender, Power and Social Change in the Argentine Prairie*, Oslo 1996; Marit Melhuus, 'A Shame to Honour – A Shame to Suffer', *Ethnos*, vol. 55, nos 1–2, 1990; Marit Melhuus 'The Troubles of Virtue – the Values of Violence and Suffering in a Mexican Context', in Signe Howell, ed., *The Ethnographies of Moralities*, London 1996; Andrea Cornwall 'Gendered Identities and Gender Ambiguity among *travesti* in Salvador, Brazil', in Andrea Cornwall and Nancy Lindisfarne, eds, *Dislocating Masculinity. Comparative Ethnographies*, London 1994. Also important are the proliferating studies in history and literary criticism, which are too numerous to list here, but for Mexico see, for example, Jean Franco, *Plotting Women: Gender and Representation in Mexico*, New York 1989; Sandra Messinger Cypess, *La Malinche in Mexican Literature: From History to Myth*, Austin, TX 1992; Carmen Ramos *et al.*, *Presencia y transparencia: La mujer en la historia de México*, Mexico 1987; Silvia Marina Arrom, *Las mujeres de la ciudad de México 1790–1857*, Mexico 1988. Obviously, the theme of gender and gender imagery is one that is central to many Latin American novels, but it is also a theme set by Latin American essayists, most notably Octavio Paz in his *El laberinto de la soledad*, Mexico 1988 [1950]. See also Melhuus, this volume, Chapter 10.

26. See, for example, Andrea Cornwall and Nancy Lindisfarne,

'Dislocating Masculinity: Gender, Power, and Anthropology', in Cornwall and Lindisfarne (eds) 1994, pp. 12 ff.

27. Except probably the vast amount of psychological literature; see, for example, Erich Fromm and Michael Maccoby, *Social Character in a Mexican Village*, Englewood Cliffs, NJ 1970.

28. The significant contrasting imagery would be that of the 'madres de la plaza de mayo', the mothers who marched in silence every Thursday throughout the years of the dictatorship, confronting the authorities with their demands for knowledge of the whereabouts of their disappeared children. This arena was (is) eminently feminine, drawing on the symbolic meaning of the mother. Yet whereas in football the relevant others are other men – whether concretely, in the form of the other players, or symbolically, in contradistinction to the men with authority and responsibility, the mothers produce and make visible a different set of relationships: they challenge the power of the authorities (that is men) in their search for their children. Thus they point simultaneously, to the betrayal of the fathers and the children's dependence on their mothers.

29. The importance of freedom and choice for the understanding of power is not new in the more general discussions of this question. Foucault saw freedom as a precondition for modern forms of power – Michel Foucault, *Power/Knowledge: Selected Interviews and Other Writings. 1972–1977*, Brighton 1980. This is also the view of Lukes, who argues that even though social agents operate within structurally determined limits, they none the less have a certain degree of autonomy and thus could have acted differently – Steven Lukes, *Power: A Radical View*, London 1974, pp. 54–5. Pierre Bourdieu claims that the most important form of domination is complicity, referring to domination based on shared values and perceptions between the dominated and the oppressors – P. Bourdieu (with Loïc J.D. Wacquant), *An Invitation to Reflexive Sociology*, Cambridge 1992.

30. S. Morgan and A. Bookmann, *Women and the Politics of Empowerment*, Philadelphia 1988; Lila Abu-Lughod, 'The Romance of Resistance: Tracing Transformations of Power through Bedouin Women', *American Ethnologist*, vol. 17, no. 1, 1990, pp. 41–56; I. Halsema, *Housewives in the Field: Power, Culture and Gender in a South Brazilian Village*, Amsterdam 1991;. K.A. Stølen, 'The Gentle Exercise of Male Power in Rural Argentina', *Identities*, vol. 2, no. 2, 1996.

31. Moore, 1994, p. 59.

32. R. Connell, *Gender and Power: Society, the Person and Sexual Politics*, Stanford 1987, p. 242.

2

Playing Styles and Masculine

Virtues in Argentine Football

Eduardo P. Archetti

Andrea Cornwall and Nancy Lindisfarne argue, with justifica-
tion, that the different images and forms of behaviour contained
in the notion of masculinity are not always coherent, and
can appear contradictory and indeterminate.[1] In this sense it is
important to try to capture the diversity of these signs and
forms of behaviour by understanding that masculinity cannot be
treated as something fixed and universal. The ability to negotiate
these differences is a function of the power of the masculine
imaginary. For that reason we must focus on certain social arenas
where masculinity is produced and reproduced differently. These
arenas are constructed as both complementary and opposed to
the feminine, but also in contexts which are eminently masculine,
where the relevant others are men – different types of men. In
many societies football is, without a doubt, one such arena. In
Argentina, football is not only an eminently masculine social
arena but it is also associated historically with the construction
of national identity through the international successes of the
national team and the 'export' of great players to Europe from
the 1920s onwards. Argentina would henceforth be not just the
country of beef, cereals and tango, the land that receives millions
of European immigrants, but also the place where splendid
football players come from. Football permits the early development in Argentina of a public masculine imagery linked to the
meaning of styles of play and their associated masculine virtues.
To explore masculine differences through football is, therefore,

a way of understanding the power of the masculine imagery in a concrete society.

In previous work on the masculine world of football I have concentrated on songs heard and transcribed in grounds, on written and oral stories and, more recently, on the moral reflections of the fans.[2] Here I will concentrate on the analysis of written material taken from the weekly magazine *El Gráfico*. Founded in May 1919 in Buenos Aires, *El Gráfico* was in the beginning literally a graphic magazine 'for men'. Produced by the Atlántida publishing house, which also brought out very successful magazines for children and for women, *El Gráfico* included, in different measures, political articles, news photos, sports, photos of artists, and reports on leisure and open-air activities. After 1921 *El Gráfico* gradually became a sports magazine, although photos of women artists and singers, and even some daring female nude photos of unknown and supposedly foreign dancers, would be published until the end of the twenties. The circulation of *El Gráfico* increased in this decade, and levelled out at some 100,000 copies in the thirties. The magazine's circulation reached its peak between the mid 1940s and the mid 1950s, with 200,000 copies published weekly.

Until well into the 1950s, *El Gráfico* was a true sports magazine. A great deal of space was devoted to football, but other sports like motor racing, polo, swimming and boxing, in which Argentines had gained an international reputation, were also well covered. At the outset, the magazine was a mouthpiece for the modernist ideology in vogue: it emphasized the importance of physical education for health, notions of hygiene, recommendations on the best diet to follow and how to avoid illnesses, the importance of developing hobbies such as model aircraft, the need to encourage women to participate in sport and, above all, the persistent emphasis on the moral and educational aspects of sport. According to *El Gráfico*, sport should be understood as the moral activity of the body, since it develops a strict code of conduct in those who play it, owing to the existence of rules, controls and sanctions. An activity of the body which is the result of individual fantasy and creativity, and is not controlled by strict rules, is defined as a game, not as a sport.[3]

El Gráfico is certainly the middle-class sports weekly which has had, and continues to have, the greatest influence in Argentina. The analysis of the content of this magazine is, therefore, an analysis of the construction of middle-class male imagery. Whether or not it was hegemonic can be discussed, but there is no doubt about its decisive influence on the definition of the different areas of masculine moral thought. The journalists of *El Gráfico*, excellent writers in the main, think as members of the middle class but, at the same time, give space to the expression and dissemination of the voices, images and the performances of football players and other sportsmen. The transformation of the latter into 'heroes' or 'villains', into 'models' to be emulated or not, and the careful analysis of their performances, are examples of the process of the symbolic construction of the 'national' through an examination of masculine sporting virtues. The term 'national' is used to indicate that in *El Gráfico*, voices, performances, successes or failures of popular actors are combined with the intellectual reflections of middle-class writers and journalists. This confluence, in my opinion, is less apparent in specialist women's magazines or in the more political or literary weeklies, where the dominant voices are those of the upper or middle classes.

Football as a Product and an Example of *lo criollo*: the Creation of a Style

This concern over questions of the nation and masculinity found in *El Gráfico* is not unique at this particular moment in Argentine history. The massive migration of foreigners, combined with rapid economic progress, the fast pace of urbanization and the growth of a big city like Buenos Aires, transform the notion of 'the Argentine' into a problem. Football is an English sport brought by the English to Argentina, as to the rest of the world. One of the differences between Buenos Aires and other Latin American cities like Rio de Janeiro and Montevideo, where football would also be important, is the importance of the British and of British culture in the construction of the city, in the definition of free time associated with sporting activities, in the modernization of the Argentine economy and its early incorporation into the world market. At the beginning of this century almost fifty thousand British people lived in Buenos Aires. There were also hundreds of thousands of other European immigrants. By the end of the century football had become the most popular sport in Buenos Aires and throughout the country. In the first decade of the century each neighbourhood within Buenos Aires and each town close by had its own football club. Each club had its own stadium and social and sports centre, which was the focus of much of the cultural and recreational activity of the neighbourhoods. At the same time, after 1904, amateur football in Buenos Aires became part of the global world of sport, with regular summer visits from some of the best British professional football teams.

In this context of the expansion and definitive consolidation of football as the masculine sport *par excellence*, *El Gráfico* developed in the 1920s the theory of the two foundings of Argentine football: the first founding is British, the second is *criollo*. One of the arguments used refers to the ethnic origins of the players in the most famous teams and also those playing for the national team. In the era of the British founding – from 1887 to 1911, the date when the hegemony of the Alumni, the 'glorious British club', was broken – players of British origin predominated:

> The English who came to the River Plate were the first to play the sport and their sons continued to do so in English schools, where other sports like cricket are also played. Thus *River Plate football had English origins in its first stages* and the first lesson in advanced technique came from Southampton and then Nottingham Forest, Everton, Tottenham Hotspur, etc. *All completely English, as can be seen and appreciated in the famous stars of our football beginnings who were called Brown, Weiss, Lett, Ratcliff, Buchanan, Moore, Mack, Watson Hutton and so many others whose names are indistinguishable from football players in the Fair Albion.*(emphasis added)[4]

The *criollo* founding began in 1913 when Racing Club, without a single player of British origin, won the first division championship for the first time. From that moment the 'British' clubs declined in importance, and their players disappeared from the national teams. According to *El Gráfico*, this change became

possible because: 'when football began to spread, the stars with British names gave way to those with purely Latin, especially Italian and Spanish, surnames like García, Martínes, Ohaco, Olazar, Chiappe, Calomino, Laforia, Isola etc.'.[5]
It is interesting to note that *lo criollo* is defined as having a predominance of Spanish and Italian surnames. *Lo criollo* is founded through the sons of Latin immigrants. The sons of 'English' immigrants were never conceived of as *criollos*, and could not become *criollo* by playing football. How can these differences be explained? Purely genealogical reasons give way to reasons based on styles of play. These styles, in turn, are based on ethnic differences conceptualized as differences in character and in the form through which feelings and bodily movements are expressed. Once, from the middle of the first decade of the century, the sons of Latin immigrants have made football their own, *El Gráfico* explains:

> it is logical that as the years have gone by *all Anglo-Saxon influence in football has been disappearing, giving way to the less phlegmatic and more restless spirit of the Latin.* . . . Inspired in the same school as the British, the Latins soon began modifying the science of the game and fashioning one of their own, which is now widely recognized . . . it is different from the British in that it is less monochrome, less disciplined and methodical, because it does not sacrifice individualism for the honour of collective values. In British football a team is not important because of its separate members but because of the uniform action of the whole group. For that reason, British football is really powerful and has the regular and impulsive driving force of a machine, but it is monotonous because it is always uniformly the same. River Plate football, by contrast, does not sacrifice personal action entirely and makes more use of dribbling and generous personal effort, both in attack and defence, and for that reason is a more agile and attractive football. (emphasis added)[6]

In the texts of *El Gráfico*, 'Britishness' is identified with being phlegmatic, with discipline, method, the collective, force and physical power.[7] These virtues help to create a repetitive style like a 'machine'. The author recognizes that this style allows one to conceptualize British football as 'perfect' – that is, industrially perfect. The *criollo*, thanks to the Latin influence, is exactly the opposite: restless, individualistic, less disciplined, based on personal effort, agility and skill.[8] Owing to these characteristics, the author concludes, one can see River Plate football as being imperfect and, therefore, open to development once professionalism is established. Later, in the 1940s, the idea of the 'machine' is opposed to the idea of 'art' in the sense of artistic musical interpretation: Argentines play football with the touch and virtuosity with which artists play the piano or the violin. For that reason, a great football team is like an orchestra made up of great individuals.[9] The most typical characteristic of Argentine football would be the touch, which could be short, slow or quick according to the tactical requirements and the intensity of the game.

The notions of opposing British and *criollo* physical virtues would remain, but become modified. The English physical virtues are associated with 'force and physical power', while the virtues of the *criollos* are those of agility and virtuoso movements. The metaphor of the 'machine' as opposed to individual creativity is a constant in the Argentine football imaginary.[10] 'Britishness' is associated with the industrial, the *criollo* with the pre-industrial social system. Faced with the machine, or the repetitive, the typical *criollo* response would be the dribble. Dribbling, which would later be called the *gambeta* (a word derived from gauchesque literature which describes the running motion of an ostrich), is eminently individual and cannot be programmed; it is the opposite of the industrial, collective game of the machine.

By 1928 *lo criollo* had acquired its own characteristics. The 'founding' of the '*criollo* style' had to have a precise date, protagonist and event: this was fixed in 1913 when Racing Club deposed the champions Alumni, the major club power for many years and the representative not only of the British 'founding' of football but also of the 'British style'. One might conceive of a personal football-playing style as something totally imaginary, but in general style develops through comparison with other playing styles, as the texts quoted above indicate. However, in the fifteen years between 1913 and 1928 the transformation from the British to the *criollo* style was a gradual process. In this transformation the gaze of the 'distant other', the Europeans, and the 'near other', the Uruguayans, would be important.

El Gráfico argues at an early date that football will become the fundamental sport in Argentina, since it allows a nation to express itself through its national team.[11] This, they emphasize, could not happen through individualistic sports. To play for the national team requires the players to have a developed sense of the nation, since they have to put aside for a time their private interests as players from different clubs. At the same time the commentator observes that national differences, the differences between styles, can be seen more clearly in a game of football than in any other sporting competition.

The Uruguayan victory in the 1924 Olympic Games in Paris and the successful tour in 1925 of Boca Juniors, a first division side, throughout many European countries would confirm the existence of a 'River Plate' football different to European and English football. Until the Boca tour, the Argentines were more English than the Uruguayans. The Europeans contributed to this change through their own perception of the differences involved, through their definition of a 'River Plate' football played by both Argentines and Uruguayans. The visit in 1926 of Real Deportivo Español, a club from Barcelona, led to the development of a theory of *criollo* football as something distinct. Without a trace of modesty, *El Gráfico* wrote about the visit of the Catalan team:

> We feel that the quality of the football played in our country is very high – so high that we consider that only the football played by British professionals is superior to it – and it is thus within a very strict definition of technique that we respect the merits of our guests . . . and we conclude that football in Spain has made surprising progress that puts it almost on a par with our own. We say almost on a par since we are convinced that our own play is technically more proficient, quicker and more precise: it perhaps lacks effectiveness due to the individual actions of our great players, but the football that the Argentines, and by extension the Uruguayans, play is more beautiful, more artistic, and more precise because approach work to the opposition penalty area is done not through long passes upfield, which are over in an instant, but through a series of short, precise and collective actions: skilful dribbling and very delicate passes.[12]

In *El Gráfico*'s perception, the Argentine players' skill in dribbling is one of the fundamental aspects of *criollo* style. Dribbling is an individual, not a collective, activity. The collective style would therefore come to depend on the qualities of the best players, those with highly developed dribbling skills. Dribbling would be the factor that enabled the transition from the 'founding' to the development of a style. Dribbling gave style a form. The gaze of the 'others', the Europeans, accelerated this process. At the same time, the Argentine and Uruguayan players who began to appear in Europe in the 1920s were great dribblers.

The Masculine Imaginary of Freedom: the *pibe* and *potrero* as Symbols of a Style

In this context, and with this accepted view of a collective style, Borocotó developed the theory of '*criollo* dribbling' in 1928.[13] This theory is based on the personal qualities of the *pibes criollos* (the '*criollo* boys') and their relation to the social and spatial contexts which allowed them to develop these qualities.[14] In the first place, the *pibe criollo* realized when he saw how the English played, that this style of play left no room for improvisation, for 'imagination'. Secondly, the *pibes* played football spontaneously in the *potreros* (empty urban spaces of different sizes, usually small, with very uneven surfaces) without any teachers, unlike in England where, according to Borocotó, football was integral to the school system. In the *potreros*, with so many other players in such a confined space, the only way to keep control of the ball for some time was by becoming an inveterate dribbler. Thirdly, Borocotó recalls that Argentine football has become known throughout the world through dribbling, and that the players leaving Argentina to play in Europe are the best dribblers. He argues emphatically that until now Argentina has been known throughout the world for exporting its valuable frozen beef and its quality cereals, 'non-popular products' – in the sense that they come from the estates of the pampa-based landowning classes – and now it is important that it should become known for its 'popular products'. One of the high-quality 'popular products' is dribbling, and its exponents are the exquisite Argentine football players.

In this theory, clearly, the *pibe* (the boy), without any form of teaching, is the inventor of the *criollo* style in the *potrero*. This image of Borocotó emphasizes not only that there was an infantile beginning, as in every game, but also the importance of the freshness, spontaneity and freedom which are associated with childhood and usually lost with the advent of maturity and its resulting responsibilities. Borocotó proposes that Argentina should raise a monument in 'any walkway' to the inventor of dribbling. This monument would have to be:

> a *pibe* with a dirty face, a mane of hair rebelling against the comb; with intelligent, roving, trickster and persuasive eyes and a sparkling gaze that seems to hint at a picaresque laugh that does not quite manage to form on his mouth full of small teeth that might be worn down through eating 'yesterday's bread'. His trousers are a few roughly sewn patches. A vest with Argentine stripes, with a very low neck and with many holes eaten out by the invisible mice of use. A strip of material tied to the waist and crossing over the chest like a sash serves as braces. His knees covered with the scabs of wounds disinfected by fate; barefoot or with shoes whose holes in the toes suggest that they have been made through so much shooting. His stance must be characteristic, it must seem as if he is dribbling with a rag ball. That's important: the ball cannot be any other. A rag ball and preferably bound by an old sock. If this monument is raised one day, there will be many of us who will take off our hat to it, as we do in church.[15]

Chantecler, another of the great writers of *El Gráfico*, would also contribute to the development of a theory of *lo criollo*. Dribbling, an expression of the body, would become a manifestation of the essential *criollo* character. Dribbling expresses the wily and crafty *criollo* as opposed to the artless British.[16] To the central tenets of Borocotó's thesis – the pure imagination of the *pibe* and the congestion of players on the field – one more component is definitely added: wiliness. Without the existence of the qualities of craftiness and wiliness, dribbling could not emerge and there would be no space for creative improvisation. Chantecler maintains that the British are cold and mathematical and, for that reason, play a 'learned' football. By contrast, the River Plate footballers, who are warm and improvisers, play an 'inspired' football. At the same time, he draws a distinction between the River Plate countries: the Argentines play with the heart, they are faster and more aggressive; the Uruguayans play with the head, they are calmer and more romantic.[17] However, he states that despite these differences, one can talk of a River

Plate football. Historically, and because it has been played in the final of 'the Olympics, which is the world championship':

> River Plate football is the most highly regarded in the world and the intelligence put to the service of sport by a bunch of virile young men has done more for our underrated South America than all the diplomats put together. *Now they consider us and praise us: now we are something.* (emphasis added)[18]

Here we can see the same argument as Borocotó's: football allows Argentines to be 'seen' in the world, to be 'remembered' and, above all, to be 'praised'. The fact that Argentines and Uruguayans reached the final of the first true world championship, played in 1930, would confirm this theory of the supremacy of River Plate football.

Chantecler continued to develop his theory of *criollo* craftiness, and came to conclusions which were quite different to those of Borocotó. Borocotó, as we have seen, talked of the *criollo* influences of the pampa. In this sense, something unique and untransferable, the pampa and its culture, becomes naturalized: the contact of the sons of immigrants with nature (including the *potrero*) allows them to be transformed. Borocotó continued to adhere to his theory of the nature of the *criollo*. In a much later article, published in 1950, he argued that the style of play is derived from nature – it is a natural gift; a *criollo* player is born so, and cannot be made so.[19] Being born a *criollo* player depends on the air, the blood and the earth, and on the products of the land: food (barbecued meat and mate tea). The 'natural', the *criollo*, appears as a barrier against cultural transference, against the importation of European styles, which was the main point of discussion in 1950. Borocotó finds a symmetry between being and feeling: the natural has to do with feelings, not with reason.[20] From this perspective, the immigrants brought nothing of substance to help this transformation: their sons, born on the pampas, became *criollos*.

Chantecler, by contrast, would develop the theory of the 'melting-pot', of a continuous process of *criollo*-ization. A *criollo* is not born but made; he is the product of a tradition that is altered by individual contributions. In an article entitled '*Viveza criolla*, The Main Characteristic of our Game', he writes:

When our immigrant country receives in its breast the great migrations of all races, it has assimilated qualities from each of them and has amalgamated them, giving them its own mark. This is the new race that European intellectuals talk about when they come to study the psychology of our people and cannot find a clear-cut defining characteristic because we have something from each civilization without belonging typically to any of them.[21]

Chantecler considers that in the development of *criollo* 'craftiness', players from the British era, like Leonard, Charles Brown, Charles Buchanan and Arnold Watson Hutton, helped to change the coldness of the British. Chantecler would define in a very precise way 'the products of *viveza criolla*' in a dictionary of *criollo* football: the feint, the 'bicycle' (a special type of dribbling), standing on the ball, forcing a corner or a throw-in, letting the ball run on to a fellow player, the *chilena* (bicycle kick), a fake attack, the *túnel* (to do a nutmeg), the *marianela* and also what he calls 'disreputable cunning'.[22] *Viveza criolla* becomes not just a list of inventive play but, rather, a quality that developed historically. Behind each one of these above-mentioned plays there is a creator, a *criollo* player who developed it.

Borocotó tried to develop a theory of national football by cleansing it of British influence, transforming it into something purely *criollo*. His 'tour de force', his modification of the theory of nationalist writers of the time, is to have linked *criollo* football with immigration and the city. The immigrants nationalize football because they become *criollos*, inheriting the characteristics of the 'authentic *criollos*'. There is no melting-pot. Chantecler accepts immigration, but the story is a story of individual wiliness where there is even room for British craftiness. Being *criollo* is not permanent, it develops over time through a sort of successful melting-pot. What is common to both theories is to have divested the *criollo* of force and courage by making supreme virtues out of dribbling – that is, a play that avoids physical contact with the opposition – and cunning, the ability to hide one's true intentions by turning life (the game) into a series of continual pretences, making the opponent believe the opposite of one's true intentions, turning deceit into victory. I do not think that nationalists of the time would have easily accepted this theory.[23]

The pacific world of the melting-pot proposed by Chantecler is problematic, as is the essentialist world of Borocotó. The idea of the *criollo* as a mixture is also problematic. The European, the European style of play as opposed to the *criollo* style, would always be present in the collective Argentine imaginary. One has the impression while reading *El Gráfico* of that period when the *criollo* style develops, becomes consolidated and is reproduced because it is successful. Their teams triumph, as do the players who go to Europe. A tradition, in the sense of a 'school' to be copied, can more easily be constructed on the basis of victories and on the recognition of 'others' who are defined as relevant. *El Gráfico* obsessively asks European players visiting the country, European diplomats stationed in Buenos Aires, Argentine players playing in Europe and Argentine trainers who are successful abroad: 'How do they see us?'; 'What do they think in Europe about the *criollo* style and its players?'. *El Gráfico* would always insist – I think correctly – that there can be no tradition based on defeats. A football tradition requires not only historical continuity but also, essentially, victories. Thus with every significant defeat, what is called into question is *criollo* style. In those moments of crisis, an attempt was always made to import the 'European style'. There was never any thought of importing the 'Brazilian style', since it was felt that this would be impossible. This impossibility was implicitly associated with the African presence in Brazilian football. To import 'European' characteristics was not, perhaps, to change the direction of the cultural mixing; it was to recognize that, after all, Argentines descended from the immigrants brought in boats to the River Plate. By importing the European, the tactics and discipline of Europe, the Argentines recognized an important part of themselves, yet experienced this 'mixing' in a contradictory fashion. The contradictions between the *criollo* and the European appear with greater clarity as we focus on the descriptions of the individual virtues of certain players.

Individual Masculine Virtues

We have seen that the space for the masculine construction of football is the *potrero*. More precisely, however, *El Gráfico*, especially Borocotó, would associate the *potrero* with the *baldío*. A *baldío* is a patch of irregular ground in the city which has not yet been cemented over. The Argentine players originate from the *baldío* and the *potrero*. They do not come from the playgrounds of primary or secondary schools, or from the clubs – that is, the spaces controlled by teachers and trainers. The *baldío* is an exclusively male free space, where there are no women. As a consequence the great players are the pure products of this freedom that allows them to improvise and create, without the norms or rules imposed by experts or pedagogues.

As part of the reflection on *criollo* style, portraits of players are presented as archetypes of these values. For Borocotó, Carlos Peucelle, a mythical player from the 1930 World Cup team, was a paradigm. Borocotó entitles his article 'Carlos Peucelle, Citizen of the *baldío*', and writes:

> he is the personification of the *potrero*, the citizen of the *baldío*, he's the wasteground in motion . . . look at him in his stride, out there in the game, his freckled, smiling face, like a naughty child, and you will agree that he is harnessed to the *potrero* . . . *He has the* baldío *in his heart*. Observe him. Look at him as he stops in the centre of the field, with his stooping gait, whirling his arms and shaking his wavy locks that are at war with hair cream. See how he seems to be telling the boys in their striped jumpers pressed against the wire fencing: 'Wait for this to finish and we'll go off to the *potrero*'. (emphasis added)[24]

To be a citizen of the *baldío* is to be a 'free man' in a world of equals. The *baldío* is presented as the democratic truth: after the game, Peucelle can go off to the *potrero* with the spectators for a kickabout. Peucelle has the *baldío* in his heart because his body reveals it: he is casual, unkempt and inelegant. The *potrero* is ground, body, the material. The unity of heart and soul is celebrated.

Peucelle also looks like a *pibe* (a boy); he seems like a 'naughty child', and for that reason he has not lost his freshness. This paradox is significant: an important masculine virtue is to preserve, as far as possible, this pure, childlike style. Through his style, Peucelle transmits the idea that football is a game and, as such, can be fully enjoyed only when one has total freedom. In the democratic world of football, players are all *pibes*, they are all children, they are not tied to the authority of their parents and they have escaped from schools and clubs, from authority and hierarchies. The *baldío* is not a world of mature hard men, of duellists, it is not peopled by the gauchos of nationalist literature or the *compadritos* of tango lyrics, prepared to fight and, if necessary, to kill to defend their stained honour. The *baldío* is a world of naughty, wilful and crafty boys.

The *baldío/potrero* is systematically opposed to the blackboard and the school. Glossing a photograph of a 'football teacher', an English international player with a ball in one hand and a pointer in the other, in front of a blackboard containing a clear outline of a football field, Borocotó comments:

> Yes sir, yes sir; English football is more technical, more effective, whatever you like, it's all the same to me. Goals are the mark of a victory, but there are victories that are very ordinary and there are defeats which are clear triumphs. I recognize that discipline is very important, but please, old man, don't come at me with a blackboard. Only the English could think of football in terms of a blackboard. We have to make a fuss . . . there they have to go to school to learn football, here you have to play truant from school. There we have an international with a ball in one hand and a ruler in the other, in front of a blackboard; here we have a leather ball and lots of boys mucking in. There we find a honed, severe, conscious technique; here we have the *gambeta*, grace and improvisation. On the one hand the coldness of numbers and hypotenuses; on the other, the joy and emotion of the spectacle: . . . *Between the blackboard and the* baldío, *between those over there and those over here, I prefer our game a thousand times over, even if we lose, because in every melee there is a touch of grace, in every conquest there is a tiny grain of emotion.* (emphasis added)[25]

This opposition can be seen in the style of one of the great defenders of the time: Fernando 'El Marquéz' Paternoster. This great Racing Club player was in the national team for the World Cup in 1930, then triumphed in Brazil before starting a successful career as a trainer in Colombia. *El Gráfico*, in one of its many unsigned articles, describes him in the following way:

There is something English about his impeccable positional play, but he becomes South Americanized in the elasticity of his swerves, the lack of urgency in beating off the attack and above all, in *his elegant indolence.* . . . *It is enough to say that he is an Argentine to know that he has not studied theory, or learned from a blackboard.* . . . He *was one of the boys from the* potrero; *his lack of physical size showed him that he would have to get on through cunning; and effective cunning is nothing less than a sign of intelligence.* . . . he has a magician's art and speed which comes from both agility and an instant reading of the game. (emphasis added)[26]

This description of Paternoster makes explicit reference to his small physical size. In this relationship between physique and styles, Paternoster makes up for his size through ability and technique. The author of this article is merely confirming with this particular example the theory developed by Chantecler some years previously about the necessary relationship between physique and style. According to Chantecler, since the European style is stolid, slow, strong, disciplined and harmonious in its collective play, it needs 'big and strong men'. *Criollo* style, which is light, quick, delicate, with more individual skill and less collective play, needs 'small and weak' men.[27]

Paternoster is a clear example of a 'small and weak' man, an example of skill. Skill is contrasted to force. The exponents of the *criollo* style have to be 'weak but very skilful men'. That does not mean that there were no 'big and strong men' playing in Argentine football at that time or that, in the event, a team might not need this type of player. The player profiles published in *El Gráfico* would be structured around these differences. In 1940, *El Gráfico* published a series of profiles of players from the past. The author, Félix D. Frascara, is another great journalist of the magazine. His articles bear the suggestive title 'Cara y seca' ('Heads or Tails'). Let us look at some examples.

The first contrast is between Perinetti, from Racing Club, and Carricaberry, from San Lorenzo de Almagro:

[Perinetti] was always a cultivator of delicacy . . . he saw football as an entertainment but also as an artistic creation. A player of exceptional quality . . . in terms of football technique, he was one of the authentic expressions of classicism. . . . [Carricaberry is the] complete antithesis . . . Perinetti is the midfield man. Carricaberry is the goal man. Perinetti is the greatest expression of the classical. Carricaberry is the clear

exponent of the material. The former is gentleness, the latter, energy.
. . . Perinetti was a traditionalist and Carricaberry is an innovator. The
former was a work of art, the latter a productive machine. He disdained
the *gambeta* and the midfield in favour of the short burst and the shot
at goal . . . Carricaberry impresses. Perinetti gave delight. Heads or
tails.[28]

The dichotomies are clearly presented: the spiritual (traditional)
classical form is opposed to the material, gentleness to energy,
art to the machine, the *gambeta* to the shot, and delight to pure
impressiveness. Frascara concludes by linking these individual
qualities to the characteristics of the teams. Perinetti's Racing
Club would be known as 'the academy' (that is, tradition and
classicism), while Carricaberry's San Lorenzo de Almagro would
be known as the 'cyclone' (that is, force).

Frascara contrasted the styles of two centre forwards of the
1930s, Gabino Sosa and Bernabé 'The Fury' Ferreyra:

[Sosa] used every means to reach the goal with the greatest elegance . . .
he had a slow, delicate, elegant build-up, he used his brain for every
move . . . he worked 'by hand' . . . [Ferreira] always went abruptly for
goal without considering the means . . . he was always a destroyer . . .
quick, instinctive. He put all his rough physique behind every shot
. . . he worked 'like a machine'.[29]

Here the dichotomy between 'by hand' and 'by machine' appears
once again. However, the context is slightly different. 'Art'
previously referred to instinct, to creative improvisation. Sosa is
presented as cerebral, as an architect, as a true artisan who
gradually develops his work. He is not necessarily an artist but,
rather, an artisan, fine and delicate, cerebral and thoughtful.
Ferreyra is instinctive in the use of his body and, in this sense, is
a destroyer. The opposition between brain and body, as if the
brain were not part of the muscular activity, appears irreconcil-
able. In some way, the fundamental opposition between skill and
force has been transformed into an opposition between brain and
body.

The following comparison is between two centre halves:
Zumelsu of Racing Club and Monti from San Lorenzo de
Almagro. It is important to remember that for the 1930 World
Cup team the choice for that position was between these two
players and that Monti was finally selected. We read:

[Zumelsu was] an aristocrat . . . he was one of the most spiritual . . . noble . . . elegant and apparently indolent of players. He himself did not reject the title of 'layabout' . . . a neat sidestep, a short passer, a beautiful action, pure intelligence . . . [whilst Monti was a] worker, a tank, forceful, nervous, he seemed sculpted out of stone . . . a true generator of energies . . . a tireless fighter, a picture of a muscular athlete, strong in bitter struggles. His arena was the fight . . . he was a battler.[30]

In this comparison there is a new contrast between the aristocrat and the worker. Zumelsu is an aristocrat because he is spiritual, elegant, does not work, and is delicate and refined. Monti, by contrast, is a worker because he uses his body and physical strength, he generates energy, he is well built, a great battler who relishes the fight. Zumelsu, the aristocrat, lives to enjoy himself while Monti, the worker, is made for the battle.

What is paradoxical about these outlines is their explicit acceptance of different types of players, each with their own style, physique and masculine virtues. Furthermore, in Argentine football of the period, as now, the two types could coexist in teams, and their divergent qualities did not hinder the public's identification with them. These portraits and their conclusions are quite clear: one's own style, the *criollo* way of playing, does not require force to assert itself. Peucelle, Paternoster, Sosa and Zumelsu appear as representatives of a different way of playing. Hence, identity is constructed through a double relationship: it is defined initially by distant 'others' (the British) and later by those closer to home. Through this double construction, the near 'others' resemble the more distant.

By Way of Conclusion

El Gráfico, as I pointed out above, was one of a cluster of modern magazines in Argentina at the time which disseminated ideas about the importance of living an orderly, healthy, open-air and disciplined life.[31] However, the narrative of Argentine football that developed in the first decade after its foundation, and the masculine virtues associated with it, acquire a clearly anti-modern tone. In contrast to the values and language of technocracy, expressed in the importance of 'work', the 'machine', 'science', and the 'collective game', the narrative of *El Gráfico* proposed 'indolence', 'art', 'intuition' and 'individualism'. These values were those that would define a national style and a *criollo* tradition. Thus, the culture of football expressed in *El Gráfico* derives to a large extent from the conflict between these modern and anti-modern aspects. The opposition and contrast to the 'British' or 'English' style of play must be seen from this perspective.

El Gráfico constructs the image of masculinity and masculine virtues through an exaltation of skill, cunning, individual creativity, artistic feeling and improvisation. The ideal football player, the faithful representative of the nation, appears to be quite removed from the dominant masculine models in the literature of the period. For cultured writers like Lugones or Borges, the dominant masculine models would be associated with the figures of the gaucho and the urban *compadrito*, in which courage, bravery and physical strength are decisive.[32] There are players, however, who might have these characteristics but who, according to the narrative of *El Gráfico*, are not central to the definition of a national style. In the narrative of the magazine, football is not considered a necessary rite of passage for an adolescent to become a true man. Quite the reverse: the privileged image of the ideal player is the *pibe*: the authentic Argentine player will never stop being a child. The 'masculinity' imagined in football does not have the force of traditional masculinity associated with paternal responsibility, the protection of the family, discipline of the body, seriousness and reliability in work associated with nationalism as an ideology.[33] Football allows a man to go on playing and remain a *pibe*. The 'purity' of the football player is not associated with the purity of the warrior and the emphasis on youth, virility and sacrifice.[34] One could say that the imaginary world of football reflects the power of freedom and creativity in the face of discipline, order and hierarchy. If men become men through discipline and a sense of responsibility inculcated in schools and military barracks, then football and the image of the *potrero* appear as counterpoint. The masculine ideal of football is the masculinity of those who never stop being children, who represent improvisation and play, and are in opposition to responsible men. The masculine styles in *El Gráfico* are based on compounding the evident contradiction between elegance and force. The writers of *El Gráfico* recognize the existence and importance of physical force in a team but argue that this should not be praised.

It is interesting to mention, by way of contrast, that in the same period the cultured Argentine nationalist writers were insisting on the opposite: on the importance of force and the heroic sense of life (the cult of physical courage) as purifying elements that allow the pride, the dignity and the moral reliability of men to be maintained.[35] In this model of masculinity, these virtues are associated with Catholic-based spirituality. The importance of physical-muscular power and Christian spiritual power are clearly represented in the exemplary role of the paterfamilias.

I hope I have shown that through these representations we can see not only the appearance of different images of masculinity but also all the ambiguity and conceptual vagueness of the idea of nation. In this narrative of football, what is *criollo* is conceived not only as excluding the British, but also as creating an exclusive masculine space from which women are excluded. To establish and, above all, to administer differences and exclusions is a function of the power of the masculine imagery. In the face of censorship, violence and economic pressure, we find constructed a parallel world of representations which supplement the ambivalences and lack of precise origins of an 'essence'. The imagery of Argentine football is a place where we can find these parallel masculine representations.

Translated by John King

Notes

A longer and more ambitiously comparative version of this essay was presented at the 48th World Congress of Americanists, Stockholm–Uppsala, 4–9 July 1994. The observations and critical comments of Kristi Anne Stølen and Marit Melhuus helped me to concentrate my arguments and avoid repetitions. By suggesting the title of the article to me, Kristi Anne Stølen helped me to avoid unmanageable comparisons.

1. A. Cornwall and N. Lindisfarne, 'Dislocating Masculinity: Gender, Power and Anthropology', in A. Cornwall and N. Lindisfarne, eds, *Dislocating Masculinity: Comparative Ethnographies*, London 1994, p. 12.

2. See E.P. Archetti, 'Place et fonctions du comique et (ou) tragique dans le "discours" des "supporters" du football argentin', in J. Ardoino and J-M. Brohm, eds, *Anthropologie du Sport. Perspectives Critiques*, Paris 1991; 'Argentinian Football: A Ritual of Violence?', *The International Journal of the History of Sport*, vol. 9, no. 2, 1992; 'Masculinity and Football: The Formation of National Identity in Argentina', in R. Giulianotti and J. Williams, eds, *Game without Frontiers: Football, Identity and Modernity*, Aldershot 1994; and E.P. Archetti and A. Romero, 'Violence and Death in Argentinian Football', in R. Giulianotti, N. Bonney and M. Hepworth, eds, *Football, Violence and Social Identity*, London 1994.

3. *El Gráfico* (EG), no. 394, 1927, p. 18.

4. EG, no. 470, 1928, p. 15.

5. Ibid.

6. Ibid.

7. It is important to point out that although in terms of style the relevant 'other' is the 'British' style, *El Gráfico* knows that one cannot play against the British but only against the national sides of Wales, Scotland, England and Northern Ireland. From the beginning of the history of Argentine football, the main enemy, in the sense of an obstacle to be overcome before reaching maturity and a supposed universal recognition, is England. Not only had she invented modern football and its rules, but her players were professionals and, for that reason, did not mix with the amateurs at the Olympic Games. On innumerable occasions, *El Gráfico* not only compared different styles but also insisted on the need to follow the same road as the English and professionalize national football. This would come about only in 1931, with the creation of the professional league. For decades, Argentines would dream of a victory over England. Reading *El Gráfico*, one always gets the impression that victories over other teams were less important.

8. Applying the term '*criollo* foundation' to a game introduced by the sons of first-generation immigrants would be considered an insult by the nationalist writers of the time. The nationalists were against the immigrants because they contaminated the 'national essence' and 'sullied the country' (see D. Rock, *La Argentina Autoritaria. Los Nacionalistas, su Historia y su Influencia en la Vida Pública*, Buenos Aires 1993, pp. 41–2). In the world of football, the immigrants and their creativity allowed the national style to appear, strengthen and be reproduced over time. National identity in football belongs to the sons of immigrants; it is a cultural form created on the margins of the nationalists' *criollismo*. The narrative of *El Gráfico* is a homage to the sons of foreigners excluding, explicitly, the sons

of the British. The exclusion of the sons of the British can be seen as a concession on the part of the writers of *El Gráfico* to the nationalists' 'anti-British imperialism'. I think, however, that *El Gráfico* also contributed in its way to defining 'Britishness' as the relevant 'other' for the Argentines in the field of sport. In this way, the magazine would defend Argentine players leaving to play abroad, even playing for national teams where they would be defined as 'native' (Italy made flagrant use of this by including four Argentine players in the winning World Cup team of 1934). These players would be considered as ambassadors of *criollo* football. *El Gráfico* writes:

> We must not be egotistical. Orsi, Cesarini, Stábile and all those crossing frontiers in search of better horizons, on the way to countries that need them, should be seen in the way that old Spain watched its Advance Guard leave. They leave to conquer other lands. The country is now a little small for us and a good football lesson given on one of our pitches no longer dazzles anyone. For many years we've held the Chair in dribbling and in scoring goals. For that reason, it is necessary to go outside, the good players that do us proud abroad are working patriotically. Stábile goes to Italy, not to defend football in the peninsula, but to defend *criollo* football, since he is a *criollo* player. (no. 589, 1930, p. 37)

9. EG, no. 1124, 1941, p. 18.
10. Kanitkar argues that the Imperial British created the image of the 'sporting boy'. The games recommended were team sports which required qualities of leadership, working together and loyalty. To be part of a team was conceived as being part of a perfect machine (H. Kanitkar, '"Real True Boys"; Moulding the Cadets of Imperialism', in Cornwall and Lindisfarne [eds] pp. 186–7).
11. EG, no. 190, 1923, p. 4.
12. EG, no. 366, 1926, p. 17.
13. Borocotó became one of the most influential sports journalists in Argentina. Born in 1902 in Montevideo, Uruguay, he joined *El Gráfico* in 1927 and retired, as managing editor, in 1955. From 1927, he was active as a radio journalist. He was author of many bestsellers, and also had success in the film world. He wrote the script of one of the classics of Argentine cinema, *Pelota de Trapo* (Rag Ball), made in 1948 (see G. Cechetto, Buenos Aires 1993, Taller Escuela Agencia – mimeo). The film describes with 'spontaneity and lyricism the world of children and their passion for football' (C. Maranghello, 'La Pantalla y el Estado', in Centro Editor de América Latina, *Historia del Cine Argentino*, Buenos Aires 1984, p. 102).
14. EG, no. 480, 1928.
15. Ibid. p. 11.
16. EG, no. 467, 1928, p. 16.

17. Ibid.
18. Ibid.
19. EG, no. 1626, 1950, p. 46.
20. Ibid.
21. EG, no. 652, 1932, p. 21.
22. EG, nos 652 and 653, 1932.
23. This argument is fully developed in E.P. Archetti, 'Estilo y Virtudes Masculinas en *El Gráfico*: La Creación del Imaginario del Fútbol Argentino', *Desarrollo Económico*, vol. 35, no. 139, 1995.
24. EG, no. 716, 1933, p. 4.
25. EG, no. 614, 1931, p. 6. This is a clear example of the way in which *El Gráfico* deals with the 'British' and the 'English'. The 'British tradition' is generic, and the players, albeit representatives of this tradition, have different nationalities. In this case, the international player in the photo is English.
26. EG, no. 633, 1931, p. 16.
27. EG, no. 467, 1928, p. 21.
28. EG, no. 1105, 1940, p. 35.
29. EG, no. 1107, 1940, p. 4.
30. Ibid., p. 50.
31. On the importance of the press in the creation of national styles and sporting events, see J.S. Leite Lopes and J-P. Faguer, 'L'Invention du style brésilien. Sport, journalisme et politique au Brésil', *Actes de la Recherche en Sciences Sociales*, no. 103, 1994, pp. 27–35 and M. Oriard, *Reading Football: How the Popular Press Created an American Spectacle*, Chapel Hill, NC 1993.
32. See L. Lugones, *El Payador*, Buenos Aires 1916; J.L. Borges, *El Tamaño de mi Esperanza*, Buenos Aires 1993 (1926) and *El Idioma de los Argentinos*, Buenos Aires 1994 (1928); and S. Bullrich and J.L. Borges, eds, *El Compadrito*, Buenos Aires 1945.
33. See G.L. Mosse, *Nationalism and Sexuality*, Madison, WI 1986.
34. Ibid., p. 117.
35. See M. Navarro Gerassi, *Los Nacionalistas*, Buenos Aires 1969, p. 43; Rock, p. 18; C. Ibarguren, *La Inquietud de esta Hora*, Buenos Aires 1934, p. 139 and *Respuestas a un Cuestionario acerca del Nacionalismo. 1930–1945*, Buenos Aires 1971, p. 31.

3

Pacharacas, *Putas* and *Chicas de su casa*: Labelling, Femininity and Men's Sexual Selves in Lima, Peru

Lorraine Nencel

This essay is a result of a study I am completing on the meanings of gender for female prostitutes who live in Lima, Peru. Since the outset of this project it has been assumed that prostitution is an expression of male sexuality. In Lima, going to the prostitutes is a commonly used sexual alternative which crosses class, age and ethnic boundaries. For generations, prostitution has served as a space for sexual initiation.[1] The open or – in some cases – tacit acceptance that an adolescent or an adult will go to a prostitute is perhaps a characteristic that does not belong solely to the Limanian setting, but is none the less essential for its understanding. To understand the cultural specificity of prostitution, therefore, it is fundamental to unravel the construct of male sexuality.

The motivation to analyse male sexuality has led me to the exploration of a broader, more profound domain: the theoretical representation of male sexuality and its implications for the notion of power. I am concerned here with Latin American theories concerning *machismo*, and the client's image in prostitution studies. These theories have contributed to the development of a Latin American feminist thought which resounds in feminist activists' political agendas. Within this constellation of theories, strategies and objectives aimed at changing women's subordinate position, men are portrayed as a homogeneous category. However, as Andrea Cornwall and Nancy Lindisfarne state: 'It is ironic that the logic of feminism as a political position has often required the notion of "men" as a single, oppositional category.'[2] The positioning of men as an oppositional, homogeneous category obstructs the construction of knowledge concerning the notions of sexuality, masculinity and power.

In Latin America, the symbolic representation of masculinity and male sexuality merge in the concept of *machismo*. *Machismo* is an all-embracing concept determining women's subordination. It is often assumed to be synonymous with male dominance; the site where gender and sexual oppression conflate. Generally, it is defined by describing attributes of men's attitudes or behaviour which make them *macho*. Evelyn Stevens considers *machismo* to be a cult of virility: 'The chief characteristics of this cult are exaggerated aggressiveness and intransigence in male-to-male interpersonal relationships and arrogance and sexual aggression in male-to-female relationships.'[3] The fact that gender and sexuality are intrinsically related in the concept of *machismo* need not be a theoretical obstruction. Judith Ennew points out that 'the structure of gender differentiation in Peru [is] a structure which has a more explicitly sexual rationale than may be observed in many other societies'.[4] Thus, it is feasible that sexuality and gender are far more entwined in Latin America than, for example, in Western Europe. However, this does not suggest that the concepts are interchangeable; each possesses its own dynamics. Since no distinctions between the two concepts have been made, it is almost impossible to capture how sexuality and masculinity feed into each other.

Very often it is assumed that the attitudes and behaviour of the *macho* are reflected in a society's structural level as institutional traits. Ana Silvia Monzón states: 'although violence is the most evident expression of *machismo*, there are a series of subtle attitudes which subordinate women and assign them a secondary status, which also originate from "male superiority" and have caused more harm to women than physical abuse'.[5] Monzón continues by showing how *machismo* is manifested in different institutions such as education, health, work and legislation. Carmen Lugo analyses *machismo* in terms of violence, and shows how it affects women and minority groups in Mexico.[6] The category *machismo* includes all 'healthy' heterosexual men. These men are allotted the entire panoply of power, and women and minorities have to do without. The analysis of power is straitjacketed into discovering the mechanisms of male dominance. Ethnic, class and sexual differences between men are barely recognizable. Moreover, there is no space to explore how men's subjective experiences inform the construction of these concepts.[7]

A similar tendency is observable in writings on prostitution. In Peru, there are two feminist stances on prostitution: those who uphold the 'sexual slavery' theory, and those who are uncertain whether this explanatory model is satisfactory but are as yet unable to offer an alternative. In the sexual slavery theory, prostitution is considered to be the most extreme form of women's subordination in patriarchal society. When and if men are mentioned, or their sexual behaviour is analysed, this is normally done in a fashion which reproduces the assumptions of the *machismo* model. An excerpt from an editorial by a Peruvian women's group which works with prostitutes[8] and proposes the abolition of prostitution illustrates this excellently:

> Prostitution is a logical consequence in a society that reduces women's bodies to an object and commercializes women's bodies. Prostitution is a logical consequence of a society that reduces women's bodies to merchandise and where men consider sex a right. As long as society instrumentalizes the woman as a sexual object, as long as men consider sex a form of merchandise acquired by force, by money or by conquest, there will always be prostitution in our society.[9]

Prostitution is placed on an equal footing with rape, abuse, and sexual violence in general. This constructs the image that all men who go to prostitutes are sexually violent and capable of abusing women in other areas of their lives. Another example is encountered in a study of prostitution in the Dominican Republic. The authors devote a chapter to the client, and label male sexuality *la miseria sexual masculina* (masculine sexual misery). Men who go to prostitutes convert them 'into one huge vulva which complacently opens in waiting for their penises. This helps them erase the faces, bodies and names. . . . Her function is to give pleasure (if you can call this sexual misery pleasure), and to achieve this she needs only three instruments which can make him ejaculate: vagina, hands and mouth.'[10]

Once again, male sexuality unequivocally expresses the oppression–subordination relationship. The portrayal of male sexuality in this theoretical current as unchanging and predetermined echoes – albeit for different motives – the essentialist notion of male sexuality in the mainstream discourse of prostitution, which perceives it as a necessary evil.[11] How can this circle of reasoning, which continually reproduces its own assumptions, be broken? Susan Edwards proposes a solution after she has analysed different prostitution discourses. She concludes:

> It is men that we need to study, to understand their desire for power, for sexual mastery. We need to address and confront why it is that men are orgasming [sic] to visual images of women's subordination, harm and abuse in pornography, and also to their use and subordination and insult in prostitution. We need to examine the social construction of male sexual arousal and the channelling of sexual arousal into a context of abuse and harm in which women are degraded.[12]

Although we tend to agree on the urgency for more research, collaboration stops when male sexuality is predefined as a complex but none the less fixed notion. Does the recognition that prostitution is a male prerogative, and thus a symbol of male dominance, give us the right to assume that all men experience this relationship in the same way? Do these experiences figure uniformly in men's construction of their sexual selves and how they act out relations of power? Is it sufficient to assume that all men use prostitutes' services for the same reason? Perhaps questions such as why, when and why not are even more important. These are just a sample of the innumerable questions which can be posed when the concepts of sexuality and gender are perceived as separate, plural, unfixed and changing. This essay is founded on this premiss.

Despite the grip that feminist thought has in the representation of masculinity/sexuality, there are signs that this is slackening. A significant number of studies are appearing which have cut the notions of masculinity and male sexuality loose from their automatically assumed position in the oppression model without losing sight of the relations of power which are produced and enacted in their construction.[13] This has revealed the multiplicity of meanings given to the constructs of masculinity and sexuality, and how they shift, contradict and coexist. Oscar Ugarteche deconstructs the concept of sexuality in the Peruvian context. He illustrates how the introduction of a repressive sexuality brought by the Spaniards, which exalted female virginity and monogamy, and prohibited homosexuality, transformed the extremely liberal pre-Hispanic notion of sexuality. He shows that one of the idiosyncrasies that characterizes the contemporary notion of sexuality – namely that everything is possible in terms of sexuality as long as it is not talked about – can be traced back to this historical period of transformation.[14] In Richard Parker's study on sexual culture in contemporary Brazil, sexual experience is perceived:

> less in a singular than in the plural, and it is thus less accurate to speak of a single, unified system of sexual meanings in contemporary Brazilian culture than to think in terms of multiple subsystems, recurring yet often disparate patterns, conflicting and sometimes even contradictory, logics that have somehow managed to intertwine and interpenetrate within the fabric of social life.[15]

Eduardo Archetti's work on Argentinian football analyses football matches as rituals in which sexual symbols of homosexuality are used to affirm the notion of masculinity.[16] These studies have severed the symbiotic relationship between gender and sexuality, making it possible to study them separately. Moreover, with their rich ethnographic analyses they contest the fixed notion of masculinity and sexuality, and the implications of these categories in the construction of power.

I intend to contribute to the growing body of anthropological literature which explores sexuality by questioning its meanings in a specific context on the basis of interviews with twenty-one men by my male assistant. The majority of the respondents belong to the middle class – a multifarious category in the Limanian context. All of them identified themselves as heterosexuals.

The respondents' recollections of their affective and sexual lives relate complex processes involved in the construction of their sexual selves. The concept of the sexual self is not assumed in advance to be 'unified, rational, coherent, bounded'; instead it is perceived as plural and as the 'potential sites for the play of multiple discourses and shifting, multiple subject-positions'.[17] The sexual self is thus a heterogeneous construct which can potentially make apparent the differences that exist between men, and the different meanings of sexuality moulded either in specific situations or through the course of time.

The construction of the sexual self is approached by analysing sexual meanings and labels produced in the continual interaction between discourse and subjectivity. The relationship between discourse and subjectivity is not antagonistic. Sexual meanings produced in this process coexist. Within these configurations, power relations become as fluid and situational as the notion of the sexual self.

The interviews demonstrate the preponderant influence of the discourse of male sexuality in the construction of men's sexual selves. The most salient characteristics of this sexual discourse are the relational construct of gender which positions men and women oppositionally, and the singular, essentialist concept of sexuality in which sexual desire is imagined to be virtually instinctual and, therefore, uncontrollable. The interviews reproduce moments in which the respondents affirm their sexual identities by embodying discursive notions. This process of affirmation is made even more explicit because of the underlying methodology which guided the interview process.[18] The respondents were asked to relate experiences of their affective and sexual lives. They selected freely from their memories to construct their story, and often chose to emphasize certain recollections, or used words which reproduced notions encountered in the discourse. Additionally, their accounts were organized along lines which made a distinction between affective relationships and sexual experiences. Their recollections of their sexual experiences expressed their pronounced desire to achieve sexual satisfaction by having intercourse. More often than not, they sought to quench their sexual thirst with women whom they considered to be sexual outlets. In these encounters sexual desire embodied a virtually instinctual quality. In their relationships with their girlfriends, sexual desire lost this quality. Their accounts did not emphasize their need to obtain sexual satisfaction; rather, sexual desire was experienced as one of the many emotions they felt in their relationship. This distinction, which I call the fragmentation of sexual desire, is an expression of the belief that sexuality is virtually instinctual. As we shall see below, men's propensity to experience their sexuality distinctly with different types of women is one of the particularities embedded in the construction of their sexual selves, and it also opens these apparently constrictive notions to multiple interpretations. Subjectivity, which is the other significant concept in this analysis, is a dimension which is rooted in the individual's circumstances and experiences, and his interpretations of them. It is through subjective experiences that discursive notions are reworked, rejected, or converge with sexual meanings that emerge from the individual's personal history. The analysis of subjectivity – of how men experience their sexuality – provides the space required to explore difference, and subsequently challenge the all-too-familiar, but none the less oversimplified, image of male sexuality.

First I explore the sexual language used in the Limanian lexicon of *jerga* (slang) which contains the strongest discursive representations. Then I go on to related terrain: the labels given to femininity. The oppositional, bounded discursive categories of femininity divide women into two groups: the good woman (the mother) and the bad woman the (whore). In practice, however, men create more than two categories. The labels given to femininity are symbols for men's projections of their sexual desires and intentions, and are in turn expressions of power. This section is followed by an analysis of men's experiences with prostitution. Prostitution is the location which simultaneously expresses the heterogeneous nature of male sexuality and stands for the most extreme representation of the essentialist notion of sexual desire. In its entirety, this essay attempts to show that the analysis of sexual meanings produced between discourse and subjectivity provides tools for understanding the complexities involved in the construction of men's sexual selves, and how this informs the relations of power between men and women.

Talking Sexuality

At a certain point in an adolescent's life, football, hanging around with the boys on the street corner and being mischievous are not the only meaningful things. Suddenly, or perhaps slowly but surely, the adolescent becomes aware of girls and sex. At this age – approximately eleven to thirteen – sex is visual, taking on forms such as porno magazines, or verbal. Conversations with mates about breasts, legs, penises and masturbation are the order of the day.

When a boy starts to like a girl and summons up enough courage to *declararse* (to declare himself), if she accepts they are boyfriend and girlfriend. They hold hands, kiss, and perhaps there is an occasional caress. They go out together, but he will not make any bold sexual advances. If it turns into a lasting relationship, they may eventually make love. In the meantime his sexual desire is growing, and in many of the testimonies the respondents told how they ended up at a brothel for their first sexual experience. It is as if their sexuality is in the fast lane, while they are limited by all the boundaries which accompany having a proper girlfriend. Thus sexual outlets are sought outside the relationship, and frequently found in encounters with other women. It is in this process that certain words, expressions or metaphors begin to take on sexual meanings. Men develop different attitudes, behaviours and ways of talking which make distinctions between women, and also between women and men.

The underlying essence of sexuality in Lima is expressed as a dualism. The words which refer to sexual encounters and practices distinguish different sexualities for men and for women. Men's descriptions of their sexual encounters have connotations of conquest, possession and sexual assertiveness. A verb such as *agarrar* (to seize, take or grab) is used to describe the act of touching a part of a woman's body – *me agarré su teta* (I grabbed her tit) – or as a metaphor which implies sexually possessing a woman – *agarré a todas* (I grabbed all of them). *Meter* (to put) is also used to denote the action of touching, but carries the connotations of shove or push – *metí mi mano en su blusa* (I shoved my hand in her blouse). It is also used to describe penetration. Another word with subtler connotations is *chapar*. *Chapar* can be defined as to catch or be caught. In sexual language *chapar* means to kiss. Although it is sometimes used synonymously for *besar*, a distinction is usually made. It refers to a kiss which is stolen in a situation – for example, a party.

The words interchangeably used to mean sexual intercourse convert sexual intercourse into a male performance. The verbs *comer, dar, planchar, montar, tirar, cachar, culear* signify making love. *Comer* (to eat), *dar* (to give), *planchar* (to iron or press), *montar* (to mount – generally used in reference to mounting a horse or a bicycle), *tirar* (to throw) are verbs which indicate an action which can be performed by both sexes. In sexual language, the man is the initiator of the action, and what was the inanimate object has now been transformed into the woman. *Cachar* and *culear* are verbs which come closest to the English 'fuck' or 'screw'. They are used quite commonly to describe coitus. On rare occasions the term *hacer el amor* (to make love) is used, usually in relation to a partner.

The oppositional character of male and female sexuality is constructed by emphasizing men's actions. Women are the receivers, the direct objects, implicitly conveying a notion of passivity. Underlying these expressions is a reified notion of sexuality which is implied in other expressions that characterize male and female sexuality.

Men's sexual desire is often described in terms of a functioning machine. A man can feel *cargado sexualmente* (sexually loaded) and need to *descargar* (unload). As one of the respondents stated, '*Necesito estar descargado porque hace una presión psicológica*' (I need to unload because it [*being loaded*] causes psychological pressure). His desire can also be warmed up, implying sexual arousal without necessarily terminating in coitus – *calentar las pelotas* (to warm up the balls). Male sexual desire is portrayed in terms that imply an impending danger if it remains unsatisfied. What happens to a machine if it overloads or overheats? It is likely to explode. Thus, male sexuality can be controlled only with regular maintenance: frequent sexual intercourse.

Women appear in this configuration as vehicles for obtaining sexual satisfaction. Sexual encounters acquire an aura of premeditation which is aimed at achieving sexual satisfaction. To get to a woman's sexuality and obtain sexual satisfaction, she has to be worked – *trabajarla*. If she is worked successfully, she can *caer facilmente* (fall easily) or *aflojar* or *soltar* (loosen up or let go). These expressions evoke an image of men who manipulate women to get them to let go of what they want, namely their 'sexual favours'.

Many of the terms are used frequently in anecdotes about parties. At certain stages of men's life cycles a party can be seen as a metaphor for a sexual battlefield in which men, especially in adolescence, chalk up sexual experience. A woman or various women are sought out to see how far they will go. As one of the respondents related about his early adolescent experiences at parties:

'They were my field of experimentation. Sexually no. . . . I used them to *calentar las pelotas* ['warm up my balls'] . . . *me las chapaba* [I kissed them] and . . . haven't I told you already that I wasn't looking for the opportunity to *culear* [to fuck]? I went out with them once or twice, *me las chapaba* [I kissed them], made my conquest and then I said so long.' (Lucho, 31, married)

In sexual language the verb *mandar* which means command or order, takes on further connotations regarding men's sexual role. *Mandar* implies seduce or conquer, making a man who is a successful seducer a *mandado*. If he does not exhibit behaviour which adheres to this image, he runs the risk of being called a *quedado* (derived from the verb *quedar*, to remain or stay behind) – a man who has not mastered the art of seduction, and therefore has not been able to conquer many women.

In a young man's early sexual experiences, when his own sexual satisfaction is his only objective, a woman who seduces becomes an object of pleasure. Since women's 'sexual favours' are seen as something which has to be obtained, a female seducer is offering herself and transgressing the appropriate behaviour outlined for women. In these situations the reaction of many of the respondents was to take what was being offered regardless of whether he was interested in the woman. One respondent recounted the first time he had sexual intercourse with a girl at a party at the age of fourteen. He was asked:

'Who seduced whom, you or her? [*Quién se mandó, tú o ella?*]'

'I think it was simultaneous, but I believe that I began, because it was also the period of *la pendejada* [bullshitting around]. Well, I mean, if you're at a party and it's like "OK what can I do to this girl?", you put your hand in [*le metes la mano*], you kiss her neck and then you begin to kiss her [*chaparla*], and everything. Well, I was playing around when I saw that she was responding and responding, so I picked her up. I felt scared. Scared because I did it at a party. She had more experience than I. How did I feel? On the one hand, it made me feel bad because they always told me that I should *mandar*. It's the man who should seduce. On the other hand, it gave me a certain amount of confidence because in some way she helped me. It was satisfactory. I didn't take the relationship any further, during this period I was seeing another girl.' (Hugo, 29, single)

In retelling his story, Hugo reshaped the incident to portray himself as the one in control. The fact that the encounter began out of mutual interest loses significance because the woman agreed to go further, transforming her sexual desire into an offer. The discomfort he felt in not being able to live up to her expectations subsided because he realized that going to bed with an experienced young woman was functional. She taught him the basics of making love, and through this one-off experience he began his 'sexual career'. Although he rejected the idea of a relationship, this should not automatically be interpreted as a rejection because the woman was not a virgin. Going to bed with a virgin is considered delightful, but virginity is a scarce and prized possession, and it is not as decisive a selection criterion as the sexual discourse leads us to believe. Asked his opinion of female virginity, one respondent stated:

'It is one of the most beautiful things that can happen, that a woman comes to you as a virgin, but this is really difficult to accomplish. I do respect women who have had previous sexual experiences.' (Eduardo, 22, single)

Thus, if having been sexually active is not a distinction which makes one woman different from another, then what is? It is whether they adhere to the expected behaviour which is associated with the label they are given. Whether a woman's sexual experience is perceived as something to be taken advantage of is greatly dependent on the man's intentions. If he is interested in the woman as a partner, his approach to the situation would be different from what it would be if he was just out for a good time. Hence, rather than reflecting a woman's perceptions of her gender identity and her expectations, the labels given to women are male projections.

Labelling Women

In sexual language the oversimplified dichotomy of mother/ whore gives way to three different types of woman: the potential partner or spouse; the one who provides pleasure and is excluded *de facto* as a potential candidate for a relationship; and, lastly, the prostitute. There are different labels which designate women as belonging to a specific group.

A widely used term for a (potential) girlfriend is *chica de su casa* (a girl of her house). The term *chica de su casa* is a commonly agreed upon label, but other words are used that do not share this recognition. Percy, for example, called potential partners *amigas cariñosas* (affectionate friends); he described them thus:

'Normally they are *chicas de su casa*, they work, study, they make something of their life, they are people who have a life, their world, their family.' (Percy, 30, single)

Lucho, whom we have already met, called them *mujeres comunes* (ordinary women). He described their behaviour as follows:

'She's simply a girl leading the life of an adolescent. At a party she's looking to enjoy herself, dance, *planchar*, or maybe to find a possible boyfriend.'

As we saw above, the apparent contradiction that this woman is sexually active need not present a problem. She belongs to the category of potential partners. Her sexual desires are placed in this context. Thus she does not exceed the boundaries of the ascribed behaviour for her group of peers. The respondents offered no criteria to explain why a woman is considered a part of this group, yet what makes a woman identifiable as a potential partner is a configuration of different subjective criteria: appearance, social class, ethnicity, sensations and emotions. Accompanying this label is a code of proper behaviour which might not be spoken about openly but is tacitly recognized by all the individuals involved. Lucho talks about his experiences with *mujeres comunes*:

'I deceived them, I could deceive them because I could make them
believe that we were going to have a relationship and that I loved them
and that we were going to develop something firm, stable and coherent
. . . although you know deep down that the relationship isn't going to
go anywhere.'

Perhaps Lucho is an exception, and other men would not
think of manipulating the situation to such an extreme. In the
interview, he reflects upon his behaviour as corresponding to a
certain stage in his sexual development, implying that he
feels that it has changed since then. Nevertheless, his strategic
behaviour shows that he was aware that certain expectations
and behaviour belonged to this category.

Most men talked about their relationship with their partners
as being an extremely positive experience, the locus consolidat-
ing different needs and desires: intellectual, affective, emotional
and sexual. Therefore, a man will act cautiously, protecting his
partner's sexuality, making sure that she is not threatened by his
sexual desires until the appropriate moment. For some men,
having a serious relationship was a sufficient motive to stop going
to prostitutes or stop looking around for sexual adventures.
Others, however, still found it possible and enjoyable to *sacar la
vuelta* (be unfaithful) or *tener plancitos* (this comes closest
to having [little] plans; however, the plan referred to is a not-so-
serious relationship with another woman). This proved possible
because of the distinction they made between their partners
and what they were looking for in a relationship with other
women. Certain feelings, sensations and emotions are reserved
for the first group of women. Sexual desire and satisfaction are
enmeshed in a conglomeration of emotions. With the other group
of women, sexual desire and satisfaction are fragmented from the
range of emotions they feel with their partner and perceived as
virtually instinctual, making it seem possible for them to have
sexual adventures without putting their relationship in danger.
This becomes explicit in their definition of being faithful. When
the respondents were asked whether they were faithful, several
did not connect faithfulness with monogamy and initially
answered affirmatively. Only after their answer was challenged
did they reformulate it.

'You never had another woman?'

'No. Well, entirely faithful, no, because once in a while a female friend comes along and insinuates something, so forget it, you can't just sit around doing nothing, something happens.' (Eduardo)

'I never *sacaba la vuelta* – well, let's not say never, but relatively no. Faithfulness doesn't mean you can't have relationships with other women.' (Hernan, 28, single)

'It's one thing to love someone and another thing to screw. You can screw with one person or another, but that doesn't mean you've stopped loving the third person. You can screw, to put it simply, because you're horny. And if there's a woman who wants to screw you, why not screw her?' (Percy, 30, single)

For some of the respondents, being faithful is a normative value with a logical rationale. It is not synonymous with mono-gamy, because what they experience with the other woman is not intended to replace their relationship but, rather, expresses another part of their sexuality. This constructs different notions of sexuality which are enacted with different women, and is one of the underlying forces behind labelling women.

Pacharaca (pacha, pachita), pampita and *ruca* are different names for women who serve as sexual outlets. Some men use these terms interchangeably, but usually there is a distinction between the *pacharaca* and the *ruca*. The *pacharaca* or *pampita* (the terms are synonymous, but *pampita* was used more often by men who grew up in the 1960s) is characterized as a woman looking for a good time with an enormous amount of sexual contacts. She is normally found in bars, restaurants and discos, making it known by the way she dresses and her behaviour that she wants to be picked up. Often a group of men will go out to pick up *pacharacas*. Although some men admitted that a *pacharaca* is not only interested in sex but is looking for affec-tion, or that some women were *pacharacas* because they were trying to find a potential partner and climb the social ladder, their attitudes and behaviour remained unchanged. The man is quick to make sexual advances – an unlikely occurrence if he considers the woman a *chica de su casa*. He is out for a one-night stand. There is no monetary transaction involved, but a material exchange is expected. If a man wants to pick up a *pacharaca*, he is aware that he has to offer her a good time. Food, drinks, and maybe drugs are expected items on the menu. The essence of a relationship with a *pacharaca* is given by one of the respondents who could never get into being a *pacharaquero* (a man who frequently picks up *pacharacas*):

> 'I couldn't get into it – you know, bringing your girl home and then going off to look for *pacharacas*. It just isn't me. Sexuality is something more than just the physical, you know? Not necessarily a greater commitment, but something more – sympathy . . . I don't know . . . enjoyment, empathy, some type of human relationship which goes further than the physical.' (Álvaro, 34, single)

The *ruca*, which comes closest to the English 'slut' or 'tramp', is a woman who goes off with a lot of men. She could be known in the neighbourhood for being 'easy'. She is the closest to a prostitute without charging for sex and is usually an acquaintance, while the *pacharaca* is normally a stranger.

The *ruca* and the *pacharaca* are distinguished from the *chica de su casa* by boundaries that restrain or let loose men's sexual desires. The *pacharaca* and her cohorts are sought out to satisfy their sexual needs. To a large extent, they are dissociated from their social identity and perceived in purely sexual terms. Men transform them into sexual actors, negating the significance their social world has for them. This enhances the notion of sexual desire as virtually instinctual and thus uncontrollable. Men are able to give vent to their sexual desire in these sexual encounters. The further a woman goes into a man's emotional world, the more she is perceived as a social actor, and other elements become decisive in determining the appropriate moment to have a sexual relationship. In this sense, a relationship with a *chica de su casa* restrains a man's sexual desire. None the less, having sex with a *chica de su casa* (one's partner) was often seen as the most gratifying.

The three categories of women are constructed through men's sexual intentions. It is most probable that a woman who is regarded as a *pacharaca* in a disco is a potential partner at work or school. Hugo showed how labelling is a male projection when he recalled his first girlfriend at the age of twelve:

'It was very Platonic, Platonic in the sense that it carried a lot of illusion and fantasy with very little eroticism.'

'You didn't desire her?'

'Of course not. At that time, the girls you desired had to be *rucas*.'

Labelling women illustrates how the meanings of men's sexual desire shifts at different moments and simultaneously constructs meanings of femininity.

The prostitute, or *la puta*, is the third category of women. It would be inappropriate to conceptualize this label as constructed like the others, since prostitution in Peru is an institution officially recognized by the State, with accompanying regulations. Needless to say, prostitutes are sexual outlets for men. Although the majority of men are aware of the social conditions in which many prostitutes live, and how these conditions contribute to their decision to work as prostitutes, in sexual encounters prostitutes are perceived as the furthest removed from their social world. They are the supreme example of the sexual actor.[19] Sexual encounters with prostitutes means paid sex: a clear-cut relationship with no emotional involvement. Paying for sex enables men to demand that their sexual desires should be satisfied according to their fancy. This is not always guaranteed with the other groups of women. At first glance, the prostitute appears to be the least ambivalent category of the three; however, going to a prostitute was experienced differently by the men who were interviewed.

Going to Prostitutes

It is a difficult task to generalize about men's experiences with prostitutes. Some never went to a prostitute; others visited them regularly. Nevertheless, for all men, even those who never used a prostitute's services, going to a prostitute is a male prerogative. In other words, there comes a point in a man's life when he must decide whether or not he should go to a prostitute. Among the men interviewed, fifteen had some kind of experience with a prostitute, six never used their services, and only three had never been inside a brothel.

What all the men who used prostitutes' services had in common is that they started young. The majority were sexually initiated (*debutar* – to make a debut) in a brothel. In general, whether it was a brothel in Lima or one in the provinces, they referred to the regulated brothels characterized by their anonymity, with huge factory-like corridors lined with small rooms and women posing in the doorways trying to entice a client to enter. This first experience was usually described as disastrous. Between being nervous and trying to conceal the fact that they were a novice[20] and the prostitutes who were quoted as saying things like 'Hurry up', 'Have you finished yet?' or 'Novices aren't good fucks', it was considered a memorable experience, though it was an experience they would rather not remember. Entangled within their accounts is a layer of disillusionment which expresses a conflict between the actual situation and their emotional expectations.

> 'It was disastrous. It wasn't the scheme I had in my head, nor the idea I had in my life about sex. At no moment did I feel fulfilled as a man, which I suppose you should feel with your first sexual experience.'
> (Percy)

> 'After we'd finished I asked the whore, "What do we do now?" – was it possible to start making love, because what we did was not making love. She turned to the friend I was with and told him I was crazy. The whore followed me to the door and caused an uproar.'
> (Carlos, 31, single)

What they wanted and what they got clashed tremendously. They were looking for a sexual experience comparable to having sex in an affective relationship. They imagined that that was what they had bought. What they got, however, was paid sex. After the first experience, many went back on a regular basis. Although it took time to internalize the differences, they eventually found satisfaction in this sexual relationship. Only one man stopped going after his first experience.

Three patterns in the use of prostitutes' services can be discerned. First there are those who never went to prostitutes. Then there is the group who used their services regularly, but eventually stopped – the majority of the men interviewed. Finally, there are those who continue to find opportunities to go to an establishment where prostitution is practised.

Two closely related factors play an essential role in under-standing why certain men never used prostitutes' services. These respondents had the hardest time accepting and acting out a fragmented notion of sexual desire. Words such as disgust, rejection, degradation and incompatibility were used to explain why they never ventured past the threshold of a prostitute's room. With the exception of one informant who said he never went to prostitutes because he was afraid he would catch a venereal disease, they could not accept this purely commercial enterprise. Having sexual intercourse meant more than simply having an orgasm. This does not imply that they withheld from having sex until they met the 'right woman', even though one man was still a virgin and did not feel the need to have sexual intercourse until he had a serious relationship. On the contrary, this decision was made easier because there were women who were not prostitutes available for a sexual relationship which allowed for a certain degree of feeling.

> 'If you put a girl in front of me who works in a brothel, it bothers me. I don't like to see the girls who are standing there in a *tanga*, or something of the sort. A sexual relation should be with feelings. . . . At least there should be pleasure, and money shouldn't come into it. I feel it degrades me to pay to be with a woman.' (Angel, 24, single)

> 'It makes me feel disgusted. I have no need or desire or curiosity. I always had good sex with my girlfriends. I didn't need to go to a prostitute. What can a prostitute give me, sexually speaking, that an *hembrita* [woman – chick in diminutive form] can't, if we have a good screw?' (Alberto, 33, married)

> 'In my group we measured our conquests at parties, not at a brothel or with a prostitute. Although there are many attractive prostitutes, in essence it is a commercial contact – that's how I always considered it. It's incompatible with pleasure.' (Carlos, 27, single)

Their motives for not going to prostitutes are voiced in similar terms to the disappointment the majority of the men felt after their first experience with a prostitute. Their thoughts on this subject contrast most strikingly with those of men who continue to use prostitutes' services occasionally. The difference lies in the way they give meaning to sexual desire. In the latter group, sexual desire, satisfaction and emotion need not go together; thus they have no problem going to a prostitute. Despite the fact that there must be many men who never stopped going, among the respondents only three still went. One of the men had severe problems making social contacts. His last relationship with a non-prostitute was when he was a teenager. He found it much easier to relate to prostitutes, and had a serious relationship with one. Even though he never stopped paying for sex, he wanted to marry her. The other two used their services occasionally. One of them claimed that his eleven-year-old marriage was stable because he had frequent extramarital relationships. He preferred to look for sexual satisfaction among the *pacharacas*. However, going to a prostitute was a last resort which he used on occasion:

> 'I still go to prostitutes sometimes. Where are you going to find a woman at one o'clock in the morning after you've had a few drinks?' (Juan Carlos, 33, married)

Finally, we come to the group of men who stopped using prostitutes' services. The frequency with which they went to prostitutes varied, and their feelings about their experience cannot be generalized. Some enjoyed it; others never stopped seeing it as a last resort. What they do share is a change in their perception of their sexual selves. At some point sex for the sake of sex became unsatisfactory, and they realized that with their partners they are able to obtain a sexual relationship which goes beyond the physical. Álvaro reflects on the change that occurred:

> 'My experiences with prostitutes can be compared with a cold shower in winter. You have to shower, you suffer, and when you've finished you say "that was that". I stopped going to prostitutes at the age of 24, when I started to have a sexual relationship with my partner. That was the age when my sexuality, my partner and affection consolidated into one thing.'

In conclusion, men's experiences with prostitution are linked with their sexual experiences in other areas of their lives. For the majority of the respondents, using prostitutes' services informed the construction of their sexual selves. Their different stances towards prostitution and their different experiences with prostitutes support the idea that the concept of male sexuality is neither homogeneous nor fixed.

The significance of going to prostitutes is best symbolized as a tug of war between sexual desire as virtually instinctual and sexual desire integrated in a range of emotions. This mirrors the distinctions made between women as sexual and social actors. For men who never used prostitutes' services, the fragmentation of sexual desire from other emotions is less pronounced than it is in the other groups. These men look to satisfy their sexual needs either with their partner or in the group of women who are conceived of as social actors. The men who continue to go to prostitutes can easily separate sexual desire from other emotions, pulling them to the prostitutes with one simple tug. The largest group of men, who are situated between these two extremes, are in a continual tug of war. They are pulled and pushed back and forth, shifting the outcome at different moments of their lives. There are moments when the fragmented notion of sexual desire appears to be more unified. At others they have less difficulty in separating it into two entities. The decision to stop going to prostitutes is a moment in their life cycles when the meaning of sexual desire changes and their perception of their sexual selves is less fragmented. It is impossible to predict if it will shift again in the future. Since they have accepted prostitution as a sexual alternative, there might come a time when they decide to go back to prostitutes. If this is not so, why were there a large group of men in their thirties and forties who frequented the establishments where I conducted my fieldwork? Do they all belong to the group who never stopped going to prostitutes? Or does this group also include men who have returned?

The continual shift in the meanings of sexual desire is most visible in the group of men who stopped using prostitutes' services; nevertheless, it is not a personal trait that belongs solely to them. It is just as improbable that men who continue to use prostitutes' services will always perceive their sexual desire as virtually instinctual as that men who have never been to prostitutes identify their sexual desire only in the emotional realm. The tug of war between sexual desire and emotion can be seen as a representation of the interplay between discourse and subjectivity. Their subjective experiences give voice to discursive notions of sexuality. At other moments these notions are rejected, or coexist harmoniously with other experience-based meanings. Although many men wrestle with their stance on prostitution, the fact remains that prostitution contains the strongest essentialist images of male sexuality. How this essentialist notion is given form in men's sexual selves is highly dependent on their subjective experiences.

Constructing Sexual Selves

The majority of the group who participated in this project could be considered typical heterosexual middle-class male inhabitants of Lima who are among the many referred to in theories concerning *machismo*, oppression and male sexuality. These theories portray their lives as the reproduction of discourse in practice. I have chosen to use the concept of sexual selves to facilitate an analysis which includes the subjective dimension. This has shown that sexuality is not singular but contains various meanings in multiple configurations which shift their positions in different situations, at different moments in time, and with different women. Some of these meanings embody the discursive notions of sexuality. Others emphasize experiences that differ greatly from cultural expectations or situate the discursive notions in a less prominent position, producing sexual meanings which contest and contradict, but none the less coexist with, the discursive notions.

The stories the men told of their sexual lives illustrate the pervasive influence of the discursive notions in affirming their sexual selves. Men's sexuality as essentialist, virtually instinctual, is embodied in the metaphors they use to describe sexual desire and sex. The oppositional constructs of male and female sexuality emphasize men's performance in sexual encounters. Women's presence and pleasure are mediated through these expressions.

Yet notions of women's sexuality are far more ambiguous than is supposed in the sexual language. It is not whether a woman is sexually active that constructs difference but, rather, if she sexually conforms to the label she is given. Underlying the labels of femininity is a fragmented notion of sexual desire which appears virtually instinctual on one level and on another as integrated into a man's emotional world. This is expressed in sexual encounters which seem predominantly aimed at pure sexual satisfaction, constructing women who serve as sexual outlets such as the *pacharacas* and *rucas*, and those with whom they can experience their sexuality, within a realm of emotions that include sexual desire. Women's gender identity is split in two: those who are social actors and those who are sexual actors. The representation of the prostitute is the most powerful expression of a sexual actor.

Thus, the simple dichotomy between the good woman (asexual, passive) and the bad woman (sexually active) is less at play in the realm of sexuality than we are led to believe. That these gender notions have significance in the construction of femininity goes without saying. However, I would argue that the sexual self is, in part, constructed through an ordering principle that distinguishes different meanings of male sexual desire grounded on men's projections of their sexual intention. The distinctions which this produces between women might conform to the gender imagery of the good and the bad woman, but even then these values are not fixed. A man, for example, who steps out of line with culturally expected behaviour and falls in love with a *ruca* or prostitute is grappling with the normative values associated with the gender imagery. It is in the aftermath, when the relationship is established or terminated, that this act of transgression will label the woman good or bad.

The significance of the partner for a man's sexual and emotional world illustrates how discourse and subjectivity continually interact. The relationship with the *chica de su casa* is the locus where different emotions are enmeshed in a social world. The woman's sexuality is perceived positively by men. This sexual relationship with a partner is considered the most gratifying. This meaning of the *chica de su casa* conflicts with the discursive gender notions which portray her as the good, asexual woman. Yet at the same time the relationship reflects the workings of the discourse. The partner remains the woman who is protected and treated with respect, and for whom certain feelings are reserved. In this sense, men continue to place their adult partner on a pedestal, as they did with their girlfriends in their teenage years. There is little difference in behaviour between the adolescent who will not push his girlfriend too far and a man in an adult relationship who continues to make a distinction between his partner and other women. The different meanings embedded in the label *chica de su casa* simultaneously express difference and conform to the discursive image. Discourse and subjectivity conflate in this symbol of femininity.

The continual motion between discourse and subjectivity produces difference between men. Some could not envision themselves as *pacharaqueros*. They had trouble experiencing sex as purely sexual. Others are able to have a relationship and maintain a sexual life outside their relationship *sacando la vuelta*. The most transparent expression of difference is found in men's experiences with prostitutes. Despite the social acceptance of prostitution as a sexual alternative, and the frequency with which men turn to the prostitute for sexual satisfaction, many of the men's experiences reshape the idea that prostitution is a pleasurable way to obtain such satisfaction. They consider it a last resort, not an erotic haven of pleasure, as it is often portrayed. Additionally, their experiences challenge the fixed representation of the client which is often found in prostitution studies. The difficulty of envisioning sex as a sole objective was decisive for the men who chose not to go to prostitutes. The initial experience with a prostitute for some men was so disillusioning that it made it harder for them to find pleasure in their encounters. Other men eventually appropriated the sexual discourse concerning prostitution as their own, and began to find their encounters with prostitutes gratifying. For those who decided to stop going to prostitutes, their decision was influenced by the gratification they obtained from their relationships with a partner on more egalitarian terms.

Although going to prostitutes may not be considered a sexual outlet for all men, nevertheless it still remains a male prerogative. Rejection of prostitution is not a rejection of the essentialist notion of sexuality. What they are rejecting, for various reasons, is its most extreme expression. Their accounts have shown that even if they did not use prostitution as a sexual alternative, the notion of sexual desire they uphold is none the less fragmented into two.

＊

Mapping out the processes involved in the construction of men's sexual selves has proved a challenging task. The challenge lies in not falling victim to the temptation to replace old, worn-out concepts with new ones that are merely a new cover for old epistemological assumptions. I have tried to avoid this trap by focusing on subjectivity – the subjective level of experience – as a potential point of convergence for discursive notions of sexuality and other experience-based sexual meanings.

The subjective dimension of men's experiences is often ignored in studies that are aimed predominantly at analysing women's subordination. There is a common unspoken belief that subjectivity is not particularly relevant to the study of male dominance, because the fact that men might be different on a personal level does not change the gender order of society. The lack of analysis of the way men construct their identities through daily lived experiences, and how these experiences filter through their subjective lens to create meanings, has contributed to the reductionist construct of power resounding through many feminist-orientated studies. The ethnographic analysis presented here gives a glimpse of the complexities of how men enact power relations through the construction of their sexual selves. Labelling women is one aspect of the power relations which construct inequality. It has also indicated areas where there is a potential for negotiating less constrictive and more equal power relations – for example, in men's relationship with their partners – and suggests moments when men appear to resist the appropriation of discursive notions into their sexual selves. This could be a possible interpretation for the position of men who (eventually) reject prostitution as a sexual alternative.

I have attempted to contest the representation of male sexuality in certain feminist currents through an analysis of men's construction of their sexual selves. It was not my intention to invent an image of the new 'Latin American man' which replaces the inherent characteristics of *machismo* with others such as sensitivity, equality and mutual pleasure. On the contrary, the analysis presented enough material to sustain the homogeneous image of masculinity. However, placing the discursive notions in a fluid, situational context reveals the significance of subjectivity for the construction of men's sexual selves. Cornwall and Lindisfarne assert:

> [e]xamining how notions of masculinity are created and presented through interaction reveals clearly the relation between a multiplicity of gendered identities and power. While the ideas of 'male dominance' and 'patriarchy' are neither sensitive nor appropriate tools for analysis, we argue that relations of power are an aspect of *every* social interaction.[21]

If we define power as constituted in every social interaction, from the most mundane to the most authoritative, an analysis of masculinity or sexuality is unimaginable without including subjectivity. Only if we include it will the concept of sexuality be open to multiple readings, making it possible to understand how men's subjective experiences really make a difference in the construction of their sexual selves and, concomitantly, how their subjective experiences affirm notions of male sexuality which make it appear singular and fixed.

Notes

This study was made possible by a grant from the Bella van Zuylen Institute (University of Amsterdam) and the Dutch Foundation for Scientific Investigation for the Tropics (WOTRO), The Hague. My thanks to Ton Salman, Anke van Dam, Kees de Groot, Magdalena Villarreal and the editors of this volume for their supportive comments and stimulating criticism. A special thanks to Rafael Calvo, who has accompanied me since the idea for this essay took shape. I am extremely indebted to him for all the times I tried out ideas on him and for the comments he gave in return, which demonstrated his extraordinary insight into his own culture.

1. There are indications that middle- and upper-class adolescents are no longer using this alternative so frequently. None the less, there is still a possibility that they will use it at some point in their lives.
2. A. Cornwall and N. Lindisfarne, 'Introduction', in Andrea Cornwall and Nancy Lindisfarne, eds, *Dislocating Masculinity: Comparative Ethnographies*, London 1994, p. 1.

3. Evelyn P. Stevens, 'Marianismo: The Other Face of Machismo in Latin America', in A. Pescatello, ed., *Female and Male in Latin America: Essays*, Pittsburgh, PA 1973, p. 90.

4. Judith Ennew, 'Mujercita y Mamacita: Girls Growing Up in Lima', *Bulletin Latin American Res.*, vol. 5, no. 2, 1986, p. 58.

5. Ana Silvia Monzón, 'El Machismo: Mito de al Supremacía Masculina', *Nueva Sociedad*, 93, January–February 1988, p. 148. My translation.

6. Carmen Lugo, 'Machismo y Violencia', in A. Koschutzke ed., *Y Hasta Cuándo Esperaremos Mandandirun-dirun-dirun-dán: Mujer y Poder en América Latina*, Caracas 1989, pp. 219–30.

7. Although this type of analysis has implications for understanding the complexities of women's agency, a discussion of this kind goes beyond the objectives of this essay.

8. The criticism which is being presented concerns the differences in political standpoints between myself and the group mentioned. It must be said that despite our difference of opinion, during the course of this investigation we developed an excellent working relationship based on mutual respect and a recognition of the value of our respective work.

9. EL POZO, 'La Prostitución, un Microcosmos de la Explotación de Toda Mujer en Nuestra Sociedad', unpublished 1990, p. 4. My translation.

10. Cristina Cavalcanti, Carmen Imbert and Margarita Cordero, *Prostitución: Esclavitud Sexual Feminina*, Santo Domingo 1985, pp. 79–80. My translation.

11. A historical analysis of the Peruvian discourse of prostitution in relation to male sexuality is presented in Chapter 1 of my PhD dissertation, title still to be decided, University of Amsterdam.

12. Susan S. M. Edwards, 'Selling the Body, Keeping the Soul: Sexuality, Power, the Theories and Realities of Prostitution', in S. Scott and D. Morgan, eds, *Body Matters: Essays on the Sociology of the Body*, London 1993, pp. 102–3.

13. See, for example, Cornwall and Lindisfarne (eds).

14. Oscar Ugarteche, 'Historia, sexo y cultura en el Perú', *Margenes: Encuentro y Debate*, vol. 5, no. 9, 1992, pp. 19–64.

15. Richard Parker, *Bodies, Pleasures, and Passions: Sexual Culture in Contemporary Brazil*, Boston, MA 1991, p. 2.

16. Eduardo Archetti, 'Argentinian Football: A Ritual of Violence?', *The International Journal of the History of Sport*, vol. 9, no. 2, pp. 209–35.

17. Dorinne K. Kondo, *Crafting Selves*, Chicago 1990, p. 44.

18. See Lorraine Nencel, 'The Secrets behind Sexual Desire: The Construction of the Male Sexuality in Lima, Peru', *Etnofoor*, vol. 7, no. 2, 1994, pp. 59–75, for a more detailed discussion of the construction of knowledge through the interview process.

19. This image is strengthened by the prostitutes. Often, they choose to

distance themselves from the client and protect their private lives. Thus they consciously assume the identity of the sexual actor.

20. It is curious not only that they attempted to conceal the fact that they were virgins, but that some men recall the attempt as if they pulled it off successfully. Imagine a thirteen-year-old boy going to a prostitute for the first time, acting as if he knows what he is doing. Did they really believe that an experienced prostitute would not be able to tell? I think this is instructive about the construction of their sexual selves rather than an accurate account of the situation.

21. Cornwall and Lindisfarne (eds), p. 3.

4

Domination and Desire:

Male Homosexuality and

the Construction of Masculinity

in Mexico

Annick Prieur

This essay explores the construction of male homo- and bisexuality in Mexico in terms of gendered categories and the production of identities. Masculine-looking bisexual men and effeminate homosexuals use the images of men, of women and, as a separate category, of male homosexuals to construct their respective identities, in distinction to each other. The gender imageries are closely linked to ideas about sexual practices where the basic question is whether one is the penetrator, the penetrated, or both. These ideas are expressed through categorizations and labelling processes, and through sexual practices and sexualized games: there are striking parallels between the practised homosexuality and the homosexuality that is staged in verbal badgering and mockfighting among men, where men attack other men's masculinity by putting them in a passive homosexual role. Value is given to the male who penetrates women or other males, and never lets himself be penetrated. His defence of his own bodily boundaries and his attack on other men's bodies may mirror and symbolize the social competition among men. This construction of a particular form of practised or played male bisexuality allows for particular male, homoerotic pleasures, where the masculine-looking participants are not labelled homosexuals, and are therefore free of stigma; but the stigma–tolerance dichotomy does not grasp the complexity of the social and sexual interactions. The different practices and games are acted out on the basis of male dominance, which implies the power to define and categorize. The dominated, however, are not passive subjects of domination; they struggle for their dignity through an alternative classification.

The Actors and their Classifications of Each Other[1]

I base my essay on fieldwork carried out in Ciudad Nezahualcoyotl, a working-class *barrio* on the outskirts of Mexico City. Between 1988 and 1991 I spent a total of six months with a group of homosexual transvestites, living with them day and night and sharing their daily lives. My host was a former male prostitute who now heads a project for the prevention of AIDS. His house is a meeting-place for the youth of the neighbourhood, so I did not have to look for my informants; they gathered where I was living. These young people have very little privacy – they seem to know almost everything about each other, and carry out most activities openly. Although they knew I was a researcher, my presence did not seem to restrict their behaviour, and I gained insight into the most intimate aspects of their lives. In addition to this participant observation, I have interviewed eleven homosexuals and seven of their bisexual partners. The homosexuals talked very freely, whereas some of the bisexuals seemed somewhat intimidated and gave shorter answers.

Most of the young men who gathered at this house were in their teens or early twenties, and were homo- or bisexual in the strictly descriptive sense of the words: some have sexual relationships with their own biological sex exclusively or almost exclusively; some have relationships with both women and men. When it comes to identities and self-definition the situation is more complicated, but they divide themselves into two distinct groups, and the distinctions between the two groups are indeed visible: some are ordinary-looking masculine youngsters; others are strikingly effeminate. All of the latter use make-up, many wear women's clothes, and some even pass as women without any problems. Most of them have given their bodies female shapes, whether by external measures like foam-rubber padding or by medical measures such as hormones or implants. All use female nicknames. Their opportunities on the labour market are limited mainly to hairdressing and prostitution. Many have had severe conflicts with their families over their appearance and sexual preferences, and many have stayed away from home for a long time, or still stay away. However, they usually return to live with their parents when the latter stop trying to change their femininity, and many contribute to the household by their earnings as prostitutes. Thus they live rather integrated socially in the sense that they have their share in family life, they live overtly as effeminate homosexuals in their local community, and participate in local events. But their lifestyle has aspects of marginalization such as drinking, drug use, theft and violence, which are part of their daily lives. They are, descriptively speaking, predominantly homosexual, and I will therefore refer to them as 'homosexuals', and to those of them who cross-dress as 'transvestites'.

The ordinary-looking masculine youngsters who hang around with the homosexuals are usually their sexual partners – or the homosexuals hope they will become their sexual partners. These men, whether clients of the prostitutes or leisure-time partners, seem to consider themselves and to be considered by others as 'ordinary' men. I am best acquainted with the leisure-time partners, working-class young men who often live in established relationships with women. They do not form a separate group, nor do they refer to themselves by any special term. But the homosexuals call them *mayates*, a local term for masculine-looking men who have sex with effeminate men. As almost all of them have sexual relationships with women as well, I shall call them bisexuals, but I stress that in so doing I refer exclusively to a bisexual practice, not to any kind of identity linked to it. (We shall see later that the homosexuals use the Spanish word *bisexual* in a very different sense.)

This pattern of homosexual relationships has been described in other Latin American societies, too,[2] and in other studies from Mexico.[3] In Mexico this pattern seems to be typical of the lower strata of the urbanized working class. Middle-class homosexuals tend to have a more discreet effeminate style, or a very sophisticated masculine style, and they usually have partners like themselves. A homosexual transvestite may even be disgusted by the sight of two men with moustaches kissing each other. In their own eyes, they behave normally: they let a man be a man and a woman be a woman. The middle-class homosexuals are often labelled as cowardly, closeted homosexuals, because they do not show clearly that they are homosexual. The taste, style, and judgements of the working-class homosexuals are particular to them; they do not try to copy the middle-class homosexuals.

The local classifications give a key to the ideas about gender that underlie the identity constructions and the sexual relationships. The efforts of Fidel – also called Fifí – to teach me the local vocabulary can serve as an illustrative example: 'A *mayate* is a man who does it with *jotos*. A *tortilla* is a man who likes to fuck a *joto*, and likes to have the *joto* fuck him. *Bugas* are those who, according to them; don't do it with *jotos* – only with women. Then there are the *heterosexuales*, who like to fuck men – which means *jotas* who like to fuck men. And *bisexuales* are those who fuck men, and the men who fuck *jotos*. They are the *bisexuales mayates*. They are *tortillas*. My experience is that the majority of men that I have been with are *mayates*. And some rare times *bisexuales*. And then *bugas*; the truth is that I don't think they exist any more. Because now any man will be with a *joto* or with a woman.' Perhaps this was not crystal clear, but there is a logic to it.

Locally, the Spanish word *homosexual* is used to denote a man in the woman's role who has sex with a masculine man – ideally, he retains the passive role. Some *homosexuales* are transvestites in the sense that they wear women's clothes, and they are called *vestidas*. Some have a less feminine appearance. They are all called *jotos* or *jotas* – the latter form has a feminine gender, thus placing a stronger emphasis on the feminine. One explanation I have been given for this term is that *joto* is the name of a Spanish dance where men move in ways that are seen as feminine. Or it might refer to a Mexican prison where homosexual inmates were placed in wing *J* – the letter *J* being pronounced *jota* in Spanish. Other words are also used, like *gay*, which is used as a synonym for *joto* or *homosexual*. *Puto* – literally whore in the masculine gender – is used negatively, like 'faggot', but the homosexuals have appropriated the term and may also use it themselves. *Maricón*, however, probably a male-gendered version of *María*, is a pejorative term that they would never use to refer to themselves.

The local use of the Spanish word *bisexual* is as a term for men who have an androgynous appearance – who do not hide the fact that they are men, but have some female characteristics: perhaps just a haircut, a flowered shirt, and a pair of trousers that are a bit high-waisted, or perhaps their movements and voice. They are expected to have sex with men who resemble themselves, then to trade off being active and passive. Masculine men who sleep with other masculine men can also be called *bisexuales*, precisely because they are expected to take part in the same changing of roles. The term, then, refers partially to appearance, partially to sexual practice, and there is an expectation that there is a correlation between appearance and practice. In the local terminology, trading off between being active and passive is called being *internacional*, perhaps because foreigners are supposed to do so, but maybe just because it implies doing an *ida* – a departure, being active – and a *vuelta* – an arrival or a return, being passive. It is also called being a *tortilla* or *tortillera*. A *tortilla* is a corn pancake made by turning the dough between the hands and patting it on both sides; a *tortillera* is the woman who bakes it. The terms express an expectation that there is a correlation between an androgynous appearance and a sexual practice where one is both penetrating and penetrated, that is, acting both like a man and like a woman.

The Spanish word *heterosexual* is rarely used, so many do not have an opinion of what it means, but some think that being *heterosexual* is being a man, or being *normal* – and a man is a man, or is *normal*, as long as he looks like a man and sticks to the active role, regardless of whether he has sex with women or men. I have, for instance, heard the term *la prostitución heterosexual* being used to denote the prostitution of young boys who stick to the active role with their male clients. According to the same logic, Fifi spoke above about *jotos heterosexuales*, meaning homosexuals who like to penetrate men.

A *mayate* is a man who looks like a man and has sex with men who are regarded as *homosexuales*, and usually also with women. He is commonly supposed to play the active part. But some *mayates* are also penetrated by the men they are with, which makes them *tortillas* even though there is nothing feminine about their appearance. They can also be called *mayates bisexuales*. I have been told that the word *mayate* originated as the name of a little beetle that makes a ball out of its own dung, lays its eggs in it, then pushes the ball in front of itself using its snout. This reflects the expectation that *mayates* are supposed to be the active party during anal intercourse. However, most of those who use the word are probably ignorant of this origin.

The term *buga* refers to men who have sex only with women, and are therefore always active. Sometimes the term is also used for men who pretend to have sex only with women, or for men whom the homosexuals find very manly, *hombre-hombre* (man-man) or *machín* (meaning very *macho*, very male), and whom they would like to seduce, even if the *bugas* would then not really be *bugas* any more.

This terminology usage focuses primarily on sexual actions and roles, which blend with appearances, because appearance is normally seen as a signal of sexual actions and roles. A man's feminine appearance is a signal that he wants to be penetrated, while a masculine appearance connotes a desire to penetrate, and those with a more androgynous appearance are expected to want both. But the choice of object also lies in these terms, because in order to be passive, men need other men; in order to be active, men need women and/or other men. Any dictionary will state that the correct way to use the terms homo-, bi-, and heterosexual is as a reference to practice as it relates to choice of object. But more vulgar usage in other languages, too, is more in line with these examples, placing emphasis on the concrete sexual actions.

Local and more generally used categorizations and understandings are mixed here: the definition of homosexuals as effeminate men who are penetrated by other men corresponds to a more general way of perceiving homosexuals in Mexico. The homosexuals take this as a point of departure, but subdivide themselves into different, smaller categories. They also label and classify their partners. But their labelling power is weak, and their classifications of their masculine partners are barely known: the masculine men's self-understanding reigns, and they do not see themselves as *mayates*, but as men *tout court*. To be active with a homosexual partner is subsumed under the more general category of being active, which again characterizes male sexual behaviour. This is a reflection of the fact that male dominance implies linguistic dominance,[4] a labelling power that consists of both the power to label and the power not to label.

The Bisexual Men

We have seen that *mayate* is the term used by the effeminate homosexuals to denote men who have sex with other men without being feminine and without seeing themselves as homosexual. Often their main interest is in women, and to the extent that they are with men, they are with *vestidas* – transvestites – or at least with manifestly effeminate men.

Anybody can be a *mayate*. Even without data from quantitative studies, I would assert that it is not at all unusual for Mexican men from the urban working class to have sexual experience with men, at least during certain periods of their lives. Qualitative studies cannot estimate how widespread this is, but may show how easy it is for effeminate homosexuals to obtain sexual contact with men.[5]

The following examples are from my own fieldwork. An effeminate homosexual can go into the underground during the rush hour and end up pressed against a man who feels him up or lets himself be felt up. I have seen men push forward the minute they see an effeminate homosexual come into the carriage, and they make sure they stand close to him. I have also been present at parties (for instance, a celebration of a daughter's fifteenth birthday) where there is dancing in the street outside the house. The men ask the homosexuals to dance, and they might also pop into the bathroom to have sex with them. In the house where I lived there were always some homosexuals who seduced the man who came to read the electricity meter or the plumber who came to do some work. In the evenings the neighbours often came knocking, hoping for sex. The homosexuals who have been in prison tell about being raped by all the other inmates, who do it together, in front of each other. Thus it seems that a man can invite another man to dance, or have sex with a more feminine man, without being labelled homosexual and without causing himself identity conflicts.

Some studies indicate that male bisexuality is widespread throughout Latin America, and this has been linked to its relative acceptability. For example, Joseph Carrier writes: 'This lack of stigmatization provides prospective active participants with the important feeling that their masculine self-image is not threatened by their homosexual behavior.'[6] Ana María Alonso and María Teresa Koreck write: 'the active role in *macho–joto* relations carries no stigma'.[7]

Observing the frequency and lack of reserve surrounding these contacts, one could easily be led to believe that bisexual practice is a non-stigmatized and unproblematic kind of behaviour. But this deduction is problematic: one cannot automatically deduce that a phenomenon is accepted merely because it is widespread, particularly not in the sphere of sexual morals. For example, in many parts of the world infidelity is no doubt fairly widespread – without there being any general moral acceptance of it.

My observations indicate that male bisexuality is neither socially accepted nor stigmatized. This polarization does not grasp the complexity of what is happening. Contacts between masculine men and effeminate homosexuals are playing fields for very complicated social games, where one does not necessarily say what one means, nor necessarily mean what one does.

I have noticed that contacts between effeminate homosexuals and masculine men in Mexico are not made too openly – unless it is in a place where everyone is initiated, where all the men do it. The homosexual men's feminine bearing serves to conceal the fact that what is happening is actually a homosexual relationship. To a certain extent, the *mayates* can have sex with men without ever being aware of it. Many *vestidas* look completely like women, even with their clothes off. If they do not let the man touch their intimate parts, they are often capable of having sex without him discovering that he has had anal instead of vaginal intercourse. But it is probably more common that the men delude themselves, rather than that they are deluded. These are intricate games where the homosexual willingly gives the man the excuses and pretexts he needs.

A common pretext is money: it is by no means unusual for the *mayates* to be the ones who 'prostitute' themselves (this goes, of course, only for leisure-time partners, attractive young men, not for clients in prostitution). But as a rule, these young men 'sell' themselves cheaply. The homosexuals give them money, drinks, food or clothes in exchange for sexual services – just enough to give the young men an alibi; they can pretend they did not enter the sexual relationship because they had a homosexual desire, but simply because they could make some kind of economic gain from it.

In conversations with men who did not know that I knew they had sexual contacts with homosexuals, they denied such contacts. This made it difficult for me to get interviews with *mayates*; they had to know I already knew. Those interviewed knew that I already knew, because they knew I was living with some of their sexual partners who might have told me all about it, and sometimes because I had had the opportunity to watch them pick up a partner.[8] Even so, they systematically downplayed their experiences with homosexuals – compared to what their partners had told me about them. They would insist that it had not happened often, it probably would not happen again, and they got more out of being with a woman. For a couple this was not consistent with my own observations of them; for others it was not consistent with what their partners told me – that these men had had sexual relationships with many of the homosexuals, and had come back for more over a long period of time. Whom should one believe? I have chosen to believe the homosexuals, as I cannot see why they should not tell the truth (they were already labelled homosexuals anyway, and a few experiences more or less would not change anything), and they have given me very plausible explanations for why the bisexual men should want to downplay their homosexual experiences. It is all about maintaining a masculine image. Furthermore, I find this consistent with the way the bisexuals excused themselves in the interviews. 'I was so young,' they would say; 'I didn't yet know about women's love'; or 'I was drunk, they paid me.' And it was not – oh no! – an emotional attachment. One even told me he reacted with nausea the first time; several said that they could do it only with the lights out, or in certain positions which did not remind them too much of the gender of the other person.

These experiences are treated with discretion, and are usually not spoken of. Pedro told me why he had not told anyone about his experiences, and why no one had ever told him about theirs: 'Maybe people would take it badly, even be repulsed by you, maybe feel so strongly that it makes them sick.' These are pretty forceful words, and they certainly show that to state that male bisexuality is socially acceptable in Mexico is a gross over-simplification.

Bisexual practice, then, is kept secret rather than being accepted. Discretion is coupled with silence. The lack of verbalization is associated with the fact that this activity is not segregated from other activities and relegated to a ghetto. Clark Taylor describes homosexual encounters at public places in Mexico. At nighttime men gather at *plazas*; they may talk a little, drink a little, smoke some marijuana and maybe engage in flirting and joking with homosexuals, and maybe go a little further. Taylor uses Goffman's terminology, and calls these encounters a game. There are players in different roles: effeminate homosexuals, homosexuals who pretend to be manly, thieves who pretend to be homosexuals, police agents who pretend to be hustlers, and so on – and a great many people who either don't notice anything or pretend not to notice anything. Contact is obtained through glances. If words are used, they are code words, indicating whether one is an insider or not. If the game is disclosed, it can be stopped immediately – and nothing has really happened. Taylor does not discuss the psychological consequences, but I believe that this tacit organization of the activity also leaves the participants free to keep it non-verbal and only semi-conscious.[9]

When he explained his reasons for not wanting to talk to anyone about his experiences, Roberto said: 'I'm not a saint or anything. 'Cause I have done it with homosexuals. And I take it as something normal. I don't criticize them, I'm not for or against. If I tell a woman that I've done it with a homosexual, then she's not going to see it as something normal. But for me it is, 'cause nowadays any man will do it with a homosexual.' What he is saying is that really he just acts like all other men, it is just that women do not know that it is like this, and that is why they would condemn it. And perhaps this is a relatively correct description of the moral climate around male bisexuality: it is a collective secret among men, justified to themselves and among themselves by the fact that there are so many who do it, not because it in itself is seen as morally acceptable. But as Roger Lancaster points out in his study from Nicaragua, this goes also for other small sins – *pecadillos* – like heavy drinking or adultery. Such acts are morally disapproved of, but at the same time they are status-markers of male honour. I would argue that Latin American masculinity is constructed partly in opposition to Christian morality, and that the virtues of humility and willingness to forgive are considered more appropriate for women than for men.

For the *mayates*, the most sensitive aspect of homosexual contacts is the sexual practice. *Mayates* usually claim that they always take the penetrator's role. Of those I interviewed, all answered that they were never penetrated. Yet again, on the basis of what their partners say, I am inclined to believe that several of them were not telling the truth. The homosexuals had told me in advance that no *mayate* would ever admit to having been penetrated, because that is something that cannot be said. This, of course, is a methodological problem, but I believe it is also a finding, as I have now learnt why they cannot admit it: to be passive means to be homosexual, and this in turn means not to be a man.

Daniel lived with an effeminate homosexual for three years. Did he ever feel like a homosexual himself? 'No, because with the guy I lived with, I slept naked, totally naked with him. And he never tried to grab me, I mean around the waist, my hips. Never.' Ricardo said: 'As long as he doesn't touch my bottom it's OK, because then I wouldn't feel like a man, but like a *gay*. Then I pass from being a *mayate* to being a *joto*.'

To be penetrated marks a transition. Ricardo states that a man who lets himself be penetrated becomes homosexual. As long as a man is the penetrator, or at least is perceived as such, having a homosexual relationship will not be threatening to his self-image, or to the image others have of him. But no one – except a direct witness – can know what actually happens in bed. Therefore there will always be a doubt connected to homosexual encounters and, thereby, a risk that a man's masculinity may be perceived as impaired. This is one reason for treating such encounters with a lot of discretion.[10]

The Symbolic Signification of Penetration

Penetration represents a crossing of the body's boundaries. As Mary Douglas[11] has shown, beliefs about pollution and danger are often connected to such crossings. In the case of Mexico, we may see how certain beliefs about penetration are connected to the perception of gender, to gender categories, and to categorizations within each gender (as virgin or woman, as man or homosexual). Men fear becoming homosexual if they are penetrated, and this implies crossing from one category to another. In this sense penetration is seen as a source of pollution – men are polluted with femininity.

In a similar way, a girl who is penetrated 'is made into a woman', according to a common expression in Mexico. She crosses from girlhood, maidenhood, to womanhood, possibly motherhood – an irreversible passage. This is reflected, for instance, in popular songs where a man claims that a woman belongs to him, even if she now lives with somebody else, because 'le hice mujer' – 'I made her a woman'. A maiden may become a woman and a mother by penetration, and thereby improve her social standing. But if the man abandons her afterwards, and she turns to other men, she risks becoming a whore – a transformation as dramatic as the one the penetrated man is subjected to. Then the penetration has implied some sort of pollution; something sticks to her. Marit Melhuus[12] describes the different representations of women that compose the Mexican imagery of femininity: the Virgin of Guadalupe; the mother; the traitor Malinche; and the bad woman, the whore. All these representations can be linked to acts of penetration or non-penetration. The unpenetrated virgin, the mother who compensates for the loss of maidenhood with motherhood, Malinche who became the mistress of the conquistador, the whore who has had too many men. As indicated, penetration is also important for the imagery of masculinity. This might be illustrated by the constant use of references to penetration in verbal badgering among working-class Mexican men. Mexican men are typically homosocial, working together and gathering at public places after work. These gatherings are – according to observers like Octavio Paz, R. Diaz-Guerrero and José Limón[13] – characterized by a wordplay called *el juego de los albures*. I will take an example from Limón, from a bar in Texas where Mexican men gather to eat *tacos* and drink beer.

Jaime greets Simón, and Simón takes his hand and holds it firmly over his own genital area as he responds to the other's 'How are you?' by saying '¡Pos, chinga ahora me siento a toda madre, gracias!' (Well, fuck, now I feel just great, thank you!). Jaime responds by grabbing Simón's genitals and squeezing them. They end up on the floor, Simón drops his *taco*, and Jaime asks him to say that he loves him. Simón finally says: 'Te quiero, te quiero' (I love you, I love you), but as soon as he is released, he says: 'Te quiero dar en la madre' (I want to beat the hell out of you), playing on the double meaning of 'quiero' as 'I want' or 'I love'. They exchange some semi-mock punches before helping each other up, and then Jaime tells Simón: 'Dejando de chingaderas, anda a traer otro taco y traile uno a tu papa' (All screwing around aside, go get another *taco* and get one for your father).

To name oneself the other's father is a common way of marking one's superiority. And it was Jaime who won this fight. First, Simón tried to put Jaime in the role of the homosexual, by letting him 'caress' his genitals. But Jaime turned the tables and got Simón into the homosexual role by getting him to say he loved Jaime.

According to Paz, the loser in this kind of sexualized game is the one who cannot answer, who has to swallow the other's words – words loaded with sexual aggression. Hence the loser is symbolically raped by the other. Limón regards Paz's interpretation as condescending, and claims that the aggression is mostly a mockery, and that the play is about solidarity between men, not about humiliation. My interpretation would be that men display their masculinity by putting their fellows in feminine or subordinate positions (which in the Mexican context are the same) – by putting them in the homosexual role. And just as in children's games, the limits between teasing and mobbing, and between mobbing and violence, are not and cannot be clear. While Limón's interpretation of the cases he has observed seems reasonable, not all cases seem to be as good-tempered as these are. In some instances the games create social bonds between all participants; in others only between the participants on the one side.

Eduardo Archetti[14] has shown how Argentinian football supporters try to humiliate and offend the other team by representing them as children or as homosexuals in their songs or their shouting. After a goal the supporters from the winning team sing: 'And now, now, they suck my balls well'. Another team gets the following message: 'Wipe your asshole, we're going to fuck you'. To make it clear that they have no intention of giving the others pleasure, they promise to burst them. Archetti interprets this as a ritual where men's identity is constructed by underscoring the difference between being a man and being a homosexual, where being a man stands for power, strength, independence and authority. Reducing the other to less than a man, to a homosexual, implies an enhancement of one's own masculinity, while showing that the other is unable to defend his masculine identity. Archetti also shows that those who are subject to this labelling do not appreciate it, and that the teasing sometimes goes together with violence.

El juego de los albures is a public ritual where references to the body are used as metaphors.[15] The ass is an area of the body through which one might be humiliated; it is a very sensitive part of the male body.[16] As Paz has put it,[17] the male body is seen as closed, and the female body as open, or as opened by a male. The ass is the place where even a male body might be threatened, might be opened – thus resembling a female body. In this discourse the act of penetration is the most central metaphor, and very often linked to violence. Mexican swear words tend to focus on rape (in contrast to the more common Latin American focus on the mother's promiscuity or prostitution). The verb *chingar* means everything from pestering to rape; a man may be characterized as a son of a raped woman, or he can be encouraged to rape his mother himself. But to be *chingón*, someone who pesters and rapes, is positive – not sympathetic but smart, cunning, someone who knows how to get along and to gain advantage from others.[18]

But not only are metaphors based on reality, a play with what could really happen, but what happens in reality also refers to metaphors. The practised male homosexuality follows the same pattern as the metaphorical homosexuality. What the men in the Texan bar and the men I have studied have in common is to have been born men, and born into the working class with scant opportunities for social mobility. The only status to be obtained is among equals. Here, among them, a man's masculinity is under constant attack by other men. His defence of his own bodily boundaries and attacks on other men's – whether symbolic attacks like the ones Limón and Archetti described, or the concrete acts of penetration I have described – may mirror and symbolize the social competition among men.

Domination and Violence

The struggle over the definitions of masculinity is a struggle between men; and given the masculine domination in Mexican society, men also have considerable power over the definitions of femininity. Forms of masculinity and femininity become symbolic capital, contributing to determine positions in the social space.

Pierre Bourdieu[19] writes about how schemes of perception and appreciation are connected to the body, and at the same time linked to a more general, cultural scheme of oppositions between up and down, front and back, right and left, wet and dry, hard and soft, and so on. The divisions of things and of activities between women and men might be seen as arbitrary if they are seen in isolation, but they are given their 'naturalness' through an insertion into this scheme of oppositions; and thereby the underlying social relations of domination are hidden. These relations are somatized, they are naturalized through an inscription in the mind's schemes of perception and in the bodily *hexis*. Bourdieu shows how the Kabyl (of Algeria) connect all that ranks highest to masculinity. The eyes, the nose, the moustache and the mouth are all elements related to a presentation of the self, and are used in ways that underline one's masculinity. To look somebody in the eyes and to speak in public places is reserved for men. It is against this background that what Bourdieu calls the Mediterranean offence *par excellence* – allusions to male homosexuality – should be understood as linked to the bottom, a feminine and degraded part of the body.

Gérard Mauger and Claude Fossé-Poliak[20] point to how the male body might be used as a principle of domination in youth gangs outside Paris. Subjected to cultural and economic domination, the young men try to impose their own principle of domination, based on physical force and on a 'capital of masculinity'. They dress up and move around like cowboys, they use tattoos, they talk *argot*, they fight, they like hard rock, football and motorbikes. Through this presentation of themselves they express, as Bourdieu says regarding working-class men, a 'practical philosophy of the male body as a sort of power, big and strong, with enormous, imperative, brutal needs'.[21] He claims that if men are forbidden every sort of 'pretension' in matters of culture, language or clothing, it is not only because aesthetic refinement is reserved for women or associated with the bourgeoisie: 'It is also because a surrender to demands perceived as simultaneously feminine and bourgeois appears as the index of a dual repudiation of virility, a twofold submission which ordinary language, naturally conceiving all domination in the logic and lexicon of sexual domination, is predisposed to express.'[22] One of the examples given from ordinary language is *pédé* – faggot. Mauger and Fossé-Poliak see this word as a marker of the distinction from a world in which working-class men have no chance to succeed – but still they claim to be superior to that world, basing their self-esteem on other values, like the male body.

But *pédé* is not merely a metaphor: there *are* homosexuals who are exposed to violence:

And if the homosexuals have been and maybe still are the prime targets of the tough guys, this is not so much a sign of 'repressed homosexual impulses' as because they sum up at the same time, from the tough guys' point of view, the cultural pretension, the financial pretension (first and foremost regarding clothing) and the sexual negation of virility.[23]

Faggot becomes a metaphor for femininity in men, including the pretentious, the refined and fancy, the verbalized and culturally educated as opposed to the strength of the body. This shows that the different social classes' representations of masculinity do not follow the hierarchy of social power, but give a certain superiority to the working-class representation of masculinity, or at least working-class men have an autonomy in their representation of themselves (they do not take over the dominant definition of them as their own definition of themselves).[24] Masculinity as a bodily principle of domination is a tool for resistance against class domination.

The homosexual occupies a central role in the definition of masculinity: in many societies, he is a cultural symbol for the opposite of the masculine man. In Latin America he is often used as a negative label in the upbringing of boys: 'Don't cry, you little faggot'. A more violent use of the expression is quoted by Bech,[25] in the context of the training of Greek soldiers to become torturers under the military junta. The term for the passive homosexual was the favourite invective used by the officers towards the soldiers or by the torturers towards their victims. To label the other a passive homosexual was a humiliation, and at the same time what justified the humiliation. The homosexual is used in the same way in verbal play and mock fights between Mexican men, and by the public at Argentinian soccer games. In the Argentinian examples it was only the masculine, penetrating party who derived any pleasure from the act in the songs, by having his testicle sucked or by penetrating the other. Yet it was only the other, the one who was forced, the one who was passive, who was homosexual.

According to Bourdieu,[26] power and domination imply mastering the categorizations and appreciations, the possibility of enforcing one's judgements as valid. It is the masculine men who define what homosexuality is and who the homosexual is, as they may also define acceptable and unacceptable sexual behaviour for women. They have the labelling power, as Lorraine Nencel puts it, and may thereby affirm their own masculinity. Their categorizations allow them to escape stigma – in Argentinian football songs as well as Mexican sexual practice. Homosexuality is defined as pertaining only to passive homosexuals: they carry all the shame and guilt, while the active part remains normal, invisible and manly. That is why violent homophobia, *machismo*, and widespread male bisexuality go so well together. The masculine domination, the subordination of the feminine, the degradation of the homosexual – these are the conditions for the homoerotic freedom of masculine men. This is evident in group rapes where men enjoy having sex with homosexuals, while ensuring that they are degraded and condemned. But I believe that relations of domination also structure the more friendly or loving relationships between masculine-looking men and effeminate homosexuals in Mexico, as it is only on the basis of masculine domination that the masculine party may enter these relationships without having his social identity or his self-image threatened. This power gives a licence to pleasure.

A Struggle for Dignity

But what, then, about the other part – the effeminate homosexuals? Why do they participate so willingly? Bourdieu[27] claims that the most important form of domination is not coercion but complicity. The dominated share the dominators' schemes of perception and appreciation. The effeminate homosexuals are victims of this symbolic violence, becoming victims of their own categorizations and appreciations. Dominance and masculinity are at stake whenever an effeminate homosexual meets a masculine man – yet these encounters might give both parties love and pleasure, just as love and pleasure are possible in relationships between women and men, blacks and whites, despite the long history of oppression and dominance. On the other hand, the dominated party probably always develops some strategies for gaining dignity from below, some sort of resistance – just as working-class men may use their valorization of physical force as a resistance against the deprivation of other resources. We may read Melhuus[28] as a description of how female subordination is compensated in Mexican gender imagery by a moral superiority given to women. This is not, of course, a revalorization available to the homosexuals, as they may be neither virgins nor mothers.

The effeminacy of the working-class homosexuals might be interpreted as a result of social pressure,[29] as a way of adapting to a *macho* society. The effeminate homosexuals themselves, however, do not perceive themselves as forced into effeminacy. Quite the contrary: they consider femininity as natural for them, and condemn all kinds of social restrictions that might force homosexuals 'to not play out that part of themselves'. As we have seen, working-class homosexual transvestites may call middle-class homosexuals closeted and cowardly. As middle-class homosexuals are less effeminate, transvestites claim that they hide their homosexuality. Middle-class homosexuals' refusal to be effeminate may be interpreted as an attempt to maintain their social status despite their homosexuality. By contrast, the young homosexuals from the working class have no status to lose. Indeed, they have something to gain by adopting an effeminate style: confronted with middle-class homosexuals, they gain self-respect by referring themselves to the same hierarchy of masculinity as the working-class men do. Transvestites cannot brag about their own masculinity, but then neither can middle-class homosexuals. But transvestites may brag about their sexual partners' masculinity, as indicated by the following example. An effeminate homosexual at a gay disco told me he had just met a middle-class homosexual in the toilet, and the latter had said with heavy contempt, pointing at the former's enormous, artificial buttocks: 'So much oil! It's horrible!' – 'You don't mean that. You'd give a fortune for that ass, even if it was just for one night.' – 'That's what you think?' – 'Of course. You've got no ass at all. And the men I get are real *machines*, while you've got to content yourself with other *tortilleras*.'

Machines means very masculine men; *tortilleras* means more androgynous gays who both penetrate and are penetrated. And actually, it is striking that at clubs frequented by working-class homosexuals there are a lot of heterosexual-looking men, together with the effeminate gays and transvestites, while at more middle-class venues there are very few heterosexual-looking men.

But how do the effeminate gays and transvestites defend themselves against the contempt of their working-class surroundings – their families, neighbours and partners? My overall impression is that there seems to be a firm belief among the working class that effeminate homosexuals are born effeminate and homosexual. They claim that even as small children they wanted to play with their sisters' dolls instead of their own toy cars, that they also played at dressing up in their mother's clothes, and that they felt the urge for sexual contact with men very early. Usually they have had severe conflicts with their families over this, but after a certain time the parents resign themselves, and stop trying to change their son's femininity and homosexuality. The essentialist view on homosexuality and effeminate style is rather tolerant: what cannot be changed must be accepted – although not necessarily appreciated. Moreover, in the area where I did my fieldwork, most transvestites lived with their parents, and contributed to the family household. Earning money and sharing it is a way of gaining respect from relatives. Most of the effeminate homosexuals also have an impressive linguistic competence, and can defend themselves verbally, often through mockery and humour.

But still, when they are with their partners, how do they respond to a situation so loaded with domination and contempt? One strategy is to show that they are smarter than their partners. They will often steal something from them. I do not think those thefts are only economically motivated. From the way they talk about them, I get the firm impression that the important point is to show their own smartness. But the most important strategies concern gender play: effeminate homosexuals use a dual-track strategy to neutralize the loss of male honour. They either refer to their femininity, or they make use of their maleness.

The first strategy is to become female as far as possible by looking like women, acting like women, and often passing as women. Then it is 'only natural' that they should let themselves be penetrated like women – they are women, or almost. An affirmation of their femininity lies in the partners' masculinity, which they may help to maintain by always taking the passive part in intercourse – or at least, pretending to. In more lasting relationships they often expect their lovers to be rather stereotypical, traditional *machos*, and they may accept a certain subordination – because the more masculine the partner is, the more feminine they feel themselves.

The second strategy is to use their own maleness to deprive their partners of their masculinity. For how can he despise them if he lets himself be penetrated, too?[30] These two strategies, although contradictory, may be combined, as the story of Pancha shows.

Pancha did not want his lover to come to the place where the homosexuals meet, but he did anyway. 'He came, he slept with Mema, he slept with Francisca, he slept with Gloria – and they fucked him. On top of the whole damn thing, they fucked him. So I was embarrassed and didn't want anything more to do with him.' Infidelity is one issue, but letting oneself be penetrated is going over the limit. Pancha had never penetrated his lover. 'I don't care if he lets himself be turned over, what's it to me? It's his asshole and his business, isn't it? But not when I can see it, and even less if it's with the people I hang around with. Because now they're making fun of me. Not of him, but of me.' I am puzzled by this, because I know that Pancha likes to penetrate. But preferably not his lover, because: 'Then I feel that he's less of a man than I am. Just think about it – a queer and me. If I go dressed as a woman with him, then I am a woman and he is a man, right? But then there is no point in me going all stuffed out or wearing a dress or high-heeled shoes or a bra or nylons. If I am to do it as a man, it's better that he wears the skirt.'

The example of Pancha illustrates that it is precisely the contradictory nature of the two strategies that makes them the perfect response to an ambiguous situation. If he juggles the strategies well, he will always be the winner. Rather than being neither woman nor man, the effeminate homosexual tries to be both; he juggles with gender. Femininity is the proof that the homosexual is a victim of his essence; consequently, he cannot be blamed for being penetrated. Still, it is a loss of male honour, and he ends up at the bottom of the pecking order, free prey for male aggression and desire. However, he can turn the tables by defending himself with his own physical maleness, and deprive other men of their masculinity. This strategy is a defence against the dominant definition of him, by labelling negatively those who label him negatively, in the same way as many other stigmatized groups have tried to disperse the stigma that is put on them.[31]

The story of Pancha also shows that clothes, physical presentation and sexual acts are signs which, taken together, constitute and maintain masculinity and femininity. Gender is composed of signs that refer mutually to each other, so why wear feminine signs if the partner doesn't respect the masculine signs he is supposed to show? The game breaks down, and Pancha must choose between taking off his bra and his foam-rubber padding and finding himself another man. When the rules of the game are not followed, there is no point playing any more.

In all societies genders are constructed through a symbol system inscribed in minds, which most of the time functions automatically and makes us take the social world, with its sexual divisions, as given. This symbolic system refers heavily to 'nature' and to the body, and thereby gives the genders their 'naturalness'. Gendered categories like 'man', 'homosexual', 'woman' and 'maiden' are based on certain ideas about the body, the body's boundaries and bodily practices and, in this Mexican example, first and foremost on ideas about penetration. In other societies the bodily rules and the symbolism connected to the body may be very different, and the specific focus on penetration may not be found. But the symbolic of active versus passive might have a wide validity for the understanding of gender, and within what has a very wide validity is male domination, so deeply inscribed in the schemes of perception and appreciation that it appears to be natural, as Bourdieu states.[32] In the representation of masculinity, the homosexual man serves in Mexico as a symbol of not-male, whether he is physically present or just symbolically represented in a game between men. Thereby, by being the negation of masculinity, he contributes to the definition of it, to the perception of malehood and to the constitution of men's self-images.

Through these representations a fundamental *difference* is created between two kinds of men which, biologically speaking, are the same, and in the homosexual relationships the two parties usually co-operate to maintain this difference. But the possibility that at any moment the other can turn out to be the same as oneself, as only an appearance separates the two, is the reason these relationships are so fragile – that they may so easily switch from love to disgust, as for Pancha; or from sexual pleasure to aggression and violence, as has happened for many bisexual men, with the homosexuals as the victims.

Notes

1. For a more detailed account of methodological and analytical issues, see Annick Prieur, *Stealing Femininity. Male Homosexuality in Mexico*, Chicago, forthcoming.

2. For Nicaragua, see Roger N. Lancaster, 'Subject Honor and Object Shame: The Construction of Male Homosexuality and Stigma in Nicaragua', *Ethnology*, vol. 27, 1988. For Brazil, see Richard Parker, 'Masculinity, Femininity, and Homosexuality: On the Anthropological Interpretation of Sexual Meanings in Brazil', *Journal of Homosexuality*, vol. 14, 1986; Richard Parker, 'Youth, Identity, and Homosexuality: The Changing Shape of Sexual Life in Contemporary Brazil', *Journal of Homosexuality* vol. 17 nos 3–4, 1989; Rommel Mendès-Leite, 'Les apparences en jeu', *Sociétés*, no. 17, 1988; Andrea Cornwall, 'Gendered Identities and Gender Ambiguity among Travestis in Salvador, Brazil', in Andrea Cornwall and Nancy Lindisfarne eds, *Dislocating Masculinities: Comparative Ethnographies*, London and New York 1994. For both Brazil and Guatemala, see Frederick L. Whitam and Robin M. Mathy, *Male Homosexuality in Four Societies, Brazil, Guatemala, the Philippines and the United States*, New York 1986; and concerning Chicanos, Tomás Almaguer, 'Chicano Men: A Cartography of Homosexual Identity and Behavior', *Differences*, vol. 3, no. 2, 1991.

3. See J.M. Carrier, 'Participants in Urban Mexican Male Homosexual Encounters', *Archives of Sexual Behaviour*, vol. 1, no. 4, 1971; J.M. Carrier, 'Cultural Factors Affecting Urban Mexican Male Homosexual Behavior', *Archives of Sexual Behaviour*, vol. 5, no. 2, 1976; J.M. Carrier, 'Mexican Male Bisexuality', in Fritz Klein *et al.*, *Bisexualities: Theory and Research*, New York and London 1985; J.M. Carrier, 'Sexual Behavior and Spread of AIDS in Mexico', *Medical Anthropology*, vol. 10, nos 2–3, 1989; Joseph M. Carrier, 'Gay Liberation and Coming-Out in Mexico',

Journal of Homosexuality, vol. 17, nos 3–4, 1989; Ana María Alonso and María Teresa Koreck, 'Silences: "Hispanics", AIDS, and Sexual Practices', *Differences*, vol. 1, no. 1, 1988; Ian Lumsden, *Homosexualidad, Sociedad y Estado en México*, Mexico City and Toronto 1991; and Clark L. Taylor, 'Mexican Male Homosexual Interaction in Public Contexts', *Journal of Homosexuality*, vol. 14, 1986.

4. See Lorraine Nencel this volume, Chapter 3 above.

5. Confirmed by Carrier 1985; Alonso and Koreck; and Taylor.

6. Carrier 1985, pp. 77–8.

7. Alonso and Koreck, p. 111.

8. Pierre Bourdieu claims that it is a prerequisite for the interviewer to already know, and that the interviewed knows the interviewer already knows when the interview deals with certain very sensitive issues where it will be too humiliating for the interviewed to admit the truth unless he or she knows the truth is already known (in Pierre Bourdieu *et al.*, *La Misère du monde*, Paris 1994).

9. If this is true, it may explain some of the difficulties involved in reaching bisexual men with AIDS education; many may not admit even to themselves that they are relevant targets.

10. Andrea Cornwall shows that while the majority of the Salvadorian transvestite prostitutes' clients probably want the transvestite to penetrate them, they are still commonly believed to be acting 'as men', as inserters.

11. Mary Douglas, *Purity and Danger*, London and New York 1966; and *Natural Symbols: Explorations in Cosmology*, New York 1982.

12. Marit Melhuus, this volume, Chapter 10 below. See also Marit Melhuus, '*Todos Tenemos Madre, Dios También*': Morality, Meaning and Change in a Mexican Context, PhD thesis in social anthropology, University of Oslo, 1993.

13. Octavio Paz, *El Laberinto de la Soledad*, Mexico City, Madrid and Buenos Aires [1950] 1980; R. Diaz-Guerrero, 'Adolescence in Mexico. Some Cultural, Psychological and Psychiatric Aspects', *International Mental Research Health Newsletter*, vol. 12, no. 4, 1970; José E. Limón, '*Carne, Carnales and the Carnivalesque*: Bakhtinian *Batos*, Disorder, and Narrative Discourses', *American Ethnologist*, vol. 16, no. 3, 1989.

14. Eduardo Archetti, 'Fotball og nasjonal etos', in Egil 'Drillo' Olsen, ed., *Fotball – mer enn et spill*, Oslo 1985; and 'Argentinian Football: A Ritual of Violence?', *The International Journal of the History of Sport*, vol. 9, no. 2, 1992.

15. Douglas 1966.

16. 'Behind' is *zona sagrada* in other Latin American societies, too, to the point where – according to Eduardo Archetti (personal communication) – while Argentinian parents commonly let their daughters use suppositories or measure their temperature rectally, they never let their sons do so – out of fear that they might enjoy it!

17. Paz, pp. 26–7.
18. On the connotations of *chingar*, see also Melhuus, this volume, Chapter 10 below.
19. Pierre Bourdieu, 'La Domination masculine,' *Actes de la recherche en sciences sociales*, no. 84, 1990.
20. Gérard Mauger and Claude Fossé-Poliak, 'Les Loubards', *Actes de la recherche en sciences sociales*, no. 50, 1983; Gérard Mauger, 'Enquêter en milieu populaire', *Genèses*, no. 6, 1991.
21. Pierre Bourdieu, *Distinction: A Social Critique of the Judgment of Taste*, Cambridge, MA and London 1984, p. 192.
22. Ibid., p. 382.
23. Mauger and Fossé-Poliak, p. 66.
24. Bourdieu 1984, p. 384.
25. Henning Bech, *Når mænd mødes. Homoseksualiteten og de homoseksuelle*, Copenhagen 1987, pp. 61–2.
26. Bourdieu 1984.
27. Pierre Bourdieu (with Loïc J.D. Wacquant), *An Invitation to Reflexive Sociology*, Cambridge 1992.
28. Melhuus 1993.
29. Lumsden, p. 35.
30. Cornwall found the same judgements of men who are penetrated among Brazilian *travestis*, but takes it simply as a fact that they are sharing the masculinists' attitudes that render them objects of abuse. I believe it is also a defence of the weak: they despise those who despise them, for not living up to their own standards.
31. For instance, drug users who condemn alcohol abuse, thieves who condemn tax fraud, immigrants who state that all are descendants of immigrants, or prostitutes who claim that all women have to sell themselves in one way or another.
32. Bourdieu 1990.

5

Masculinity and the Political
among Dominicans:
'The Dominican Tiger'

Christian Krohn-Hansen

Two sets of claims are supported in this essay. First, notions of masculinity among Dominicans have played, and continue to play, a central part in the everyday production of political legitimacy – inside and outside the political parties, and the state.[1] Ideas about masculinity among Dominicans constitute a dominant discourse – or what is summed up by Pierre Bourdieu's notion of a 'legitimate problematic'.[2] A legitimate problematic helps to produce a field of what is politically thinkable, and a particular set of power relations. Among Dominicans, the legitimate problematic of masculinity has entailed a particular confinement of society's hegemonic political imagination, that is, the reproduction (albeit a changeable one) of a certain vision of what has constituted political reality. Or – to put it another way – a number of verbal expressions that are used in daily life in Dominican society in order to classify and shape different forms of male behaviour (like 'courage', 'generosity', 'eloquence', 'seriousness', and so forth) represent political categories and expressions:[3] relations between leaders and followers, or patrons and clients, are given meaning in terms of ideas about masculinity – far more than, for example, in terms of a version of a thinking about Weberian bureaucracy.[4]

Second, since the 1930s a particular term for labelling and classifying certain men's behaviour has established itself as a common one among Dominicans. The central meaning of this label, the *tíguere*,[5] is 'survivor in his environment'. The term is used to classify men in a wide spectrum of positions (for example, a wholesale trader or a street trader; an engineer or a worker; a doctor or a magician; a Congress deputy or a lower-level public employee; and a professor or a student). According to the first book to be published on the subject of the Dominican uses of the word *tíguere*, a collection of essays by the Dominican journalist and author Lipe Collado, this label may, at present, be one of the most frequently employed words in the country. As he says, Dominicans abroad

> are often called 'Dominican *tígueres*', for that word is always on their lips; and why not? For they are characterized by 'a tone', a personal style that makes them different from the other Hispano-Americans, and . . . from the other inhabitants of the earth. . . . Hence, in order to know the Dominican, one must know the *tíguere*, that magnificent expression of the 'creole'.[6]

The *tíguere* can be seen as the essence of any successful pragmatism: he is a type who acts according to the situation, is cunning, and has a gift for improvisation. I shall argue here that the image of the *tíguere* represents both an everyday hero and a sort of trickster (difficult to classify fully in terms of conventional moral notions on which people draw to interpret and debate men's behaviour). Common to most of those men referred to by this label is that they appear to embody a moral and political power which is ambiguous. The Dominican mythology of the *tíguere* has shaped, and continues to shape, a man who is both astute and socially intelligent; both courageous and smart; both cunning and convincing; and a gifted talker who gets out of most situations in a manner that is acceptable to others, while he himself does not at any time step back, stop chasing, or lose sight of his aim (be it women, money, a job, a promotion, etc.). Like the other labels and categories used by Dominicans to classify and interpret masculinity, the label of the *tíguere* is mobilized in order to answer questions about what happens politically – that is, in order to construct legitimacy.

The Dominican production of the cult of the *tíguere* – or of a highly situational and pragmatic approach to relationships with others – has to be situated as part of a protracted national history of political turbulence and repression. As I hope to indicate

briefly towards the end of my discussion, the most important
formative period in the history of the image of 'the Dominican
tíguere' overlaps with the regime of Rafael Trujillo, the general
who ruled the country on the basis of military terror from 1930
to 1961. Ordinary men in the capital, oppressed by the Trujillo
state, first shaped the male type who became labelled the *tíguere*;
later the use of the image spread to the rest of the country.

I shall deal only with the categories and labels Dominican
men use in order to construct differences between themselves as
men. The issue of how the man–woman relationship could be
said to feed into the masculine relations I consider lies beyond
the scope of this discussion; so do specifically female Dominican
perspectives. Having said this, however, I also believe that the
verbal expressions on which men typically draw in daily life
when they classify and evaluate each other as men are the ones
that explicitly structure masculinity in this society as a dominant
political discourse or as a central legitimate problematic. The
bulk of my data was collected during fieldwork in 1991–92 in a
village which I call San Antonio, on the southern Dominican–
Haitian border. The notions with which I deal, however, ought
to be understood as representative of a Dominican national
pattern; masculinity is a dominant political discourse across the
country, and is produced, reproduced, and modified by ordinary
people in everyday life.[7]

At this point, it is worth commenting on the issue of what may
account for the high relevance of daily-life notions of masculinity
as a sort of shared 'language' for constructions of power and
legitimacy among Dominicans. While no satisfactory answer can
be provided at this stage, two points of a comparative, historical
nature should be noted. First, from the sixteenth century
onwards, Spain's colonies in the Caribbean (i.e. Cuba, Santo
Domingo and Puerto Rico) saw the development of continuums
of social definitions of race; these societies also saw the development of a relatively common culture in terms of language and
religion. In short, the degree of social and cultural mixture in
these societies provided a basis for the production of a relatively
homogeneous 'creole' (and later national) culture.[8] Another way
of putting this is to say that in general the elites in the Spanish
colonial settings of the New World were more 'creole' – or what

Sidney Mintz, in the Caribbean context, has called more 'insular' – than the elites in the British, French and Dutch colonies, whose self-identifications remained more like those of 'foreigners' and 'guests'.[9] While, for instance, the British West Indies contained relatively divided social worlds before and after Independence, the Hispanic Caribbean's historic patterns of (relative) fluidity and intermingling entailed that, as in a number of Hispanophone areas of the Latin American mainland, elites and ordinary people together produced a set of important, overlapping ideas and values – not least ideas tied to gender and masculinity. While the sharp internal discontinuities of the British, French and Dutch colonies meant a withholding of political power and responsibility from the masses there, ordinary people in Santo Domingo, from early on, helped to shape political culture.

Second, the Dominican Republic was founded in 1844 (i.e. only shortly after the new republics on the Latin American mainland had been established; and, with the exception of Haiti, long before the other states in the Caribbean) – and then only after a half-century which saw much political turbulence and a Haitian occupation (from 1822 to 1844).[10] A crucial meaning connected with these facts is that the Dominican state did not 'benefit' from modern colonial governance or from a transfer of contemporary systems and practices from a retrenching colonial power[11] (unlike, for example, the relatively newly independent states in the former British West Indies). At the very least, these circumstances entailed that specific notions of masculinity *could* establish themselves as a central political discourse in the new state once Independence had been gained in 1844.[12]

While the next section seeks to sketch how specific notions of masculinity are mobilized by men in San Antonio in order to articulate and evaluate the exercise of power, the rest of the essay will concentrate on the attempt to shed light on the use of the image of the *tíguere*.

Classifying Men

Men's categories for reflecting on, and judging, each other's and (local and national) politicians' maleness may be discussed in terms of five sets of ideas:[13] notions (1) of *valentía*, or courage; (2) of men's visibility in public spaces; (3) of the man as seducer and father; (4) of the power tied to a man's verbal skills; and (5) of a man's seriousness and sincerity. Let us consider each of these items in turn.

1. A central image of masculinity is that of the *hombre valiente*, the spirited, courageous, and brave man. People in the Dominican Republic use two words, *valiente* and *guapo*, largely as synonyms; as a man in the village explained:

> 'The man who is *guapo* is he who knows how to defend himself when he is presented with a problem. For example, it is not that I come threatening you, saying "I'm *guapo*". It is when you come to me that I know how to answer you and that I prepare myself to die defending this [or what is mine]; he is the *guapo*. It is not the man who walks about talking nonsense, it's not that kind of man. He is a boaster [*bocón*]. The man who fights when it is necessary to fight, he is the *guapo*, the *valiente*; yes, the same man who is *valiente*, a man who is *guapo*, he is the one.'

The fact that people use the word *guapo* in this way emphasizes that fighting is not viewed as necessarily destructive or evil. In Spanish, *guapo* means 'beautiful' or 'handsome'; in short, some men engaged in fighting seem beautiful. There is an image here of the beauty of certain forms of male fighting and violence, the forms said to express *valentía*, or courage.[14] However, Dominicans do not assume that respect is derived from giving rise to or provoking a fight; what is cultivated is a man's practice of fearless, active defence if he is challenged or attacked by a rival: 'He who is *valiente* waits for you to fall upon him. Then he will fight.'

The ideal which says that a man ought to be *guapo* or *valiente* is used not only to shape views of the actions of ordinary villagers and local leaders, but also to explain and justify the practices of national leaders and presidents. Leaders' ways of acting in political conflicts and rivalries – such as election battles – become evaluated in terms of these categories. For example, a man explained that he had once been a follower of Juan Bosch,[15] but had changed his political loyalty; as he said: 'I was a follower of Bosch in the 1960s. But I don't like Bosch, because Bosch cackles a lot, and the politicians must be *guapos*, like the

men in the pueblos. . . . Bosch is supported by all the good
people of the pueblos, but he suffers from two things, that he
isn't *valiente*, nor does he "turn loose the peso" [or distribute
money among his followers].' In 1990, Bosch's party received
more votes than Joaquín Balaguer's; Balaguer won the presidency only on the votes of tiny allied parties. But Bosch and
many others claim that Balaguer stole the victory by fraud.[16] For
example, a San Antonio man said laconically: 'Bosch won in the
ballot boxes, Balaguer won in the computers.' The same man
who criticized Bosch above claimed that Bosch 'had gone to
sleep' on election day rather than practising ruthless vigilance
(unlike what the *guapo* would have done), and had let them take
what belonged to him. As he chose to formulate it: 'There are
moments for eating, and there are moments for sleeping.'

2. Another set of ideas revolves around an image of the man
as one who should *dejarse ver* or make himself visible in public
spaces. Men's 'physical movements' are given different meanings
according to the cultural and moral horizon of the interpreters.
The same has to be said for men's 'public visibility' in the pueblo
or city landscape.

A San Antonio man's critical perspective on the typical daily
movements of two of his co-villagers should make this clear.
First he criticizes the mayor of San Antonio, comparing him to
the (in his, and many others', opinion much better) mayor in the
provincial capital. Thereafter he lets an ordinary villager (like
himself) have it:

> 'In the provincial capital things are like here, there are no
> resources. But if you go there, you get envious. That park is nice, and
> the man who is doing it is the mayor . . . with resources that he
> obtains from absentee villagers: he goes to the capital . . . he writes to
> them in New York. . . . He himself has contributed economically. . . .
> L. [the name of the mayor of the provincial capital] goes out [*sale*];
> L. moves [*brinca*]; but not this one [San Antonio's mayor], he has
> gone to bed and that's what we find bad, a bad mayor, because he
> doesn't let himself be seen [*no se deja ver*]. . . . He doesn't participate
> in social life [*no comparte*]. One must go to the public places. Look,
> I don't go to the cockfight arena, for I'm not a cockfighter. But I go to
> the park. . . . But he doesn't go anywhere, nowhere. L. is seen, he is
> here . . . he is everywhere, he is a good mayor.'

This same villager draws a portrait of a man who died a couple of years earlier, the father of two of my friends in the village:

[Speaking first about drinking] 'Well, if you don't drink and don't dance, but are around [*está en el medio*], it is acceptable, for I can't force you to drink or dance if you don't like it; . . . but [you should] not [stay] at home all the time. Let yourself be seen in the park . . . go to the wakes, go to a club. Because here there lived a man who died [recently]. Well, you know his sons. That man was "from home to work" [*era 'de la casa a su trabajo'*, i.e. never socialized]. People called him "mad", [and could say] "that man only works. He doesn't even have two drinks". [Others said] "No, let that man alone, for he doesn't bother you in the streets." [That may be so] but neither does he bother you in the bar or in the cockfighting arena, not even in your home, because he is "from work to home"!'

Stories of ordinary men's and politicians' visibility in public spaces draw meaning from a discourse on the need for, and 'naturalness' of, a certain generosity. The good man spends time and shares resources with his friends [*es un hombre que comparte*].[17] In other words, to characterize a man's 'visibility' (in the park, in the streets and in the bars) is to speak directly about his will to enter into and use friendships (without which there would be no 'politics' in the established sense of that word). Basically, moral evaluations of a man's 'public visibility' say something about that man's willingness to do others a favour. A man in San Antonio put it like this: 'They don't see you, you don't go out, you don't give money.'

Given these notions of the value of ostentatious male giving and generosity, we may see a politico-moral dilemma for the followers of Juan Bosch: Bosch's aim has been to help the common man – or the poor Dominican masses – on the basis of a reformed state bureaucracy. However, many ordinary Dominicans probably interpret Bosch's way of 'making himself visible in the public space' as a disquieting sign – precisely in terms of notions such as (personalized) 'generosity' and 'help'. When Bosch ignores established concepts of giving in politics (or Dominican patronage ideals), and thereby refrains from 'making himself visible', he lays himself open to a collective reading of himself which argues that he does not provide the support which good men should always offer in order to develop society. A villager whose son has worked for Bosch in San Antonio since 1973 said:

'Bosch's party [or the Party for Dominican Liberation] has many young men, who are good men. But what I'm saying is that he doesn't give. . . . They read a lot, are intelligent, but they don't have pesos, and then how do they convince? I have a son in that party, and when was that poor man given anything? Nothing. He doesn't make money, there's nothing. Juan Bosch is a very methodical man [*un hombre muy metódico*]; no one sees the money, he never has any.'

The word 'methodical' seems apt in such a context. Basically, this man's argument is only an underlining of the value of the kind of political authority that comes 'naturally' when a man is seen as *un hombre suelto*, or as a man who is 'loose'; the argument says that legitimacy in politics is derived precisely from producing the kinds of relationships which mix 'friendship', 'kinship', 'business', and 'the public'. In short, discourses which produce a difference between those men who 'make themselves visible', and those others 'who can hardly be seen' condense an entire political vision. Men who choose *not* to strive to promote their own personal visibility in the public spaces can challenge a good man's idea of what *any* politics – or, for that matter, all society – should be about.

3. Another powerful concept of masculinity, recognized by both men and women, is that of a man as moving from one woman to the next, changing partners. Such a concept may be said to correspond to an image of man as 'nomadic'.[18] An extension of this image is the man as *mujeriego* or a womanizer, engaged in the sexual conquest of women even when he is married or living in a stable union. An image of masculinity closely linked to that of the man as a womanizer is that of him as one who is always ready to party with his male friends, drinking rum, listening and dancing to music, and telling stories: a man should be a *bebedor* (drinker), a *bailador* (dancer), and *fiestero* (fun-loving).

There is, however, a second rather different notion of what it means to be a good man: men say that the man has to be a good father, providing for his *mujer*, or woman, and children. When a union or marriage breaks up, a man continues to have provider responsibility for his children, even if in practice his fulfilment of that responsibility may often be extremely limited, or completely token. This concept of masculinity presupposes that a man should sacrifice himself for his family, be loyal and supportive – in a word, prefer a 'settled' life to a 'nomadic' one. The tension between these two rather different sets of discourses on what constitutes masculinity has also been noted for the Caribbean in general. A good deal of men's constructions of male identity can be understood as continuous attempts to strike a viable balance between these two sets of moral ideals.[19]

The difference between the notion of man as a 'nomadic' seducer, and the concept of man as a 'settled' father, is mobilized in order to make sense of politics. This may be seen, for example, from a conversation I had with a man in San Antonio, a former local leader and the father of twenty-three children. Thinking back on his life with women, he said: 'I think I was a bit careless regarding that issue. To be frank, I married a good woman. But we got separated because I was a *machista*; I had another woman elsewhere. Because of that I don't really fulfil the conditions [as a complete man], for there I made some errors.' However, his recognition that he had committed 'errors' because he had been a womanizer may not have been profound. In the same conversation he stressed the value of moving from one woman to the next. Such a life, the 'nomadic' life, means that one acquires friends (who may be converted into trusted political allies; voters; and recruiters of local votes) in a large area. As he said: 'The fact that I was a womanizer did not harm my reputation. On the contrary, it helped me in my political leadership. For it meant that the fathers of the women became my friends, and their brothers and all those people. We became friends, and I was introduced to different family networks.'[20] To put it in different terms: having had relations with women in several communities, this man has been able to form, and use, ties of *compadrazgo* (or sanctified friendship) – the cement of Dominican politics – in the same communities.[21]

In short, men acknowledge a political advantage derived from drinking and womanizing. These strategies help to construct extended networks anchored in exchanges of 'trust', 'services' and 'loyalty', without which the dominant forms of the exercise of power in this society seem impossible.

4. Men and women here also associate the exercise of power with particular men's gifts for manipulating words. As Roger Abrahams says in *The Man-of-Words in the West Indies*, people in African-American settings often place a high value on verbal control and eloquence.[22] Both Dominican President Balaguer and his main rival since the early 1960s, Bosch, are intellectuals and prolific authors; and time and again, authority in politics is explicitly related by ordinary people to evaluations of verbal skills.[23] In the light of this, two points should be noted. First, the cultivation of the use of words has a practical aspect. Villagers reflect on the use of words because they have an interest in communication as a political activity; they think about the use of specific words, expressions and texts as a means of achieving tangible ends, such as a public job for someone in the household, or a public works project in their own community. The next speaker, a village politician, illustrates this. He prides himself on being a local man-of-words, and shows his understanding of the manipulation of words as a means of obtaining actual benefits (in this case, the construction of a new *barrio* or set of houses for the villagers, funded by the state). The day before these words were put on tape, he had delivered a speech at a political meeting, held by Balaguer's Reformist Party in San Antonio. Present at the meeting (apart from the village's crowd of Reformist supporters) had been his local leader, the province's Reformist Deputy to Congress (here called C.), and one of the party's top figures, the General Secretary (Luis Toral), who had arrived from Santo Domingo. Here he reproduces images from his speech the day before:

'Yesterday Luis Toral was in San Antonio. I spoke to him, and sought to motivate him. I said that the President of the Republic [Balaguer] is a man who rules the country sitting. But he has twenty-nine "thoughts", and twenty-eight of those twenty-nine he has given to each province; they have been given to the senators so that they govern, and the richest thought, the one containing most resources, he has given to [the city of Santo Domingo, i.e. the capital]. . . . But I also said [to Luis Toral] that the thought of this province hadn't worked entirely satisfactorily, for the housing situation of the poor [of San Antonio is disheartening. I said to him that] the thought of the president has "dressed" [meaning that it has constructed a *barrio* of new houses in] San Pedro, it has dressed Santa Elena, it has dressed La

Victoria, it has dressed Santiago, and it has dressed La Palma [names of villages in the province]. So it seems that the entire province beyond La Palma has God's clothing, and that San Antonio has been dressed by the Devil. And I said to Luis Toral that I had nine candles and that I had already lighted eight asking the Saints for this *barrio*, but that I had one left and that I wasn't going to light any more but that I was going to light the ninth for his saint so that he would talk with the President of the Republic and arrange a new *barrio* for San Antonio.

'Immediately after the meeting, C. [the province's Reformist Deputy to Congress] says to Luis Toral [while the man quoted here is with them and listens to them]: "Well, Luis [Toral], this man puts you under pressure, this man has an engagement." Says Luis Toral: "C., the first thing I will tell the president is this: this *barrio* of San Antonio; for this man has already said that the last man with whom he will speak about it is me. He says that he had nine candles and that he has only a single one left, which is mine, and that he will not light any more. The man has made me commit myself. C., who is this man? What sort of man is he?" He [Luis Toral] says: "That man has a natural knowledge." . . . Yes, I was born with this [gift of speech].'

Another village politician said: 'The language should be natural and plain . . . without inventing anything; in accordance with the countryside. It ought to be adapted to the surroundings. . . . For example, there are technical words which one cannot use, since . . . they [the local peasants] would not understand them.'

What is at stake here is what words can produce in social and practical terms. A few men's fame across the country for their words and books (that is, the national making of 'verbal excellence') represents a thoroughly necessary part of all this. But, more than anything, the control of speech is attractive because it is useful – a source of power.

Second, what Dominicans classify as being *político*, or politic, has largely to do with verbal skills. In his classic study *The Dominican People, 1850–1900*, Hoetink comments on Dominicans' extended use of the word *político* as an adjective. As he writes: '"Un hombre muy *político*" [a very politic man] indicates (even today) of someone that he knows how to move ably and successfully among many, sometimes antagonistic, groups.'[24] The concept of being *político* can be said to attach itself to the man who is a gifted user of words. This is so because few of the other qualities covered by the label *político* – for example, what people call *'mucho tino'* or 'a good feel for things' – can exist in a Dominican who is seen by others as a man who often lacks the right words – as a man who 'doesn't know how to speak'. The skilled use of words represents both 'ammunition' and 'protection' at all levels of society; it makes politics and leadership possible.

5. A basic concept is that of the person as *serio* (or, if used about women, *seria*), that is, serious.[25] To claim that a man isn't serious is to imply that he is shameless. Used of men, the label *sinvergüenza*, or shameless, most often connotes 'wrongdoer' or 'thief'. Bosch and his followers consistently argue that the other political parties – in particular, that of Balaguer – are in the hands of men who lack seriousness and are *sinvergüenzas*, or shameless. This discourse is a powerful one because it mobilizes key concepts used frequently in everyday life in all sectors of society; in saying that the other parties' leaders 'rob' the state, this discourse (the *Boschista* discourse) attempts to deprive them of any legitimacy. Another basic concept-pair used to characterize actions of both men and women is one that marks a distinction between *buena fe* and *mala fe*, between good and bad faith, or between sincerity and insincerity. This distinction, which expresses a thinking about good as different from evil, is also shaped in terms of differences in people's 'purity' – or their blood. People and hearts are metaphorically spoken of as *sucios* (dirty) or *limpios* (clean), implying evil or good; and the blood of evil and good people respectively is said to be *pesada* (heavy) and *liviana* (light), or *agria* (sour) and *dulce* (sweet). The saints also are contemplated through such language. Some mysteries (a common expression for 'saints' or 'spirits') are said to be sweet, while others are sour. The classification of people's *buena fe* or *mala fe*, their sincerity or insincerity, is reproduced through everyday encounters. Everything social should develop from the respect signalled by an acceptable greeting. As a man in the village said about the connection between sincerity in people and the proper greeting: 'The person who greets you without knowing you, that person has good faith, but if he doesn't greet you, he isn't completely good. He should pay attention to you, that's good faith, for if he doesn't give you the greeting – damn! He isn't complete.'

The politics of masculinity is shaped in conjunction with the daily reproduction of these most elementary notions that structure people's classifications of individuals as moral beings. Everyday classifications of men in terms of seriousness and sincerity are constitutive of the formation of relations between friends and *compadres* in local contexts, and between local leaders and followers – relations that in turn give unmistakable form to Dominicans' public life and politics.

So far I have sought to sketch the basis for drawing a conclusion which states that specific ideas and categories which structure discussions of masculinity among Dominicans correspond to a dominant political discourse – or to a legitimate problematic which helps to structure and give form to particular power relations in Dominican society. The legitimate problematic of masculinity has entailed a certain confinement of Dominican society's dominant political imagination, that is, the reproduction of certain visions of what has constituted political reality, and what has represented the politically thinkable.

In the remainder of this discussion I shall consider Dominicans' use of the tiger image. I hope to show why, and in what ways, Dominicans have put this image to use in order to give form to what many of them now see as a sort of essence of what it means to act as a Dominican male – and not only that, but as 'a Dominican' *tout court*. In the words of Collado: '[I]n order to know the Dominican, one must know the *tíguere*, that magnificent expression of the "creole".'[26]

Masculinity as Ambiguity: Men as 'Tigers'

To say of a man that he is a *tíguere* is automatically to say that his behaviour evokes several of the images of masculinity at which we have already looked. Basically, the man who is called a *tíguere* is a man who is cunning, and knows how to survive in his particular environment. As Collado has written: 'his law is "to emerge well" from every situation'.[27] At the same time, the image of the *tíguere* evokes a man who is a fighter, doesn't give in, and defends himself, and is therefore *guapo* or *valiente*. The *tíguere* is also said to be the man who 'knows everything' because 'he is everywhere'; he is a man 'who is seen' – in the streets and among his friends. He also uses seduction, and is a womanizer. The *tíguere*'s most effective tool for 'emerging well' from every situation is his 'tongue'. *Tíguere* therefore typically evokes the image of the man who is *labioso* (from *labio* [lip]), a gifted manipulator of verbal encounters.

The *tíguere* is not only a dominant symbol that flourishes on, and condenses different notions of masculinity (so that it may be used in a wide spectrum of situations, and with highly flexible meanings). It is also a sort of 'meta-image' or an image of a kind of masculine 'daily hero': an image of a man who is able to resolve, in an acceptable way, the dilemmas which have to be faced as a consequence of a tough environment and the ideals of masculinity.

I shall now attempt to substantiate these claims about the *tíguere*. I hope also to make three further points. The first is that the moral classification of the *tíguere* has to be viewed as an ambiguous one. I shall argue that *tíguere* evokes the notion of a 'trickster' – that is, an image of the kind of masculine practice that seems difficult to shape fully as 'order'. To some degree, the man who is called a *tíguere* seems to be able to transcend the limitations imposed on acceptable masculinity by the usual understandings of the categories for discussing men's actions with which I have so far dealt. The second is that the use of this symbol, the *tíguere*, is associated with political consequences: Dominicans make use of the image of the *tíguere* in order to shape legitimacy. Third, I hope to demonstrate that the production of the tiger image has to be grasped as a historical one – as a cultural production which has been related to broad transformations of Dominican society in this century.

The roots of the *tíguere* are in the city: the *tíguere*'s 'ancestors' were young men, men who lived in popular sectors of the city of Santo Domingo in the 1940s and 1950s. These men drank together, played dominoes, competed in sports, and cultivated fashion, music, and womanizing. From the capital, the label of the *tíguere* spread to the rest of the country.[28] Today the word is applied not only in the streets, but also in homes and offices. Expressions such as *tigueritos* (or 'little *tígueres*'), *mi tiguerito* (or 'my little *tíguere* son'), *mi tiguerona* (literally 'my tigerwoman' [used, for example, about a woman friend or partner]), and *los tígueres de mi trabajo* (or 'the *tígueres* at my workplace') – these expressions are employed in order to address and refer to one's family and friends. Common greetings are *¿Que tal tíguere?* ('How are you, *tíguere*?') and *¡Adiós tíguere!* ('Goodbye, *tíguere!*'). When someone arrives 'dressed to kill', he may hear the exclamation *¡Ese es un tiguerazo!* ('That man is a gigantic [or smashing] *tíguere!*'). The tough but irresistible work (or talk) of a bargainer in a bus or taxi – or anywhere else (such as in a bar, a firm or a political party) – may be summarized by others as that of a *tíguere*.

On the other hand, while uses of the label *tíguere* often mean approval, to be called a *tíguere* may also imply that one's behaviour is censured. In some contexts, to describe a man as a *tíguere* is a communication of disapproval – or, worse, a stigma. The moral 'disorder' inherent in the use of the image of *tíguere* is evident from the fact that for some time Dominicans have employed the word with two sharply dissimilar ethical connotations. One view emphasizes that *tígueres* are wrong-doers and delinquents; they are dangerous men who must be avoided and criminalized. As an old man in San Antonio said: '"Being a *tíguere*" ['*el tigueraje*'] is a big word! When they call one a *tíguere* and one isn't a *tíguere*, one should complain and say, "Why do you call me a *tíguere*?" Being a *tíguere* is a criminal thing!' Another villager, a woman of about fifty, may illustrate the other perspective. According to her, the man who is a *tíguere* is not an outsider to society but the man 'who knows how to live', a spirited and cunning man, a smooth talker. Society doesn't reject him. Instead, he is 'everywhere' and 'typical'. He is the kind of man who knows how to take advantage of circumstances yet always remains all right. In short, this is the type who knows about everything. He is also, she said, the man who may wear a large golden chain round his neck; the man who is serious is not like that, but the *tíguere* is: he loves fashion and perfume, and gets one woman after the other. But he is not bad. He is in politics, too, she added, for the *tíguere* is precisely the type who is everywhere.

Both the concept of the *tíguere* as the man who is a delinquent and therefore 'on the outside', and the moral approval which says that the *tíguere* knows public life's essence and is in the middle of everything, represent widespread views. Since the 1950s, however, it must be social 'admiration', and not social 'disapproval', that has been most strongly on the increase. This is also the view which Collado's book on the *tíguere* emphasizes and attempts to 'canonize'.[29] Yet even if we choose to look only at this 'majority' perspective on the *tíguere*, we can see ambiguity. As my woman informant said, the man who is a *tíguere* both knows about everything and is everywhere, is not 'serious', but not 'bad' either. A man in San Antonio defined this ambiguous male as follows:

> 'Wherever the *tíguere* arrives, he arrives playing tricks and making trouble, looking to find out how you button yourself behind, to find out where you put your money. They ask for a bottle, then go without paying. They walk about looking. Wherever the *tíguere* arrives, he walks about waiting. The *tíguere* arrives neither with shame nor is he shameless, for the *tíguere* lies in ambush. The *tíguere* is very dangerous and very wise, completely able.'

The *tíguere* seems to swallow the ethical evaluations of his peers. He is a man seen as both without and with 'shame', as not completely 'serious' but not 'bad' or 'evil' either. Above all, the *tíguere* offers an elastic symbol with which to make sense of men's actions by verbalizing them – that is, by talking them over in ways that shape them in terms of ethical concepts. The symbol of the *tíguere* (precisely because of its semantic and moral complexity) makes it possible to express what otherwise seems difficult to grasp and classify: paradoxes and ambiguities associated with the exercise of power in relationships. This is so because – according to people themselves – the essence of the image of the *tíguere* seems to be one of ambiguity. Being cunning but not a criminal, the *tíguere* stretches what is socially permissible and orthodox, but without losing his moral balance. As the image literally suggests, the man who sees himself, and is seen by others, as a 'tiger' is dangerous, tough, flexible and irresistible; even so, this man, this 'animal', is not rejected by society – on the contrary, he often arouses others' admiration.

Here we can see a version of the comparative theme of the 'trickster': Dominicans cultivate an image of a male who seems to be a champion of daily life because his bold movements, his cunning tricks and his pragmatic improvisations have shown themselves in practice to represent a social route worth travelling. Living with the day-to-day dilemmas of money, friends and women, a man should not only 'hunt' but also be 'good' – and that in what can look like a social jungle. Small wonder, perhaps, that many say to each other that the man who manages has to be a hero – or a tiger. The image of the 'tiger' is attractive among Dominicans because it offers a view of the exercise of power in relations which is not only pragmatic but also mystical. This image can look both like masculine power's true and essential nature, and like its notorious ambiguities and inconsistencies.[30]

Situating the Image of 'the Dominican Tiger' in History

Anyone who reads Hoetink's *The Dominican People, 1850–1900*, will realize that nearly all the important notions of masculinity that have been discussed here, also existed at that time. I have already mentioned the frequent uses of the term *político* in the past century. However, this applies equally well to the notions of *valentía*; of 'making oneself visible' and of sharing [*compartir*]; of being fun-loving [*fiestero*] and a womanizer [*mujeriego*], and eloquent; and of having *compadres*. While the uses of these concepts, and consequently their practical meanings, have most probably undergone some transformations over the last hundred years, there is none the less considerable continuity with regard to the common thinking about the politics of masculinity.[31]

The existence of a certain social and moral basis for the subsequent enormous spread of the use of the symbol of the *tíguere* can also be read from Hoetink's study. As we have seen, the cult of the *tíguere* expresses first and foremost a cult of the social type who is flexible and pragmatic, the man who acts according to continuously changing contexts. Hoetink has underscored that society itself (with its high degree of political violence and turbulence, and shifting governments) nourished what he seems to describe as a climate for markedly 'situational approaches' to one's peers:

The absence of clear ideological motivation as well as the rapid succession of the majority of the regimes in the nineteenth century created a general feeling of incertitude and instability reflected in the key words of the political vocabulary of that time. Here we have the word *situación* (or situation), which indicated the government as well as the period of government and which reflected the fluid character of alliances and formations. One was a friend or an enemy of the *situación*; a *situación* was developing; one spoke of the first days of a *situación*. The term *reaccionario* (or reactionary) had no ideological connotation. That anyone who acted against the reigning *situación*, the government, belonged to the forces of reaction fit into the neutral, mechanical interpretation of political activity.[32]

Yet irrespective of this continuity with regard to society's dominant notions of masculinity and the political, the current uses of the symbol of the *tíguere* indicate a change – that is, an example of transformation of a people's ways of communicating about maleness. The image of the *tíguere* as a source of the social production of legitimacy has been shaped mainly from the early decades of this century onwards. Collado concludes:

both the word *tíguere* and the person existed and were in popular usage at the beginning of the Trujillo tyranny, at the beginning of the 1930s. . . . [I]n the 1940s and 1950s, but more exactly in the 1950s, a 'culture of the *tíguere*' seemed to reign, a culture which then served as a model at the national level.[33]

Gendered concepts and their uses are related to, and woven together with, social history in a broad sense; such concepts and their uses may be related to processes such as state-making, urbanization, modified patterns of communication and migration, and the production of a nation. I shall round off my discussion by attempting, in three stages, to link the spread of the symbol of the *tíguere* further to Dominican changes.

First, a social basis for the construction and spread of the image of the *tíguere* has been the capital's growing urbanization since the beginning of this century. That urbanization was itself a product of the development of a large-scale sugar industry and the accompanying national growth which began in the late nineteenth century.[34] In other words, the most important formative period in the history of the image of the Dominican *tíguere* overlaps to a considerable extent with Santo Domingo's

transformation into a national capital and a large city, and with
the Trujillo regime from 1930 to 1961. It takes little imagination
to see that increased urbanization meant that many men and
women in the capital faced new types of situations, relations,
networks, and personal dilemmas. These people drew on what
was already at their disposal for making sense of masculinity and
femininity – that is, established concepts and classifications.
However, in addition, the notion of the *tíguere* was obviously a
useful one for understanding the existence of a particular urban
type (by naming him) – the man who knew how to 'emerge
well from every situation' in these more urbanized contexts. In
addition, changes in the development of the mass media have
played a part in the formation of the image of the *tíguere*.
The word *tigre* was used extensively by Cubans until the 1959
revolution; one implication of this was that Cuban dance music,
which was popular in Santo Domingo in the 1940s and 1950s,
helped to spread the use of *tíguere* among Dominicans. This
development was related to the beginnings of mass consumption
of music based on the radio. From the 1930s and 1940s onwards,
radio listening in the streets of Santo Domingo gradually grew,
and became commonplace.[35] Finally, we should bear in mind
the significance of the Trujillo regime's repression, censorship,
and control of emigration and immigration. The political
climate generated by Trujillo's terror must have strengthened the
notorious preoccupation among Dominicans with 'the reigning
situación' – that is, the social cultivation of the sort of highly
situational approaches to one's peers which Hoetink has pointed
to under the Heureaux dictatorship. In addition, it may be
assumed that the generally strong insulation of Dominican life
from its surroundings under Trujillo provided fertile ground for
the construction of a special, Dominican reading of the image
of the tiger; that reading could be challenged only to a very
limited extent through interactions with foreigners, and through
travelling abroad, before 1961. On the other hand, after 1961
the military state's restrictions on all citizens' movements (such
as between rural areas and cities) were abolished, and this must
have helped to diffuse the image of the *tíguere* throughout
national territory.

    Second, the historical production of the Dominican *tíguere* illustrates the sheer potential which may be built into practices that can be said to shape 'politics from below'. The image of the *tíguere* was made by ordinary men – the kind of men who liked to hang around in certain areas of the capital during the Trujillo regime. To such men, the army was often one of the few opportunities to build a personal career; and, ironically, Trujillo's army often preferred recruits from the countryside. Given these circumstances, men instead competed through, and consequently cultivated, politically 'innocent' activities in the streets, the activities of the *tíguere*: drinking, dominoes, sports and dancing. In so doing, they shaped an image of a man which was to grow enormously in its relevance and significance: today, this image of masculinity is in the process of becoming a nationally hegemonic one, an image used by men and women across the country, and also abroad, even in order to answer the question 'what does it mean to be Dominican?'. Or – to put it differently – ordinary men in Santo Domingo, controlled and oppressed by the Trujillo state, forged an image of masculinity that is now put to use even for the purpose of making sense of the Dominican imagined community – or Dominican national identity. To quote Collado one last time: '[Dominicans abroad are] called "Dominican *tígueres*". . . . For they are characterized by "a tone", a personal style that makes them different from the other Hispano-Americans.'[36]

Third, however, we should not feel tempted to exaggerate the degree of change that Dominican concepts of political masculinity have undergone in this century, because the construction of the Dominican *tíguere* has been 'rooted' in the country's previous history of – and already established thinking about – masculinity; that is, the image of the Dominican *tíguere* builds on a set of older notions of what it means to be a man.

The people in Santo Domingo who shaped the *tíguere* from the 1930s onwards used old 'raw material' in their production of ideas about male and female. A lot of this 'raw material' was closely linked to the existing imagery of masculinity and femininity in the countryside; while the population of the city of Santo Domingo was estimated at 20,000 in 1898, it was over 1.3 million in 1981, an urban demographic growth which means that many in the capital during the formative years of the image of the *tíguere* were either from rural areas themselves or had close relatives in such areas.[37] When people reflect on and discuss what it means to act as a *tíguere*, they use concepts and classifications that have very long trajectories – that is, the notions and verbal constructs that were discussed in the first part of this essay. To put it another way: the common meanings of the symbol of the *tíguere* can be said both to flourish on and help to reproduce (a) basic conceptual boundaries between 'sincerity' and 'insincerity' [*buena fe* and *mala fe*], and between 'serious' and 'shameless' [*serio* and *sinvergüenza*]; and (b) a set of other, central images, such as those of the man as 'courageous' [*valiente/guapo*], as a 'drinker/dancer/womanizer' [*bebedor/bailador/mujeriego*], as one who 'is seen' [*se ve*], one who 'talks easily' [*tiene un verbo fácil*], and is 'politic' [*político*].

An implication of this is that when the image of the *tíguere* travelled from the capital to, for example, the southern Dominican border and San Antonio, it was not necessarily a strange one to the people who lived there. On the contrary, the image articulated closely with their established concepts for making sense of masculinity. In addition, the image has provided villagers with an additional resource for making sense of phenomena which thrive on growing urbanization – a growing urbanization that is visible to villagers both in this part of the country and on their frequent travels elsewhere.

Conclusion

Throughout this essay I have attempted to add support to an assertion which states that notions of masculinity among Dominicans have played a central part in their routine production of political legitimacy. A number of verbal constructs that are used in everyday life in order to name, classify, and shape different forms of male behaviour and the exercise of power represent a dominant political discourse – or a crucial legitimate problematic, a problematic which helps to define and give form to what represents the political. I have also sought to show how Dominican ideas about what it means to be a man have been tied to, and are expressed through, uses of an animal metaphor.

Dominicans see masculinity's dissimilar and paradoxical faces in a single image – that of 'the Dominican tiger'. This in turn sheds light on why we can say that the shaping of the image of 'the Dominican tiger' corresponds to a cultivation of a 'trickster': the sole image of 'the Dominican tiger' represents a male whose practice seems notoriously difficult to classify fully as semantic and moral 'order', and who provokes both approval and rejection, both attraction and fear, because his law is to emerge successfully from every situation.[38]

Notes

I am grateful to this volume's editors for their critical comments on earlier versions of this chapter, and to Simon Rye for very helpful suggestions (any errors and omissions are, of course, my own). I thank the University of Oslo and the Fulbright Foundation for funding my research on Dominican society.

1. Christian Krohn-Hansen, *From Violence to Boundaries: The Production of the Dominican Republic in the Dominican–Haitian Borderlands*, PhD dissertation, Department of Anthropology, University of Oslo, 1995.
2. Pierre Bourdieu, 'Structures, Habitus, Power: Basis for a Theory of Symbolic Power', in *Outline of a Theory of Practice*, Cambridge 1977; Bourdieu, 'Political Representation: Elements for a Theory of the Political Field', in *Language and Symbolic Power*, Cambridge 1992, p. 172. See also Jean-François Bayart, 'Finishing with the Idea of the Third World', in James Manor, ed., *Rethinking Third World Politics*, London 1991, p. 64.
3. See also Andrea Cornwall and Nancy Lindisfarne, 'Introduction', in Cornwall and Lindisfarne, eds, *Dislocating Masculinity: Comparative Ethnographies*, London 1994, p. 10.
4. On the extremely high relevance of relationships of patronage and clientage to the shaping of Dominican political life and state-making, see H. Hoetink, *The Dominican People, 1850–1900*, Baltimore, MD 1982; Richard C. Kearney, 'Spoils in the Caribbean: The Struggle for Merit-Based Civil Service in the Dominican Republic', *Public Administration Review*, March/April 1986; and Christian Krohn-Hansen, *From Violence to Boundaries*, pp. 107–234.
5. The word *tíguere* is spelled the way Dominicans typically pronounce *tigre*, the Spanish word for 'tiger'.
6. Lipe Collado, *El Tíguere Dominicano*, Santo Domingo 1992, pp. 16–17, 25.

7. None the less, masculinity represents only one of the dominant discourses of Dominican politics. Another legitimate problematic, one which has been just as central to the definitions of 'the politically thinkable' among Dominicans, has been a broad nationalist problematic focused on the Dominican fatherland as a nation born to share an island with another nation, that of Haiti. See, for example, H. Hoetink, 'The Dominican Republic in the Nineteenth Century', in Magnus Mörner, ed., *Race and Class in Latin America*, New York 1970; Frank Moya Pons, 'Los Historiadores y la Percepción de la Nacionalidad', in *El Pasado Dominicano*, Santo Domingo 1986; Doris Sommer, 'Starting From Scratch: Late Beginnings and Early (T)races in *Enriquillo, Cumandá*, and *Tabaré*', in *Foundational Fictions: The National Romances of Latin America*, Berkeley, CA 1991; Lauren Derby, 'Haitians, Magic, and Money: *Raza* and Society in the Haitian–Dominican Borderlands, 1900 to 1937', *Comparative Studies in Society and History*, vol. 36, 1994; and Christian Krohn-Hansen, 'Magic, Money and Alterity among Dominicans', *Social Anthropology*, vol. 3, no. 2, 1995.

8. H. Hoetink, '"Race" and Color in the Caribbean', in Sidney W. Mintz and Sally Price, eds, *Caribbean Contours*, Baltimore, MD 1985, p. 58.

9. Sidney W. Mintz, *Caribbean Transformations*, Columbia University Press Morningside Edition, New York 1989, pp. 307–12.

10. Frank Moya Pons, 'Haiti and Santo Domingo, 1790–c.1870', in Leslie Bethell, ed., *The Cambridge History of Latin America, Volume III*, Cambridge 1984, pp. 237–75; Moya Pons, 'The Land Question in Haiti and Santo Domingo', in Manuel Moreno Fraginals *et al.*, eds, *Between Slavery and Free Labor: The Spanish-Speaking Caribbean in the Nineteenth Century*, Baltimore, MD 1985, pp. 181–214.

11. Kearney, pp. 144–5.

12. In addition, we should note the following. Since the early 1880s, the Dominican Republic has seen three long-lasting *caudilloist* leaderships: those of General Ulises Heureaux (between 1882 and 1899); General Rafael Trujillo (from 1930 to 1961), and Joaquín Balaguer ('elected' President from 1966 to 1978, and from 1986 to 1996). All three were raised in relatively modest conditions before they rose to central power; these leaderships seem to testify to the close connections that have existed until today between notions shaped and reproduced in daily life by ordinary Dominicans, and the political control of the state.

13. I shall present examples which indicate how ordinary men evaluate and discuss the masculine strength of Juan Bosch and Joaquín Balaguer: Bosch was the winner of the first presidential elections celebrated after the Trujillo dictatorship; but Bosch's government was overthrown by a coup after only seven months, in 1963; in 1966, Balaguer 'won' the presidential elections (with the aid of the USA, which had invaded Santo Domingo in 1965, and terror imposed by the Dominican Army); Balaguer was 're-elected' until

1978 (when an end was put to the military terror), and later in 1986 and 1990; Bosch has been Balaguer's main rival since the 1960s, and has founded and headed two large national parties (the Dominican Revolutionary Party, and the Party for Dominican Liberation) which have struggled against Balaguer's party (the Reformist Party) in the (often fraudulent) presidential and municipal elections that have been held every four years since 1966.

14. A villager once emphasized that a leader has to be a man who acts as a seducer: 'If you arrive where there are five or six girls and have a drink, soon you flirt with all of them. But if you don't drink and dance, you cannot do that. Nothing. Nor do they as much as look at you. A man has to be a drinker and a dancer; if he isn't, he isn't *valiente* [*no tiene valentía*]. The man must be a spender, a drinker, clean, he cannot be dirty.' Such a use of the word *valentía* directly links the *hombre valiente* or the *hombre guapo* (or the image of man the courageous fighter) to notions of male use of seduction and ideas about male beauty.

15. See Note 13.

16. See, for example, F.N. Cabrera Febrillet, *Elecciones y Fraudes Electorales Dominicanos 1974–1990*, Santo Domingo 1991.

17. The image of the generous man (the man who shares rum, stories, money, and other things with his male friends) is characteristic of most Caribbean societies. See, for example, Peter Wilson, *Crab Antics*, New Haven, CT 1973; Roger D. Abrahams, *The Man-of-Words in the West Indies*, Baltimore, MD 1983; and Peter Wade, 'Man the Hunter: Gender and Violence in Music and Drinking Contexts in Colombia', in Penelope Harvey and Peter Gow, eds, *Sex and Violence: Issues in Representation and Experience*, London 1994, pp. 115–37.

18. Wade, p. 117.

19. Both these discourses, of course, seem to be related to notions of masculinity among Europeans and North Americans. See also Wilson's classic study *Crab Antics*, which was one of the first analyses to focus on how masculinity in some Caribbean societies is produced in tension/balance between two sets of discourses – those on womanizing and drinking (in Wilson's terms, 'reputation aspects') and domestic stability ('respectability aspects').

20. The interaction between drinking and womanizing and the building of relations with the women's kinsmen in such a case is conditioned: the same man who is a womanizer offers services. For example, the man quoted here helped his women to establish and run small stores – that is, a basis for household viability and the upbringing of their children – and made himself useful to many in the local areas in question, for he acted as a broker *vis-à-vis* others, such as state representatives (helping people if they needed a loan for agricultural purposes, for example, or a public document).

21. On the significance of *compadrazgo* among Dominicans, see Hoetink,

The Dominican People, pp. 193–212; and Krohn-Hansen, *From Violence to Boundaries*, pp. 107–209.

22. Abrahams 1983.

23. For example, villagers may say about a certain man that 'he doesn't know how to speak' [*no sabe hablar*], or about another that 'his words come easily' [*tiene un verbo fácil*].

24. *The Dominican People*, p. 136.

25. *Serio/a* is used with dissimilar connotations according to gender: The classification of a woman as either *seria* or *sinvergüenza* (serious or shameless) is typically focused on the issue of sexual/marital fidelity.

26. Collado, p. 25.

27. Ibid., p. 11.

28. The information in this essay about the genealogy of the social classification of the *tíguere* in the Dominican Republic is based on Collado's brief discussion of the term's linguistic and social origins; ibid., pp. 13–24.

29. In this connection, the word 'canonization' is not chosen at random. The preface to Collado's book is written by Francisco Comarazamy, editor and book reviewer of the traditionally most prestigious newspaper in the Dominican Republic, the *Listín Diario*.

30. The daily construction of the image of the *tíguere* has political implications. The symbol of the *tíguere* plays a part in the daily shapings of meaning (or of popular and elite answers to the question of 'what happens') in the state's offices and enterprises; in the exchanges between leaders and followers; and between friends and *compadres*. Collado's book suggests that the image of the *tíguere* is even used in the attempt to make sense of the country's (incomprehensible) political history – that is, of its past of state violence and repression. In the book, reference is made to the regimes of two Dominican generals and dictators, Ulises Heureaux (who ruled the country between 1882 and 1899) and Rafael Trujillo (1930–61), as those of two 'ferocious Dominican *tígueres*' (ibid., p. 7).

31. For some illustrations, see, for example, Hoetink, *The Dominican People*, pp. 125–6, 193–212.

32. Ibid., p. 136.

33. Collado, pp. 30, 36.

34. Hoetink, *The Dominican People*, pp. 1–93; José Del Castillo, 'The Formation of the Dominican Sugar Industry', in *Between Slavery and Free Labor*, pp. 215–34; Frank Moya Pons, ed., *El Batey*, Santo Domingo 1986.

35. Collado, pp. 30–31.

36. Ibid., p. 25.

37. For the demographic data, see Hoetink, *The Dominican People*, pp. 43–4; and (for the year 1981) Dominican public census data.

38. In a different setting, that of the Bolivian Andes, people shape the

ambiguities of masculinity by using two important animal metaphors: a man can be symbolically represented as being both bull and condor (Olivia Harris, 'Condor and Bull: The Ambiguities of Masculinity in Northern Potosí', in *Sex and Violence*, p. 57). There is a contrast between the Andean case of thinking about maleness with the aid of bulls and condors, and this Dominican case. While the people of the Bolivian highlands reflect on the central ambiguities of masculinity with the aid of two different animals, the bull and the condor, the Dominican data illustrate that several of the ambiguities of masculinity can be condensed into, and expressed through, the use of one animal metaphor.

6

The Gendering of Ethnicity in the

Ecuadorian Andes:

Native Women's Self-Fashioning

in the Urban Marketplace

Mary M. Crain

Within the recent anthropological literature focusing on identity construction in the Andes, several scholars have argued that it is primarily the everyday practices of indigenous women which mark the social boundaries that distinguish particular ethnic groups from one another.[1] Such distinctions depend on a certain conflation of gender and ethnic categories in which indigenous women of the Andes serve as visual icons of 'Indianness'. The physical bodies of these Andean women become sites of 'practical social control', sites which provide a symbolic template upon which the collective identities of the entire social group are inscribed.[2] Or – to borrow from the more general arguments advanced by several French feminist theorists – female bodies are signs in a symbolic economy governed by males.[3]

With regard to the specific case of Andean women, much of the preceding anthropological literature claims that as a result both of their conservative linguistic practices (more native women retain an autochthonous language, such as Quichua or Aymara, than do their male counterparts) and of their frequent preservation of community-specific dress codes and styles of bodily adornment, indigenous women serve as the primary vehicles of ethnic identity.[4] Demarcating their community's 'difference' *vis-à-vis* the dominant national society, through their routine practices these women create identities which are vital to the cultural reproduction of the group. Ethnographers have investigated Andean women's everyday practices of boundary-making as keys to understanding identity formation. However, the analyses of ethnic identity and of native cultural history which ethnographers produce are often at variance with the accounts which diverse members of native groups offer regarding who they are as a people.[5] Such divergences in perspective are only to be expected, given differences in the respective audiences and constituencies which scholarly and nativist accounts address.[6] While ethnographic analyses frequently call attention to the constructed nature of all representations of identity (in both their anthropological and nativist variants) and note the inventedness of all cultural forms, the accounts elaborated by indigenous auto-ethnographers may, on occasion, essentialize cultural forms, or attempt to claim a natural association between a specific cultural heritage and a particular place or territory.

An example drawn from the Andean peasant community of Quimsa, Ecuador, illustrates this tendency to evoke a homogeneous ethnic identity, thereby concealing internal debates and differences within indigenous culture. In Quimsa, dominant masculine discursive practices which articulate much of what passes for local expressive culture frequently rely on 'the image of the native female peasant'. Within masculinist collective representations, it is the figure of the female peasant which is assigned a central role as the guardian of group identity. The female body is laden with a great deal of symbolic weight, and the demeanour as well as the dress codes of individual Quimseñas are highly regulated by societal prescriptions. In local cultural representations associated with diverse activities, ranging from political meetings to dance performances, the native female body is depicted as the unchanging purveyor of 'the authentic Quimseño tradition'. Alternative viewpoints which either reveal the manner in which the female body is culturally constructed, or demonstrate that Quimseñas' dress codes are creolized forms which have been subject to persistent modification, are suppressed from the realm of public discourse, in order to provide an image of Quimseño identity which emphasizes the purity and continuity of an authentic cultural heritage. Within these same cultural representations, the figure of the female peasant is frequently portrayed as occupying a stable position in space. Assuming an unproblematic relation between identity and place, the female peasant remains steadfast, as a custodian of the land, and she is depicted as a ballast, fixed within existing family structures and domestic units. These 'nativist' images of the female peasant are rhetorical figures. The female peasant serves as a metonym for an 'authentic' indigenous identity and cultural heritage uncontaminated by historical processes of colonization, hybridization and geographical displacement.[7] The deployment of these images within nativist political discourse must be explained in the light of contemporary demands placed on indigenous communities by the Ecuadorian state. Today, in the Ecuadorian Andes, proof of being 'indígena' (a person of indigenous descent) and of belonging to one of the officially recognized 'comunidades indígenas' is a necessary prerequisite for ensuring the survival of many minority groups, inasmuch as state-authorized definitions of ethnicity determine which groups may either obtain legal title to contested territory, or be eligible for special state services and resources specifically allocated for indigenous groups. Faced with external pressures to establish their cultural difference vis-à-vis the non-Indian world, Quimseños, as well as members of many other native communities in Ecuador, often have no other recourse than to invoke 'strategic essentialism' in order to acquire a political voice that will ensure them recognition in both national and international arenas.[8] Thus, in their dialogues with representatives of the Ecuadorian nation-state, native strategists in Quimsa frequently resort to static, essentialist portrayals of their culture which resonate with 'official views of appropriate Indianness'. In these nativist portrayals the female peasant, confined to a permanent and unproblematic location on the land, represents the unity and boundedness of Quimseño culture.

While I am equally concerned with tracing elaborations of Quimseño identity, my ethnographic analysis directs attention away from an exclusive concern with culturally homogeneous and bounded identities which are anchored solely in one territory.[9] Juxtaposing dominant constructions of indigenous femininity alongside divergent forms of self-representation fashioned by

Quimseña migrants in various settings in metropolitan Quito, I shall highlight the way in which identities are shifting, situational, and negotiated within fields of power relations. Investigating the reconfiguration of the gender and ethnic identities of native Quimseñas in the light of their migratory experiences in urban Quito, I pose the question of what happens when the traditional icons of ethnic identity are displaced, and become moving borders.

Following Quimseñas through space, this analysis problematizes unitary conceptualizations both of identity and of community by drawing attention to 'border zones', diverse spaces of cross-cultural interaction in both rural and urban Ecuador where communities are not tightly bounded and identities are neither stable nor homogeneous.[10] I examine the ways in which such crossings between cultures influence the construction and negotiation of subordinate identities.

I begin by considering a 'border zone' initially established by the Rodríguez, the prominent Ecuadorian elite family who have been the subjects of my research in Ecuador since 1982. During the late 1950s Don Rodríguez, the senior patriarch, promoted ethnic tourism, an undertaking that linked native women, formerly tenants on his hacienda in Quimsa, to new positions in the tourist trade in an international hotel in Quito, the capital. I demonstrate that aspects of the unfree servile relations characteristic both of the colonial era and of the subsequent hacienda system in rural Quimsa provided a symbolic model for the contractual labour relations established between these Indian women and the foreign management operating the international hotel. Rodríguez's initiative stimulated the first widespread out-migration of peasants from Quimsa.[11] And unlike the rural-to-urban migratory patterns characteristic of many neighbouring peasant villages at this time – in which the emigrants were primarily male – as a result of this initiative, female peasants also participated in early migration to urban centres.

I shall also examine the way in which dominant elites tailored aspects of native women's gender and ethnic identities to dovetail with colonialist-inspired images of 'Indianness' which would appeal to cosmopolitan audiences in metropolitan Quito. I shall describe the ability of 'the powerful' to reconfigure subordinate identities according to dominant definitions, and demonstrate the agency of native Quimseñas who, despite considerable constraints, created their own compromised sense of identity, thereby extending their employment opportunities far beyond the confines of the tourist hotel.

Before considering the Quimseñas' case in greater detail, however, I shall provide an ethnographic contextualization which describes the community of Quimsa as well as traditional agrarian relations prior to 1960. I shall then delineate significant changes in rural society during the 1960s and subsequently which opened a space for various touristic ventures.

Transformations in Agrarian Society

The research site under consideration is the peasant community of Quimsa and the neighbouring Hacienda La Miranda. The total population of this unnucleated settlement is 1,800. Approximately two-thirds are *indígenas*, or indigenous peasants, and the remaining third are 'mestizos' or people of mixed descent, both Hispanic and indigenous. There are at most four people who refer to themselves as 'Blancos', or Whites. Fluent in Spanish, they are descendants of European immigrants. All these individuals are affluent members of the local landed elite associated with the Hacienda La Miranda. Quimsa is located within the larger rural parish of Angochahua, province of Imbabura. A narrow, one-lane cobblestone road built by corvée labour connects Quimsa with the provincial capital and major market centre of Ibarra, which is bisected by the Pan-American highway. Both of these are approximately one hour away by bus. Quito, the capital of Ecuador, is approximately two hours from Quimsa by public transport.

During the late nineteenth century three large haciendas, including the Hacienda La Miranda owned by the Rodríguez family, controlled the bulk of the land in the parish. These estates were characterized by a form of servile labour relations known as the 'huasipungo tenancy system'. Hacienda peasants, or, 'huasipungueros', tied by various forms of debt peonage to the estate, worked for the landlord, and in exchange they held use rights to 'huasipungos', small plots of hacienda land which they used both as dwelling sites and for subsistence agriculture. Not until the 1950s were there public debates about the abolition of this highly stratified land tenure system. Agrarian reform legislation sought to release indigenous peasants from these labour obligations and require landowners to begin paying wages and redistributing some of their land to former tenants. Mounting demographic pressure, as well as a scarcity of land within the peasant sector, created a tense social climate. Many estate owners were fearful that their own properties might be subject either to land invasions or to state expropriation on behalf of impoverished peasant communities.

It was during this particular historical conjuncture that a remaking of the Ecuadorian landscape occurred in which touristic ventures became a prominent feature, both in several parishes of the northern highlands lying in close proximity to Angochahua and in other parishes situated further to the south, in the regions of Cañar and Cotopaxi.[12] For example, in the context of impending agrarian reform (finally instituted in 1964) and the growth of an urban economy with an industrial base, as well as shifting investment strategies, several hacienda owners sold the bulk of their estates, retaining only a small core area of land surrounding the large manor house of each hacienda. This space was converted into 'hosterías', country inns, destined for ethnic and historical tourism. Modern conveniences, such as central heating and indoor plumbing, were installed in these old colonial homes, and rooms were refurbished to receive a foreign clientele. Quito-based travel agencies offered package tours to these sites in which guests were given a feel for pre-existing colonial relations, with Indians serving sumptuous feasts in extensive formal gardens.

As we saw above, Don Rodríguez, an influential Ecuadorian politician and prominent landowner in Quimsa, promoted luxury tourism as an innovative development strategy, designed to provide economic alternatives for land-poor peasants whose families were bound by relations of debt peonage to his estate, the Hacienda La Miranda. Wanting to avoid the creation of a tourist attraction in the rural home community (as occurred in the cases of the *hosterías*), he was intent on relocating a portion of the now-surplus Indian population which was heavily dependent on his resource base. He assumed the role of cultural broker by fostering contacts with the owner of a large luxury hotel under construction in Quito, and eventually secured employment for twenty Quimseñas in the tourist trade at the Hotel Rey.

Adept as an interpreter of Indian culture, Rodríguez was able to translate native traditions into a language the hotel management was able to decode. He was also knowledgeable about the aesthetic tastes of the North American, European and Ecuadorian touristic and business clients who would frequent the Hotel Rey. A member of an aristocratic Ecuadorian landowning family, he had held various political positions of national and international prominence. All these experiences familiarized him with the lifestyles of 'the rich and famous', and enabled him to formulate certain assumptions about the preferences of this new class of tourist. Ideas about native culture figured prominently in all his formulations, and he sought to tailor Quimseñas gender and ethnic identities to conform to 'stereotypical images of Indianness'.

Rodríguez persuaded the hotel owner that a backdrop of 'Indianness' would be beneficial for hotel culture, and suggested that the natives from his hacienda could form part of the hotel's staff. During his consultations with the hotel owner, Rodríguez favoured indigenous women as the main vehicles for the representation both of 'exotic otherness' and of 'racial difference', and argued that the former should be given preference for hotel jobs over native men. As a partial consequence of the 'forced acculturation' imposed under colonialism, an experience which affected native men more directly than native women, Rodríguez claimed that indigenous women were more 'native', and therefore more 'authentic', than their male counterparts in Quimsa.[13]

Other gender ideologies also influenced Rodríguez's assessment, as he regarded the entrance of native women into the professional hotel trade as a logical extension of the gender-prescribed roles traditionally assigned to Quimseñas in the households of the rural aristocracy. Associated metaphorically with 'the inside' under the *huasipungo* system, which remained in effect until

1962, 'servicio', or obligatory domestic service performed within the colonial manor house of the Hacienda La Miranda, was primarily defined as 'women's work'.[14] Indian women also worked as milkmaids and in the fields as agricultural labourers, performing tasks which complemented men's work in these two sectors. As for their *servicio* duties, unmarried peasant girls as well as older women were required to undertake domestic chores, such as washing, ironing, sweeping, cooking and maid service, on a rotational basis for a period of two weeks.

Within peasant households a gendered division of labour also prevailed, and patterns of gender complementarity as well as gender hierarchy emerged, depending on the context. For example, both men's and women's labour were deemed necessary in order for cultivation to occur. Women's skills were required in order to plant the seeds of the primary crops, such as potatoes, ocas, wheat and barley. These were complemented by the men's skills in the actual ploughing of the fields. Both genders participated in weeding and in the harvest. Women were also active in animal husbandry and in the marketing of a limited amount of produce, in a domestic economy otherwise devoted to subsistence. In addition, peasant women exercised control over the household purse. Yet despite the important participation of indigenous women in economic life, traditional gender ideologies did not conceptualize their productive activities as 'work', whereas men's activities were frequently regarded as synonymous with the sphere of work. While the identity of the male peasant was seen to be derived from his work, the identity of the female peasant stemmed primarily from her role within the family as daughter, and later as mother.[15] Although there were exceptions to this rule, female peasants were expected to marry and to bear children. To a greater extent than the male peasant, the female peasant's behaviour reflected upon her family's standing within the community at large, and her conduct was closely scrutinized by her brothers, her father, and later her husband.

Returning to the case of the Hotel Rey and Rodríguez's assessment of the Quimseñas' capacity for employment there: he argued that the Quimseñas' facility for undertaking the repetitive tasks associated with *servicio* at the Hacienda La Miranda made them highly suitable for their new assignments as waitresses and hostesses at the hotel. During their period of rotational *servicio* duties in his household, Quimseñas had occupied a 'border zone' in which they acquired first-hand experience of upper-class mores and forms of etiquette characteristic of a cultural milieu vastly different from their own. Under the care and tutelage of both the 'patrona' (Doña Rodríguez) and resident nuns of the hacienda, Quimseñas' bodies became sites of social intervention in which negative attributes associated with their 'Indianness' were subject to reform. For example, Quimseñas received extensive instruction regarding personal hygiene, and the values of self-discipline as well as deferential comportment. Such instruction instilled codes of conduct which would prove beneficial upon their arrival at the hotel.

Finally, generational and aesthetic factors also influenced Rodríguez's selection of employees for the Hotel Rey. More than half the female servants he initially dispatched to work in Quito were attractive adolescent girls of seventeen to twenty. These young women had parental attachments, but were without families of their own. The 'youthfulness' and 'unmarried' status of these girls, selected to cater to the whims of the hotel clientele, only accentuated their 'availability', and gave rise to rumours regarding their promiscuity.

The Hotel Rey as Cultural Production

In 1959 twenty indigenous Quimseñas left their homes and were escorted by the Rodríguez family to Quito, where they were instructed to work with the management in order to prepare the Hotel Rey for its inauguration the following year. Just as the 'sirvientas', or Indian girls and women who served as domestics at the Hacienda La Miranda, had lived periodically in the servants' quarters within the confines of the manor house to ease their transition to urban life, the Quimseñas were initially assigned 'live-in' arrangements at the hotel.

A member of the Inter-Continental hotel system, a multinational chain of luxury hotels, the Hotel Rey was completed in 1960. A towering monument to modernity, and the largest luxury hotel of its kind to be constructed in the 'new Quito', it was conveniently located along one of the wide thoroughfares spanning the cosmopolitan capital, away from the crowded, winding and dilapidated streets of the old colonial city centre. While the hotel projected a progressive, modern exterior, particular spaces, objects, and tasks ensconced within its corridors were allocated to the 'bearers of tradition': that elite service corps of native women from the community of Quimsa.

The Hotel Rey depended on the visual alterity provided by native women to establish a corpus of meanings that underscored its distinctiveness *vis-à-vis* a range of competing hotel establishments. No other hotels in Quito followed suit by hiring native Ecuadorians as part of their permanent staff. One of its managers proudly told me about the exclusive ambiance encountered solely at the Hotel Rey:

> 'We strive to offer our guests a certain feel for a genteel way of life. In more common hotels one may not encounter the "gente de categoría" [people of certain pedigree] that you find here. Among our clientele, both foreign and Ecuadorian nationals, are those who can appreciate certain distinguishing features, that minute attention to detail that makes our hotel stand out as unique. Beyond a doubt, the warmth and hospitality of our cheerful women of Quimsa, arrayed in their folkloric apparel, enrich the hotel environment, adding a colourful, personal dimension to all our services. And for any of our guests who may be unfamiliar with our nation's ancient heritage, the Quimseñas' presence provides them with an instant lesson on Ecuadorian history.'

It was not just the Quimseñas' labour but, above all, the cultural meanings they embodied that were appropriated by the hotel. The incorporation of the Quimseñas underscored the hotel management's desire to capture such coded differences as 'the rare' and 'the exotic'. Quimseñas were the authentic cultural products conspicuously exhibited to demonstrate the hotel's high standards of taste. As an ideological construct deployed in this hotel discourse regarding native women, 'authenticity' carried connotations of cultural purity and rurality, as well as 'a timeless tradition' often equated with Ecuador's distant pre-Hispanic past. The Quimseñas' daily presence evoked images of rusticity and a slower way of life rooted in the rural peasant village. Such imagery provided a point of contrast with the dynamic hustle and bustle of a modern business and touristic enterprise such as the Hotel Rey. This hotel discourse of authenticity served as a colonialist discourse which sought to fix Quimseñas' identities both in time and in space. It erased from public view the fact that these women had crossed borders and were now members of a multicultural urban world during the second half of the twentieth century. While the residential quarters of most of the Quimseñas were located nearby but 'across the tracks', in Runawi, these quarters were downplayed in the hotel's representations of native women. Runawi is a lower-class residential *barrio* (neighbourhood) of whitewashed buildings stacked against one another and trimmed with a smattering of colonial blue. This ethnically heterogeneous neighbourhood abuts an enormous cliff which also serves as the ground floor of the Hotel Rey. Many of the Quimseñas working at the hotel resided in overcrowded quarters in Runawi, in the company either of their husbands or of other family members.[16] The community of Runawi was composed of diverse groups such as *mestizo* families as well as migrants from other indigenous communities in the highlands.

Daily operations at the Hotel Rey depended on a gendered and racial division of labour in which the visibility of the native female body was particularly salient, and formed a stark contrast to the hotel's predominantly upper-class, male clientele. In 1982 the number of Quimseñas employed by the hotel rose to as many as thirty, but this was out of a total hotel staff of approximately three hundred. Thus, Quimseñas constituted a relatively small but highly visible 'folkloric' component of the entire staff. While the majority of men in the community of Quimsa have abandoned 'traditional' ethnic dress and replaced it with Western apparel, such as cotton shirts or T-shirts and polyester trousers, Quimseñas have been more inclined to preserve native dress codes. Therefore, in the rural home community it is not the men but the native women, with their elaborately embroidered blouses, layers of billowing skirts, and 'huallcas', imitation gold beads that wrap the full length of their necks, who constitute the highly charged visual signs of ethnic identity.[17]

On duty at the hotel, however, the 'authentic dress' Quimseñas were required to wear did not conform to any of the everyday dress codes commonly encountered in the peasant community.

Instead, 'authentic dress' as mandated by the hotel management was an aesthetic purification of tradition. It most closely approximated the extravagant, regal dress that only wealthy Quimseñas can afford, an attire reserved solely for festive occasions in the home community. This festive uniform was combined with the starched white apron that once symbolized the Quimseñas' status as *sirvientas* at the manor house of the hacienda.

Quimseñas were concentrated in the hotel's two restaurants and adjacent bars, while all other jobs undertaken by women – which were less subject to the male tourist gaze, such as that of the chambermaid – were reserved for non-Indians. In each restaurant, Quimseñas worked as hostesses and as 'saloneras' (waitresses). The former welcomed and seated customers, while the latter were responsible for serving the finest cuisine and beverages. Quimseñas could also be seen on the ground floor, plying their silver carts and trays down the long corridors and into the large meeting-rooms where national and international business deals were often hammered out and press conferences occurred. They served coffee and tea in several of these salons, whose walls were decorated with elaborate tapestries.

By the 1970s three men from Quimsa had joined the hotel staff, and they also were concentrated in the restaurant trade. In contrast to the native women, however, who were privileged as part of the hotel's visual display, the men's labour was unmarked and hidden. Employed as cooks and as pastry chef, these men were confined to the kitchen; thus no mandatory ethnic dress code was imposed on them.

Performances of an 'Authentic' Self

Many of the women working at the hotel, whom I first interviewed in 1982, actively denounced the period of servile relations and their forced migration. Their recognition that coercive elements governed their transition to modern hotel life are highlighted in the testimony of Mama Juana: 'We went from being *sirvientas* in the big house of the *patrón* to become *sirvientas* in the biggest house of all, the Hotel Rey, and there we passed our time in Quito, attending to all the foreign *patróns*.'

Despite feelings of estrangement upon their arrival in an anonymous urban setting during a time when no other 'paisanos' (villagers from the natal community) resided there, as a result of elite preferences which equated indigenous femininity with 'cultural authenticity', Quimseñas were able to take advantage of new employment opportunities in sectors of the Quiteño job market which were scarcely available to the Quimseño.[18] Furthermore, their training at the hotel and subsequent experience in cosmopolitan Quito exposed these female employees to new ways of life unknown to the Quimseñas who remained in the village. As professional wage-earning women in the nation's capital, Quimseñas acquired a new identity as 'salaried workers' and gained a new empowering sense of self-respect and personal autonomy. As the years in Quito passed, several experienced tensions with either their spouses or members of their extended family, as their new self-images as working women came into conflict with traditional gender roles as practised in Quimsa. For example, at least four of the married Quimseñas later divorced their husbands while they were still working in Quito. Two of the divorcees indicated that instances of physical mistreatment and their spouse's drinking habits, as well as the latter's unwillingness to accept changes in the gendered division of labour within their urban household, had prompted them to dissolve their marriage ties. For many of these working women, the traditional gendered scripts in which the female peasant's conduct was closely monitored by her senior male kin, and her identity as a worker was eclipsed by her familial identity and attendant responsibilities as daughter, 'ama de casa' (wife) or mother, no longer provided meaningful guidelines for the changing realities of their lives in a metropolitan setting.

Commenting on the character of Quimseñas, male indigenous peasants who are residents of neighbouring communities maintain that 'las Quimseñas tienen mas entrada en la sociedad nacional que nuestras propias mujeres' (Quimseñas are more readily accepted by the dominant national society than the indigenous women from their villages are). However, these male neighbours also claim that metropolitan Quimseñas are reputed to be 'loose women', whose moral standards are lower than those of neighbouring indigenous women. According to this masculine commentary, an indigenous woman should ideally be both honourable and virtuous, a person who maintains her family's reputation by regulating her own behaviour, thereby earning the respect of the community.[19] She should behave with discretion even in urban environments such as Quito which, according to this masculine discourse, are riddled with a moral decay conducive to sexual abandon. On the one hand, Quimseñas are admiringly labelled 'mujeres vivas', women who are aggressive, streetwise, and therefore not taken advantage of by anyone. On the other hand, however, this male commentary also deplores the Quimseñas' flirtatious exchange of looks, as well as their salty banter across racial and class lines, as hints of potential sexual liaisons are rumoured to underlie these exchanges.

Quimseñas are aware that the commodification of their gender and ethnic identities constituted part of the Hotel Rey's successful marketing scheme, deployed to entice tourists. Just as the hotel, following Rodríguez's advice, appropriated visual images both of their 'Indianness' and of their femininity, and utilized these as an aesthetic scheme designed to further its own commercial agenda, Quimseñas have resorted to a series of counter-appropriations that advance their own interests. For example, they actively appropriate the history of the Hotel Rey, and weave this history into their own labour narratives. As the only members of the hotel's current staff who were present during its inauguration and have actually resided within its premises, they often refer to themselves as 'the founders' of the hotel, and proclaim their 'labour rights' to employment there. In the words of Doña Aneta, a hotel employee for almost thirty years: 'We opened the doors of that hotel in 1960. We breathed the very life into it. Because of that, we will always have our rights; they can't deny us our jobs at the hotel.' Having established a socioeconomic niche that is currently reserved for them alone, Quimseñas have been able to monopolize the bar and restaurant trade at the Hotel Rey. Furthermore, senior Quimseñas have fought to maintain their steady jobs at the hotel, and have not been replaced by younger women.

Urbanized Quimseñas have also wielded their influence beyond the confines of the hotel by securing service positions for close relatives in the homes of national and foreign elites, both in the nation's capital and abroad. New forms of self-representation have emerged in conjunction with the experience of deterritorialization. Labour narratives such as the preceding one, as well as stories about their illustrious association with the Rodríguez family, are pronounced every time Quimseñas seek employment, or attempt to market their products. As 'border crossers', Quimseñas are currently engaged in 'the sale of self' in an urban setting in which they mediate between diverse zones of cross-cultural interaction. Their identities take on an increasingly hybridized form, and they undergo subtle shifts depending on the particular context, such as urban Quito, rural hacienda, or the rural community, and the presence or absence of 'dominant others' within these contexts.[20] Facing stiff competition from other indigenous women and from *mestizo* women who are also in search of employment in the nation's service sector, among members of the upper class, Quimseñas realize the importance of constructing a public identity that calls attention to their exclusivity and fashionability. Thus, in their public presentation of self, they tactically manipulate appearances for their own ends by laying claim to Rodríguez's name and fame as part of selfhood and a politics of identity. They also deploy the 'cultural capital' they have accumulated as a result of their service both at the Hacienda La Miranda and at the *de luxe* Hotel Rey to persuade elites of their superiority as employees, and hence of their desirability.

Quimseñas are aware that prospective employers are not only buying their labour but also procuring emblems that bestow prestige, as by employing many Quimseñas elites demonstrate that they exercise a monopoly over certain signifiers of caste and class in Latin America, such as a cultivation of idleness and a disdain for manual labour. Quimseñas have acquired a fine-tuned appreciation of upper-class lifestyles and tastes, and they enact stylized performances that reveal their familiarity with these life-worlds. In their 'onstage' performances addressed to future employers, they emphasize their 'ethnic difference' as 'indígenas', as an aesthetic preference which, they presume, such elites desire.[21] At the same time, however, their performances feature a 'constructed Indianness' in which they have taken elements of native tradition and reassembled them within a white cultural frame. They acknowledge that even many worldly, upper-class Ecuadorians continue to associate 'the indigenous race', and native women in particular, with physicality and proximity to the natural world, as well as sloth.[22] Consequently they promote traits, such as cleanliness and industriousness, which they learned from their training with the Rodríguez elites. Quimseñas also downplay the negative connotations of their ethnic affiliation by emphasizing their superior social status, manifested in their intimate historical ties with the households of aristocratic Ecuadorian families. Such intimacy, commonly expressed in the idiom of kinship, is suggested in the following remark: 'As servants in the *casa grande* of Señor Rodríguez we were all part of one large family.'[23]

Acutely aware of the elite obsession with the acquisition of 'the authentic', as opposed to abhorrence of 'the imitation' or 'the fake', during interviews with prospective employers Quimseñas exacerbated this preoccupation by staging performances of their own authenticity. These performances were often a parody of elite expectations regarding what an 'authentic Quimseña servant' should really be like. Although the majority of individuals of indigenous descent who left the rural highlands and migrated to Quito were quick to shed the visible attributes of 'Indianness' in order to avoid racial discrimination in the job market, Quimseñas, because of their putatively higher social status, have often acted otherwise, by reasserting markers of their ethnic identity.[24] Although the cultural boundaries demarcating a unique sense of Quimsa as a community have gradually weakened (the results of out-migration and the invasion of global media images), a more self-conscious construction of ethnic identity as a rhetorical strategy has emerged, particularly *vis-à-vis* non-Indian audiences. Thus Quimseñas, in their encounters with prospective employers, pay careful attention to an outward show of appearance by dressing to produce an 'authentic look' that will meet with elite approval, such as promenading in the Hotel Rey uniform. Such dress codes are maintained for the benefit of potential employers even though the total cost of native dress is increasingly prohibitive – currently at least three times higher than that of Western dress.

That this presentation of an 'authentic self' is a performance, one strategically designed to prove their identity to elites, is made clear by the fact that it is a context-bound construction of ethnic and gender identities. 'Offstage', relaxed inside the privacy of their own homes in Quito, or during a return trip to Quimsa, these same women may, on occasion, adopt the much cheaper Western style of dress, such as polyester stretch trousers made in Taiwan and a T-shirt with an Iowa State logo stamped on it, bequeathed to them by a Peace Corps volunteer or, nowadays, marketed by multinationals.

The 'authentic' dress and acquiescent demeanour of several Quimseñas whom I accompanied during job interviews mirrored the ethnic stereotyping of Indian culture perpetuated by the Hotel Rey more than it conformed to any of the contemporary codes that govern either dress or behaviour in Quimsa today. In Quimsa, such codes are frequently subject to subtle modifications and, therefore, 'reinvention'.[25] Aware, however, of the elites' concern for the expression of a unique self as a tactic for securing jobs, Quimseñas launch into a discourse about threats to their own 'authenticity', which, they argue, also constitute threats to the reputation of elites, as the latter are anxious to maintain a monopoly over all things considered 'authentic' and 'rare'. Thus they warn elites that there are Quimseña 'impostors' roaming the streets of Quito who have surreptitiously gained entrance to the domestic service trade. They explain that because 'they' are in such high demand, and thus not always readily available, Indian girls from other communities disguise themselves as Quimseñas in order to acquire the jobs in upper-class homes that Quimseñas had imagined to be reserved for themselves.[26] Unwilling to be upstaged by such impostors, peasant women of Quimsa go to Quito prepared to prove their identity as 'authentic Quimseñas'. To impress potential employers, they are usually accompanied by an entourage of female relatives, women who have worked either at the Hotel Rey or at another prestigious watering-hole in Quito, and are able to vouch for their 'authenticity'. Quimseñas also carry bags stuffed with official papers, including birth certificates verifying their origins, and certificates from the community's primary school. They often amass their own visual documentation of dominant settings, such as photographs of the Hacienda La Miranda which show them engaged in some laborious task inside the manor house, or posing beside a member of the Rodríguez family. Quimseñas are aware that most elites who can afford to do so buy their sales pitch. In the elite construction of self, most notables want to emulate the aristocratic Rodríguez family and be equally commended for their good taste. Many elites complain that it is now difficult to find a Quimseña to work for them, as merely establishing contact with the network of Quimseñas already employed in the capital does not always lead to success in procuring a native servant girl. Consequently, sophisticated Quiteños now drive to Quimsa at the weekends and cruise the hillsides, scouting for maids and for an occasional 'huacchiman' (male watchman hired by elite families to protect their homes or cars from theft).

Although Rodríguez's initial idea was to promote peasant migration out of Quimsa by stimulating ethnic tourism in the nation's capital, this noble plan partially backfired, as upon retirement several female employees from the Hotel Rey invested their savings back in Quimsa, both in the construction of homes and in artisanal co-operatives. These enterprises provided new sources of employment for local peasants, and partially curbed the flow of out-migration. Meanwhile, the weekend search for maids by cosmopolitan Quiteños is frequently combined with different forms of rural tourism, such as exploring the natural beauty of the area, buying embroidered goods directly from local artisans and enjoying a weekend getaway at one of the nearby hosterías. Thus, despite Rodríguez's best intentions, Quimsa, too, has the potential to rival the Hotel Rey as a tourist attraction.

Concluding Remarks

Both through projects of moral reform associated with obligatory *servicio* duties in rural Quimsa and later through the institution of new regimes of representation at the Hotel Rey which exoticized native peoples, the Rodríguez elites sought to hegemonize Quimseñas' identities so that they might conform to elite-endorsed images of indigenous femininity. And while Quimseñas internalized aspects of this elite imagery as components of their own identities, it is also true that elite efforts to reform Quimseñas' identities were incomplete and had unintended consequences.

As migrants, Quimseñas entered interstitial border zones in metropolitan Quito. There, they came into increasing contact with the non-Indian world and with ethnically heterogeneous groups. As a result of these experiences of border-crossing, their identities were partially deterritorialized and reshaped in ways which eluded the control of the rural elites. In their daily interactions in urban Quito, Quimseñas' identities were both strategic and selective assertions. Rather than a unitary self characterized by attributes that remained constant in all settings, Quimseñas fashioned diverse styles of self-representation which they tailored to particular audiences. In encounters with potential elite employers they mimicked the dominant stereotypes regarding 'Indianness', providing a specular image of those qualities which they imagined future employers desired when they were hiring a household servant.

Although they occupied subordinate positions, urban Quimseñas were not without their own agency. Via performances which emphasized their 'cultural purity' and fed into the elite's obsession with 'authenticity', they appropriated the Rodríguez family's name and fame, as part of selfhood and group identity, in order to gain privileged access to positions in upper-class homes in Quiteño society.

By tracking Quimseñas' self-representations in light of their formative experiences on the rural hacienda as well as their subsequent experiences in metropolitan Quito, I hope I have demonstrated that native women's identities are historically produced, multiple and shifting, rather than being either hermetically sealed or existing in a pure, uncontaminated state. Relations with the Rodríguez elites and with urban *mestizos*, as well as processes of emigration, deterritorialization, and an onslaught of global media images, have all played a part in the construction and reconfiguration of Quimseñas' identities. Identity construction is revealed to be a reciprocal process, produced as a result of the mutual interaction between dominant representations of the subject and the subject's own self-representations.

Notes

Earlier versions of this essay were delivered as papers at the 48th International Congress of the Americanists in Uppsala, Sweden, during July 1994; at the 117th annual meeting of the American Ethnological Society, devoted to 'Border Anthropologies', held from 26 to 29 April 1995 in Austin, Texas; and at the seminar 'Género y Política en América Latina', sponsored by the Interdisciplinary Seminar Mujeres y Sociedad, at the University of Barcelona, 12 to 16 June 1995. The basic field research was undertaken in highland Ecuador from 1982 to 1984, and during the summer of 1992. Funding was provided by an American Council of Learned Society grant, the Doherty Foundation at Princeton University, and by the Institute of Latin American Studies at the University of Texas at Austin, Texas. I am indebted to all these institutions for their financial support. Finally, I would like to thank Eduardo Archetti, Jeremy Boissevain, Stephanie Kane, Kristin Koptiuch, Lola Luna, Marit Melhuus and Kristi Anne Stølen for their generous suggestions and critical commentary on earlier versions of this essay.

1. For a more extensive review of the literature on identity construction in the Andes which also examines the manner in which the domains of gender and ethnicity intersect, see Mary Crain, 'Unruly Mothers: Gender Identities, Political Discourses and Struggles for Social Space in the Ecuadorean Andes', *PoLAR (Political and Legal Anthropology Review)*, vol. 15, no. 2, 1994; Marisol de la Cadena, 'Las Mujeres Son Mas Indias: Etnicidad y Género en una Comunidad del Cusco', *Revista Andina*, vol. 9, no. 1, 1991; Blenda Femenias, 'Clothing and Ethnicity in the Colca Valley: Daily Practice as Social Process', paper delivered at the 47th Congress of Americanists, New Orleans 1991; Sarah Radcliffe, 'People Have to Rise Up – Like the Great Women Fighters: The State and Peasant Women in Peru', in Sarah Radcliffe and Sallie Westwood, eds, *Viva!: Women and Popular Protest in Latin America*, London 1993; Linda Seligmann, 'Between Worlds of Exchange: Ethnicity among Peruvian Market Women', *Cultural Anthropology*, vol. 8, no. 2, 1993; Mary Weismantel, *Food, Gender, and*

Poverty in the Ecuadorian Andes, Philadelphia, PA 1988. Jill Dubisch also addresses similar issues in her discussion of gender relations, space, and social boundaries in rural Greece; see both the 'Introduction' and 'Culture Enters through the Kitchen: Women, Food, and Social Boundaries in Rural Greece', in Jill Dubisch, ed., *Gender and Power in Rural Greece*, Princeton, NJ 1986. And for a detailed discussion of gender, ethnicity and cultural reproduction among the Emberá in Panama, see Stephanie Kane, *The Phantom Gringo Boat: Shamanic Discourse and Development in Panama*, Washington, DC 1994. Finally, Weismantel's research in the indigenous community of Zumbagua, Ecuador, focuses on the everyday practices of cooking, dress and speech. While issues of identity are not her primary concern, this excellent analysis certainly sheds considerable light on aspects of identity formation in Ecuador's central Andean region, revealing the gender and ethnic dimensions of everyday practice in Zumbagua.

2. Susan R. Bordo and Alison M. Jaggar. 'Introduction', in Susan R. Bordo and Alison M. Jaggar, eds, *Gender, Body, Knowledge: Feminist Reconstructions of Being and Knowledge*, New Brunswick, NJ 1989, p. 5. For a more extensive discussion of the notion of bodily boundaries as sites of social control, see Mary Douglas, *Natural Symbols*, New York 1982; Pierre Bourdieu, *Outline of a Theory of Practice*, Cambridge 1977; and Michel Foucault, *History of Sexuality*, vol. 1, New York 1978.

3. For further elaboration of these issues, see Luce Irigaray, *This Sex Which Is Not One*, Ithaca, NY 1985; Hélène Cixous, 'The Laugh of the Medusa', in Elaine Marks and Isabelle de Courtivron, eds, *New French Feminisms*, New York 1981.

4. As in many other regions of the world, in Andean Ecuador there are important instances in which indigenous men also maintain ethnic dress codes which are unique either to the community or to the region. For example, the dress codes both of the indigenous men and of the indigenous women of the Andean community of Otavalo, Ecuador, are recognized around the world. Otavalo is approximately one hour from Quimsa by public transport.

5. Jean Jackson offers a more comprehensive analysis of this point. She outlines differences between ethnographic and native accounts of 'Indianness' in the Vaupés region of southeast Colombia, and reveals the dialogic interplay between these two fields. Discussing an array of 'outside' parties which have had historical contacts with the Tukanoan Indians of the Vaupés, Jackson describes how these external groups have influenced Tukanoans' thinking about their own heritage. In many instances, contacts with external agents have prompted Tukanoans substantially to revise their own conceptions of the constitutive features of Tukanoan culture and history. See Jean Jackson, 'Culture, Genuine and Spurious: The Politics of Indianness in the Vaupés, Colombia', *American Ethnologist*, vol. 22, no. 1, 1995. And for a review of recent indigenous political practices in Ecuador

as formulated in relation to dominant state policies, see Lynn Meisch, 'We Will Not Dance on the Tomb of Our Grandparents: 500 Years of Resistance in Ecuador', *The Latin American Anthropology Review*, vol. 4, no. 2, 1992.

6. For further treatment of the issues surrounding the particular audiences, communities, and constituencies which writers associated with different discursive fields inevitably address, see Edward W. Said, 'Opponents, Audiences, Constituencies and Community', in Hal Foster, ed., *The Anti-Aesthetic: Essays on Postmodern Culture*, Port Townsend, WA 1983, pp. 135–59.

7. My thoughts on hybridity, creolization and displacement have been influenced by the excellent discussion of these processes in the introductory chapter of *Displacement, Diaspora and the Geographies of Identity*, ed. Smadar Lavie and Theodore Swedenburg, Durham, NC, in press.

8. For a thorough discussion of 'strategic essentialism', see Gayatri Spivak, 'In a Word: Interview', in G. Spivak, *Outside in the Teaching Machine*, New York 1993, pp. 1–23.

9. For a critique of traditional anthropological conceptions of culture which posit a naturalized association between culture and place, see Akhil Gupta and James Ferguson's seminal article, 'Beyond Culture: Space, Identity and the Politics of Difference', *Cultural Anthropology*, vol. 7, no. 1, 1992.

10. Placing his analysis of the migratory experiences of workers whose lives oscillate between Aguililla, Mexico, and California's Silicon Valley within a transnational framework, Roger Rouse demonstrates the limitations of the earlier community studies literature, with its paradigm of the stable and bounded village community. He proposes terms such as 'the border zone' and 'the transnational migrant circuit' as more adequate conceptual tools for conveying the sense in which many communities today, such as Aguililla, are lived at multiple sites. These sites are interconnected on a daily basis through flows of migratory labour, multinational capital and electronic information, as well as commodities. See Roger Rouse, 'Mexican Migration and the Social Space of Postmodernism', *Diaspora*, vol. 1, no. 1, 1991.

11. Important migratory movements which occurred in highland Ecuador during both the colonial and the early Republican periods are beyond the scope of this essay.

12. In 1992, the travel section of the women's fashion magazine *Elle*, which has a wide circulation both in France and in the United States, featured an article promoting rural tourism at *hosterias* in highland Ecuador. See 'The High Life in the Andes', *Elle*, 1992, pp. 220–24.

13. During the colonial period most native women remained in their home communities, while the economically active indigenous male population left to perform obligatory *mita* service in the mines, in the 'obrajes' (textile workshops) or in agriculture. *Mita* service involved aspects of 'forced

acculturation'; as a result, many native men abandoned the visible markers of their ethnic identity, such as their unique dress codes and hairstyles. For a case study which examines the gendered character of ethnicity in Andean communities through an exploration of local perceptions which posit that indigenous women are more 'native' than their male counterparts, see Femenias, 'Clothing and Ethnicity in the Colca Valley'.

14. In Quimsa the position of 'huasicama' or houseboy, was one notable exception to this gendered division of household labour. The *huasicama* was responsible for ensuring the wood supply of each household.

15. I have discussed the construction of female identity in Quimsa in earlier publications; see Mary Crain, 'Poetics and Politics in the Ecuadorean Andes: Women's Narratives of Death and Devil Possession', *American Ethnologist*, vol. 18, no. 1, 1991; Mary Crain, 1994.

16. Approximately 75 per cent of the Quimseñas who went to work at the hotel in 1959 later married, and all of them married men from Quimsa. When this female cohort group had children, they pursued diverse options which allowed them to combine employment at the hotel with their child-rearing obligations. For example, several received help with childcare from family members who also lived in Quito. Three other mothers hired a non-family member to mind their children while they worked. Yet others explained that family members back in Quimsa had cared for their children for extended periods of time.

17. The 'ethnic dress' worn by Quimseñas is made of store-bought materials which often receive further elaboration in the home. For example, Quimseñas purchase both rayon and cotton cloth, as well as imported Italian threads of variegated colours, to make their blouses. The most labour-intensive aspect of blouse-making is the elaborate embroidering that women stitch on to each blouse, particularly on blouses reserved for festive occasions. It is not uncommon for a Quimseña to devote a whole month to the completion of embroidery work on a particular blouse. *Huallcas* are an entirely store-bought accessory. Quimseñas purchase their *huallcas*, currently imported from the Czech Republic, in the Ibarra market.

18. While both men and women participate in wage labour markets outside Quimsa, male participation is greater than that of women. Most Quimseños find temporary work throughout Ecuador, either in the construction industry or in other areas of the informal economy. A few indigenous men also own small businesses in Quito. Quimseñas' involvement in extra-local labour markets is largely restricted to employment in Quito's service sector. For example, they work both at the Hotel Rey and in a wide array of Quiteño restaurants (in snack shops, in cafeterias inside commercial establishments, and in 'folkloric restaurants' which specialize in ethnic cuisine). While numerous Quimseñas are employed both as domestic servants and as cooks in the homes of Ecuadorian and foreign elites in Quito, only a reduced number of Quimseños find work in these

households. The majority of male household workers are employed as cooks, butlers, or gardeners.

19. During the course of my research I heard few comments from male indigenous peasants regarding the ideal moral behaviour expected of a non-Indian woman. Therefore, I cannot comment on male perceptions of appropriate behaviour for Ecuadorian women who self-identify as either 'mestizo' or 'white'.

20. For further discussion regarding power relations and the manner in which contextual cues provide parameters for both defining and negotiating identities, see Homi Bhabha, *The Location of Culture*, London 1994; Dorinne Kondo, *Crafting Selves: Power, Gender, and Discourses of Identity in a Japanese Workplace*, Chicago 1990.

21. I have borrowed the term 'onstage' from James Scott. Examining the politics of relatively powerless groups, Scott uses the term 'onstage' to refer to those settings in which hegemonic conditions prevail. According to Scott, the 'onstage' conduct of subordinate groups is typically acquiescent, and peasants are unlikely to reveal their disagreements with elites or other authority figures. In contrast, 'offstage' refers to more private social settings in which the discourse and actions of subordinate groups are not subject to direct observation by elites. In 'offstage' contexts, the public conformity which orientates the peasantry's 'onstage' behaviour often gives way to a vocal critique of 'officialdom' and the status quo. See James Scott, *Domination and the Arts of Resistance: Hidden Transcripts*, New Haven, CT 1990.

22. In his analysis of ethnic identity in highland Ecuador, Stutzman argues that 'el mestizaje', or *mestizo*ness, is the racial ideology espoused by Ecuador's dominant national culture. It is diffused through diverse media, such as school textbooks and political speeches. Notions of *mestizaje* are based on ideas of racial mixture and an ultimate whitening or 'blanqueamiento' of the diverse national populations. Denying the existence of racial heterogeneity in highland Ecuador and the cultural specificity of both indigenous and Afro-Ecuadorian communities, the ideology of *blanqueamiento* posits that all Ecuadorians who accept the goals of national culture can become *mestizos* (the only legitimate ethnic category from the vantage point of the nation-state). See Ronald Stutzman, 'El Mestizaje: An All-Inclusive Ideology of Exclusion', in Norman Whitten, ed., *Cultural Transformations and Ethnicity in Modern Ecuador*, Champaign–Urbana, IL 1981.

23. For a contrasting case study, in which female migrants who obtained employment as domestic servants were forced to deny aspects of their ethnic heritage as they became integrated into urban households in Peru, see Sarah Radcliffe, 'Ethnicity, Patriarchy and Incorporation into the Nation: Female Migrants as Domestic Servants in Peru', *Environmental and Planning D: Space and Society*, vol. 8, 1990a; Sarah Radcliffe,

'Between Hearth and Labor Market: The Recruitment of Peasant Women in the Andes', *International Migration Review*, vol. 24, no. 2, 1990b.

24. In dominant accounts of the colonial era, as well as subsequently, native peoples from the Otavalo culture area (of which the community of Quimsa forms a part) were always regarded as a superior 'race' of Indians. For further information on this topic, see Frank Salomon, 'Weavers of Otavalo', in Daniel Gross, ed., *Peoples and Cultures in Native South America*, New York 1973; Lynn Walter, 'Otavaleño Development, Ethnicity, and National Integration', *America Indígena*, vol. 41, no. 2, 1981.

25. On 'the reinvention' of identity and culture, see James Clifford's discussion in Chapter 1 of James Clifford, *The Predicament of Culture: Twentieth-Century Ethnography, Literature, and Art*, Cambridge, MA 1988.

26. Several elites, who owned large estates in the environs of Quimsa, also confirmed that there were 'Quimseña impostors', or indigenous women who pretended they were Quimseñas, working in Quito.

7

The Power of Gender Discourses

in a Multi-Ethnic Community in

Rural Argentina

Kristi Anne Stølen

I would like to explore the relationship between gender discourses and gender relations – that is, gender as it is represented and gender as it is lived – on the basis of anthropological fieldwork in Santa Cecilia, a multi-ethnic rural community in Argentina. I shall start my discussion of this relationship by drawing attention to gender discourses among the farmers who constitute the dominant ethnic group, locally called 'gringos'. Their discourses on gender stress the importance of the family, and reveal a particular preoccupation with male and female virtues associated with the division of roles in the family, and with sexual morality. These gender discourses are close to those transmitted by the local church as well as by the Holy See of the Catholic Church. At the community level they are constituted through mutual imbrication with differences of class and ethnicity. The subordinate ethnic group, locally called 'criollos', whose members also belong to a different social class, being employed as seasonal labourers by the farmers, express contrasting discourses on gender, valuing sexual desire, pleasure, and spontaneous emotionality. Their discourses are condemned by their patrons as well as by the Church.

The differences in perceptions of gender qualities between the two groups highlight the multiplicity of gender discourses. Recent work in anthropology has demonstrated that cultures do not have a single model of gender or a single gender system but, rather, a multiplicity of discourses on gender which can vary both historically and socially.[1] These different discourses are frequently contradictory and conflicting – as in the case presented here, where the female is associated respectively with chastity and sexual voracity – and they are hierarchically ordered.[2]

In order to understand the power of gender discourses, it is necessary to explore the links between the represented and the lived. Gender discourses do not exist independently of social relations. Even though the discourses do not directly reflect the social and economic conditions of men and women, they are constituted within these conditions. At the same time, the power of gender ideas and stereotypes is not just in people's minds. They have a material reality, which helps to reinforce the social and economic conditions within which they are developed and used.[3] I shall explore how the dominant position of the farmers' gender discourses is associated with their dominant economic and social position in relation to women of their own ethnic group, as well as to men and women belonging to the other ethnic group.

An important argument is that the dominant gender discourses help to legitimize and perpetuate not only relations of dominance and subordination between men and women, but also ethnic and class inequalities. The high valuation of motherhood, female domesticity and sexual chastity expressed in these discourses contributes to the maintenance of a particular sexual division of roles that secures the male farmers' control of material and organizational resources and, through this, control of women. At the same time this valuation is used to distinguish and devalue their employees, and thereby contributes to the maintenance of ethnic and class inequalities. This implies that there is a mutual determination of gender and ethnicity, the ethnic categories being highly sexualized.

I shall present the local context, paying special attention to the social and sexual division of roles on the farm and in the local community. I shall then examine the contrasting discourses on gender – how *gringos* and *criollos* see themselves and each other. Finally, I shall examine the relationship between these discourses and the gender notions transmitted by the Catholic Church in order to explore the linkages between gender, class, ethnicity and religion.

The Local Community

Santa Cecilia is a community composed of middle-class farmers, descendants of European immigrants who arrived in the 1880s, and seasonal labourers, descendants of indigenous people who arrived in the community with the introduction of cotton in the late 1930s. Due to its origin, Santa Cecilia is called a 'colonia' (colony), a residential unit based on neighbourhood and on participation in ceremonial, educational and recreational activities. The colony has its own church (since 1906), a primary school, two bars, a police station and a football field. Together they constitute what is referred to as 'el centro' (the centre), where most public events take place. The farms (34 altogether) are quite big, and scattered throughout the relatively flat and open landscape. Agricultural production (mainly soya beans, sunflowers and cotton) is highly market orientated and, with the exception of cotton, mechanized.

Santa Cecilia is surrounded by other colonies sharing similar ethnic, social and economic characteristics. The colonies are interconnected through kinship ties, and members of different colonies attend each other's fiestas and sports events. The distance from the centre of the colony to 'el pueblo' is 25 kilometres, while the Department capital is approximately 27 kilometres from the community. The relationship between the colonies and the urban centres is close. The pueblo (approximately 15,000 inhabitants), where we find the closest links, provides most of the business and cultural infrastructure for the countryside. Moreover, owing to rural–urban migration, people have extended networks of relatives there.

Sexual and Social Division of Labour

Today most farms are run by a nuclear family, and work is organized along gender lines. In the sexual division of labour within the farmer household it is the husband's role to ensure the material welfare of his wife and children. This implies having access to land and planning, cultivating, and selling agricultural produce (some also raise cattle). Since incomes are obtained from the sale of agricultural products or cattle, and the men are the ones who do the work, they also control the money. Currently, most women receive money only to cover particular expenditures, which have to be accounted for in detail. Because of the long distances between farms, and between the farms and the local and urban centres, a car (normally a pick-up truck) is considered indispensable. The car is defined as an instrument of farm work, and is thus the man's property. Moreover – as in many other societies – the car is also a source of male prestige.

Domestic work and childcare are women's domains, and defined as complementary to agricultural work. 'Atender y ser mantenida/mantener y ser atendido' (To attend and be maintained/to maintain and be attended) summarizes the way *gringos* talk about their marital arrangement. The farmer/husband considers himself – and is considered by his wife and his community – head of his farm, household and family unit. This gives him a position of authority over women and children. Generally, both men and women agree on the content of this division of roles. A farm and home should have both adult male and female members in order to function 'properly'. This sexual division of labour gives men control over the most important material resources in the community: the land and its produce, money, and the means of transport. Women's lack of direct access to money – in a context with a high level of market integration, where consumption is very important in both economic and symbolic terms – makes the farmer women highly dependent on men, and restricts their opportunities for movement and action. Men's control over the means of transport also tightly restricts women's activities and movement. I observed, for example, that the women who participated in local organizations were almost exclusively wives, daughters or sisters of male members who had unlimited access to a car, with whom they could go to the meetings.

If the farmer grows cotton, there are also seasonal labourers on the farm, the *criollos*. There are two categories of worker, the permanent ones, who live in the colony throughout the year, and the 'golondrinas' (the swallows), cotton-pickers who live in Santa Cecilia for three to five months during the cotton harvest. The resident workers are dependent on a farmer, who provides a low-standard house and, in most cases, a small plot of land to grow vegetables for household consumption. They are obliged to work for their patron whenever he is in need of manual labour. This work obligation is mainly concentrated on the weeding and picking of cotton, which are done manually on a 'piecework' basis and paid according to officially determined rates.

Among the cotton-pickers there is no rigid sexual division of roles. Women are not maintained by their male companions. Together with their children they work in the fields alongside the men. All do the same work, irrespective of sex and age. Even though women shoulder the main responsibility for housework and childcare, men, both companions and sons, often give a hand, for example, in cooking and feeding small children, and even washing clothes. In contrast to the farmers' wives, who have to ask their husbands for money, the *criollas* are often the ones who administer the household income. This is seen as a necessity by the women, and is generally accepted – more or less reluctantly – by the men, who otherwise might be tempted to spend too much drinking in the bar.

There are big differences between the two groups in material standard of living. The farmers' houses are much larger, of superior quality, and better equipped than those of the workers. Since the introduction of electricity in the late 1970s the farmers have acquired modern household equipment such as washing machines, refrigerators and freezers as well as TV sets, which are also found in some of the resident workers' houses. None of the workers has a car. If they have to go to the pueblo they must hitch a lift; for shorter distances they walk or use a bike. The children of the resident workers attend the local school, but their performance is poor. During the peak seasons their school attendance is interrupted because their parents need to mobilize the family's labour capacity to its limits.

When the cotton harvest starts, the number of cotton-pickers may increase up to tenfold. The *golondrinas* come from neighbouring districts where they are partly unemployed, partly work as casual labourers during the rest of the year. They live in 'ranchadas', clusters of small mud-and-pole houses placed at some distance from the main farm buildings.

Categorizing Difference

In Santa Cecilia people distinguish between two categories of people: 'colonos/gringos/blancos' on the one hand and 'cosecheros/criollos/negros', or 'morochos', on the other. A *colono* is a settler who lives in the colony, is a landowner, and works as a farmer. A *cosechero* is a landless cotton-picker employed on a temporary basis by a *colono* patron.

All the *colonos* in Santa Cecilia are *gringos*, which means foreigners. In this area, to be a *gringo* means that one is a descendant of Friulian immigrants from what today is the Friuli–Venezia Giulia region of Italy, has a Friulian surname and a light skin. It also has a class connotation. No *gringo* is a rural wage worker. If his *gringo* son does not become a farmer, which is quite common today, he leaves the countryside. The ideal urban adaptation is to become a 'profesional' (professional) or to establish some kind of independent business and become self-employed. However, since this cannot be achieved by all, *gringos* are also employed as ordinary wage workers both in private and public enterprises in town. Their daughters marry and become wives, mothers and housewives. Even though it is increasingly common for *gringo* women to have some training beyond primary school, most of them aspire to find a husband who is able to secure their well-being and that of their future family.

All the *cosecheros* in Santa Cecilia are *criollos* which, in this area, means indigenous, possibly with some Spanish blood. The *criollo* has a Spanish surname and dark hair and skin, the latter drawing attention to the third distinguishing category, *blanco* (white) and *negro* (black) or *morocho* (darkie) – which is also commonly used, but only by the farmers. The other categories are used by both groups as well as by people living in the pueblo.

Not only do the *gringos*, through their ownership of land and equipment, control the material resources of the community, they also control all local institutions and organizations, such as the church and school committees, the Neighbourhood Commission and the farmers' organization. As at farm level, they hold a dominant position not only in relation to *criollos* but also in relation to their own women. All influential positions at community level are occupied by *gringo* men. In some cases women are not admitted – for instance, in the farmers' organization (GEAC), where only farmers – that is, *gringo* men – can be members. The same happens with the group of 'comulgueros' (those who assist the parish priest in giving communion), where only men are admitted and only *gringo* men are appointed. In other cases anybody is eligible, but only *gringo* men are elected – as in the Neighbourhood Commission, which has eleven members. When women do participate in local organizations (e.g. school or church committees) and public events, their participation is normally an extension of their domestic activities. They do the 'background' tasks, such as decoration, cooking, cleaning, and serving, while their husbands, sons and brothers occupy the 'foreground'. They plan and chair meetings, give speeches, or make announcements on the microphone. *Criollos* do not participate very actively in formal community activities, but if they do, as in some church committees, their place is also in the 'background'. Through their control over local organizations the *gringo* men are in a position not only to define an immediate situation but also to define the ideals to strive for, as well as plan for the future – all important elements of power.

In order to understand the current ethnic composition of the community, a brief historical account is necessary. The colony of Santa Cecilia was founded in the early 1890s by sons and daughters of the Friulian immigrants who had arrived ten years earlier to settle in Avellaneda, the first colony established in this part of the country.[4] Owing to scarcity of land in the mother colony, people had to move further out on the prairie in order to have access to enough land to establish new farms. For the first fifty years after its establishment, Santa Cecilia was ethnically homogeneous. The indigenous population which lived in this region before the arrival of the Europeans – scattered groups of hunters and gatherers – was almost completely relocated by the Argentine army to areas less suitable for agricultural colonization, leaving the land open to the immigrants. This expulsion did not take place without violent resistance from groups of indigenous people, who had acquired horses and arms. During the first few years of settlement, the farmers felt threatened and were afraid of being attacked. They went to the fields armed, and did not hesitate to shoot if they saw something moving in the bushes. Thus from the very beginning the farmers – sharing the dominant view in Argentina at the time – conceived of indigenous people as uncivilized barbarians, their inferiors, whom they were allowed to exterminate if they felt threatened.[5]

Before the 1930s the *gringos* had only marginal contact with *criollos*. The farmers were highly self-sufficient as far as agricultural production was concerned. They obtained ownership of land, and production was based exclusively on the use of family labour and animal traction. The produce that was not consumed by the family was sold, mainly for export, and commercial relations were largely confined to people of European origin like themselves. Their social interaction outside the farm was also limited to the immigrant community, and revolved to a large extent around the church. The priests – Friulians who arrived with the immigrants – played a crucial role in the building of the farmer communities of the region, especially contributing to create a sense of citizenship and social identity among these immigrants who had been transplanted from densely populated villages in Europe to isolated farms scattered throughout the Argentine prairie. The church was the first public building to be raised in the colonies, and it served as a meeting-place for the farmers. The Church also played an important role in linking the different colonies of the region, especially through the patron saint fiestas, which were (and still are) important events in the religious calendar. Finally, the priests were central actors in the Co-operative Movement which led to the establishment of the first farmers' co-operative in the region in 1919.

The *criollos*, whether residents or *golondrinas*, have their roots in more marginal areas of Santa Fe and Corrientes provinces, where there have been no *colono* settlements. A good portion of them are probably descendants of those who were expelled from the colonized areas. Their actual presence in Santa Cecilia is a result of the introduction of cotton in the late 1930s. Cotton is a labour-intensive crop which, because of the climatic characteristics of the region, is harvested manually. As cotton soon expanded beyond a few hectares per farm, the farmers could not cope with the labour requirements of the harvest, despite mobilizing family labour to its limits. Since there was no market for hired labour in the community at that time, the harvesters had to be brought in from outside. During the first years after the introduction of cotton, almost all the cotton-pickers were *golondrinas*. Over the years an increasing number of them have taken up residence in the community. According to a census carried out by the local Neighbourhood Commission in 1987, Santa Cecilia had a total of 376 residents, of whom 177 were categorized as *gringos* and 199 as *criollos*. The *gringo/criollo* proportion has changed considerably since 1974, when the number of *gringos* was twice the number of *criollos*.

Discourses on Gender

The *gringos* are proud of their dominant economic and social position, and consider it absolutely deserved. They see it as a result of hard work and observance of Catholic values and practices. They consider themselves the moral superiors of the *criollos*, whom they depict as lazy, wasteful, addicted to drinking and 'sin moral' (without morals). Sexual behaviour – particularly female sexual behaviour – is an important distinguishing factor. The ways *gringos* conceptualize inter-ethnic relations are therefore closely linked to their view of the relationship between men and women.

In the farmer discourses of gender, men and women are depicted as essentially different both physically and psychologically. The differences are conceived as being of biological origin. While the woman is represented as the bearer of the heart and the emotions, whose natural vocation is marriage and motherhood, the man is portrayed as the bearer of physical strength, rationality and authority. He is protector and master, responsible for the economic needs of the household, with the woman as his faithful and devoted companion. The *gringos* emphasize that these innate attributes have to be properly enhanced and guided in order to develop into appropriate masculinity and femininity, thus preventing deviations such as homosexuality, exorbitant sexuality or other forms of 'abnormal' or immoral behaviour.

From the time they are small, *gringo* boys and girls are taught to act out culturally defined male and female personality differences. What is considered appropriate behaviour for boys, such as manifestations of tenacity and physical strength, is disapproved of in girls, who are expected to be sweet, soft and neat. If a boy exhibits what are defined as feminine qualities his parents become anxious about possible homosexual inclinations, and punish him with jokes and mockery. Even though I did not find anxiety about potential lesbianism, girls who behave in a 'boyish' way are exposed to similar treatment. Gender differences are enhanced through the children's gradual incorporation into work on the farm. The boys will accompany their fathers in the fields and beyond, while the girls stay with their mothers at home, helping them with their multiple tasks.

Criollos are less concerned about gender difference in the upbringing of their children. From an early age *criollo* children have to help their parents, and since there is no rigid sexual division of labour between the adults in the household, the same applies to the children.

In the *gringo* representations of gender there is a close association of men and women with 'la calle' (the street) and 'la casa' (the house) respectively.[6] Female domesticity is highly valued. 'Ser casera' (to be of the home) is a characteristic often cited when *gringos* talk about the ideal woman, but it has various connotations. It refers to a woman's ability as mother, wife and housewife, which are seen as the principal attributes of womanhood. According to their standards, to be a proper mother, wife and housewife requires full-time dedication, and they see themselves as fortunate in being able to realize this. Even though the *gringas* claimed that they would like their own money, this does not mean that they aspire to wage employment. They believe that a woman's participation in the labour market is undesirable because it competes with her 'natural vocation' of maternity, and because of the negative consequences for the family. They accept that some women, like the *criollas*, are obliged to work outside the home to make ends meet, and say they feel pity for them, and especially for their children who, they believe, suffer the consequences of negligence and chaos at home. They are less understanding when it comes to women who work outside the home without being in need. Two farmer-wives have wage incomes, one works as a teacher at the local school, the other cleans the school. In spite of paying maids who take on part of the housework and childcare, they are favourite objects of gossip. As far as men are concerned, paid work is presented as a non-alienating right, a way of realizing oneself as a man.

At the same time as femininity is represented as opposed to masculinity by the *gringos*, it is seen as complementary to it. A real man is definitely not *casero*, but he should have a wife who is. He should be occupied outside the home to provide for his wife and family. Thus, if his wife has her own income it should be used for 'lujos' (luxuries), which means for other purposes than to meet basic needs, otherwise it may be interpreted as proof of unmanliness, of his incapacity to maintain his wife and children in a proper way. On the other hand, a good wife should be attentive to her husband's well-being. She should be at home, prepare his food, look after his clothes, and keep the house clean.

The rigidity in the conceptualization of the sexual division of labour becomes clear when we look at role encroachments. In this connection, more flexibility is permitted for women than for men. A woman who carries out what is defined as a man's work may be characterized as skilful and hard-working, positively valued qualities, as long as she does not neglect her house and children. However, if a man lets his wife participate too much in his agricultural chores, he may lose respect. It will most probably be interpreted as an incapacity to provide properly for his family.

If a man carries out what is defined as female work, such as cooking or cleaning, he is exposed to mockery and humiliation. Some 'female activities' are considered more threatening to a man's prestige than others. Looking after children is acceptable to a certain extent. Preparing the 'asado' (barbecue) is definitely a male job (only men can actually make a 'real' *asado*!). Male informants classified the washing and ironing of clothes as the most stigmatizing jobs they could think of. In their view, a

man who does housework (except in emergency situations)
is 'dominado' (oppressed), a 'maquina de lavar' (washing
machine), because he – like this type of machine – is 'run by a
woman'; or a 'pollerón' because he hangs on the 'pollera' (skirt)
of his wife. If he likes to do housework he is called 'putonesco'
(gayish). Consequently, *gringo* men are not involved in housework. If they give a hand – which, according to some female
informants, may happen from time to time – they are careful not
to be observed by people outside the nuclear family.

Moreover, it is just as important that a man who does
housework may also represent a challenge to the prestige of his
wife, who may then be talked about as incapable of doing her
share without the help of a man. Some of the younger women
said they would like their husbands to be more involved in
activities at home, especially in the upbringing of children. They
are, however, rather ambivalent about this issue. They want
more participation at the same time as they advocate that 'males
should not become females and vice versa'.

These notions are closely linked to notions of sexuality
and sexual behaviour. The *gringos* have an ambivalent view of
sexuality. Sex is simultaneously licit and illicit, permitted and
forbidden. When it is uncontrolled it is an evil and dangerous
force; when it is properly controlled it is a positive and creative
one. As I have indicated, this is especially important as far
as female sexual behaviour is concerned. If a woman is *casera*,
surrounded only by her family, she is not exposed to carnal
temptations. Her sexuality is under control. Thus, being *casera*
also says something about a woman's moral qualities, about
her chastity and respectability, which are also pivotal female
qualities among the farmers.

The *gringos* distinguish between two main categories of
women, the one being the negation of the other: 'mujeres
decentes y respetables' (decent and respectable women) and
those who are not, their sexual availability being an important
distinguishing criterion. From an early age *gringo* boys and
girls are taught that these two categories of women exist. Girls
themselves, their mothers, sisters, and other close kinswomen
belong to the first category, as do *gringo* women in general
– unless they have made a 'mal paso' (bad step) and proved the

contrary. Thus, *gringas* are by definition decent until the opposite has been demonstrated; they deserve respect and should not be approached sexually. The opposite is true of the *criollas*, who are deemed 'fáciles' (loose/indecent). This is seen as related to their nature, their 'sangre caliente' (hot blood), and to their poor upbringing, which means that they have not learned to control their sexual urges. Consequently, they are sexually voracious and available. Therefore, they do not deserve the same respect as the *gringas*; they can be approached sexually (they ask for it!); and they do not belong to the category of 'marriageable' women. Mixed marriages are extremely rare.

Unlike the situation in many other Latin American contexts, the *gringos* maintain that men as well as women should not have sexual relations outside marriage. However, they also believe and accept that for men this is hardly possible, especially before marriage, because men have stronger sexual urges than women and, therefore, often lack the strength to resist when they meet 'temptresses' (read *criollas*) who arouse their desire. Moreover, a rupture of this chastity ideal has very different consequences for women and for men. While a man's premarital sexual behaviour has little or no influence on his opportunities to make a good match or realize other roles later in life, such experiences inflict on a woman an everlasting 'mancha' (stain) which to a large extent determines her social value, her chances of a good marriage, and her possibility of becoming a respectable mother and housewife. At the same time, her sexual behaviour will influence the social position of her husband. 'Real' men marry virgins, and have chaste and faithful wives.

The strong concern among the *gringos* about female virginity and chastity is reflected in their upbringing of children. Girls are much more protected than boys. Most of the time they stay in and around the house, except when they go to school in the company of other children. Mothers told me that they are afraid of sexual abuse. Their anxiety is directed especially at the *criollo* migrants, adult men as well as young boys. In addition to their *sangre caliente*, *criollos* are believed to be marked by their upbringing. The fact that they sleep in the same room as their parents and supposedly witness their sexual intercourse, which is believed to be quite frequent, was often used as an argument to underpin the belief that *criollo* children develop 'abnormal' sexual urges, which they do not learn to control. Consequently, they are dangerous.

My observations fully support the view held by the *gringos* that *criollos* are not much concerned about virginity and chastity. If you ask a *criollo* man if he will marry a virgin, he will probably laugh and answer no, because in that case he would have to marry a child. *Criollos* share the vision of their hot blood, but they see it as a precious attribute of which they are proud. *Criollo* women contrast their *sangre caliente* (hot blood) with the *sangre fría* (cold blood) of the *gringas* who, they consider, are able neither to feel sexual pleasure nor to satisfy a man sexually. They tell picturesque stories about how *criollo* women have aroused their *gringo* patron to the extent that he is willing to run very high risks to pursue erotic encounters.

Criollos are not much concerned about the formalization of male–female relations either. They openly refer to themselves as 'juntados', which means that they live together without being married, and their unions do not necessarily last until death doth them part. If they do not get along any longer, or 'llevarse' – which is the expression they use – they separate. This may happen as a consequence of heavy drinking, wife-battering, or falling in love with someone else, for example, which may happen to both women and men. It is not uncommon for a woman to have children with more than one man, or for there to be children in the household who are not the offspring of adult household members, without there necessarily being any familial drama behind this. 'Se encariñó con nosotros, y quiso quedarse' (he became fond of us and wanted to stay), one woman explained to me when she introduced a little boy who lived with her, her companion and two children. The little boy was the son of her cousin, a migrant cotton-picker, who returned with her companion and other children to her home after he had finished the harvest. This is unthinkable for *gringo* couples, who do not separate, divorce, or adopt children. There has been no separation or divorce among the *gringos* since the establishment of the colony in the 1890s.

Even though 'society' also defines *criollo* men as heads of household, if the household has an adult male member, this is not a concept shared by the *criollos* themselves. A woman may often be referred to as 'la jefa' (the boss), and act as such.

Criollos talk about the *gringos* as 'beatos' (hypocrites), and 'amarretes' (avaricious). They say that *gringos* live only to work and save their money. According to the *criollos*, the *gringos* are so concerned about what is suitable or not, and what their neighbours will think or say, that they don't know how to enjoy life ['no saben gozar de la vida']. They look upon themselves as more genuinely human because they are more concerned with their feelings, their likes and dislikes, and the present rather than with conventions, formalities, and the future.

We can see from this that the dominant gender discourse not only allocates women a subordinate position in relation to men, but also explicitly or by implication devalues the *criollos* who are not up to the moral standards established in this discourse. 'Falta de moral' (lack of morality) is an expression often used by the *gringos* to characterize *criollo* behaviour, and even to explain their poor living conditions. I shall return to this later.

By characterizing men and women as essentially different physically and psychologically, embodying mutually exclusive principles of agency, *gringo* gender discourse contributes to the legitimation and perpetuation of a sexual division of roles that grants *gringo* men control over the most crucial material and institutional resources of the community, and limits women's opportunities for influence, movement, and action. Women's use of space and time is highly restricted in terms of the domestic imperative, at the same time as full occupation in and around the house is seen as an indication of feminine qualities. 'Gringo' women who do not keep up standards of housekeeping – especially if they also frequently leave the farm – are gossiped about in the community because they are considered bad mothers and housewives, and their sexual morality may also be questioned. Most *gringo* women carefully adapt to the standards of behaviour that are believed to express the attributes associated with being a decent woman, at the same time as they keep an eye on their kinswomen and neighbours. Through raising children, which today is primarily the mother's responsibility, the women themselves have become the immediate guardians of virginity and chastity, as they are of the maintenance of the sexual division of labour.

It is worth noting that the gender differences legitimizing and perpetuating male dominance among the *gringos* are not associated with conflicts or grievances. Women largely embrace their role in the existing order of things – not because they cannot see or imagine alternatives, but because they see it as natural, morally correct, and beneficial. Broadly speaking, men's control over women is based on a discourse which is shared by the farmers and their wives, but not by the *criollos*, who advocate contrasting discourses on gender and reject the dominant view of their moral inferiority.

Gender, Ethnicity and Religion

I suggest that this value consensus among the *gringos* is achieved by contact with and interaction within institutions which are important producers and transmitters of gender values. In Santa Cecilia the Catholic Church is a core institution in this sense, both because of its important role in the *gringo* community and because Catholic gender values penetrate other institutions of civil society such as the legal system, the educational system and, to a certain extent, the media.[7]

I shall now look at gender images transmitted by the local church.[8] The following quotes are taken from the parish bulletin 'Carta a los Cristianos' (Letters to Christians), a monthly four-page handwritten communication from the priests to the parishioners. Even though the selections presented are rather limited, they are representative of the gender images transmitted by the local church.[9]

In the issue announcing the celebration of Mothers' Day in 1987, parallels are drawn between the secular and the divine mother. On the front page there is an illustration of the Virgin and child with the following text:

> MADRE [mother] is the most sacred name, synonymous with affection, surrender and sacrifice, merged with the life that is born and grows. Jesus wanted a mother who now is also ours. Let her bless our family, whose heart is the mother.

The second page is illustrated with a drawing showing the profile of a pregnant woman. The text goes as follows:

It is not enough to give birth to become a mother. It is not enough to have a child. It is necessary to be receptive to the will of God and be at his disposal. In this way life will become fecund and complete.

In the issue announcing Fathers' Day the same year, the front page is covered with a poem, 'Credo al padre' (Credo to the father), in which certain parallels are drawn between the secular and the divine father:

I believe in you, father, because you gave me life. I believe in you, father, because you resemble God in your love. I believe in you, father, because you, together with mother, teach us that God is our Father and that we are all brothers. I believe in you, father, because you provide us with the daily bread. I believe in you, father, because you, with your big and calloused hands, teach us the dignity of work. I believe in you, father, because your firm and gentle voice teaches us the right course. I believe in you, father, because you are in solidarity with the needs of the neighbours. I believe in you, father, because your life is sharing with others.

On the second page we read:

God the Father loves everybody and wants us to be brothers and constitute the grand 'family of God'. Therefore, to be a father means to take care of the family and, together with the other fathers, contribute to the fraternity of the community.

The cover page of the bulletin published to announce the celebration of Workers' Day in 1988 is illustrated with a pair of robust male hands surrounded by cogwheels, an axe, a screwdriver and a sledgehammer. On the next page is a picture of a strong-looking man with a plough, and on the third page an invitation to bring farm equipment to 'La plaza de los colonizadores' in Avellaneda to be blessed by the parish priests, who will celebrate a Mass there. The slogan for the day is:

Work is a benefit of Man, because through work Man not only transforms nature, but also realizes himself as Man – what is more, he *becomes* more Man.

Since women's activities are not defined as work but, rather, as care or help, expressions of love, they do not appear in this bulletin.

The local church promotes the family as the true Christian community of love and work, where the woman is the heart of home, the bearer of emotions, fidelity, sacrifice, and true love, and the man is the provider, the (only) one who works, the guide and protector of women and children. Moreover, he is the (only) one who contributes to the community. The comparisons with the divine family are explicit. Historically, the Catholic Church has promoted two models for understanding divine relations. The first is a hierarchical model of servants' feudal relations to lord and king. The Church hierarchy, with the Pope at the head, and the cardinals, bishops, priests and laymen, mediate the relationship between the unapproachable God and the Christian community. This model has now been replaced to a large extent by a nuclear family model where God is the father, Mary is the mother, and the Christian community are the children. The deity in this family is male, and coupled with the feudal model in which God is master and king. It has been suggested that the family model is by association a patriarchal one.[10]

I found a high level of confluence between the *gringo* concept of the ideal family and the one preached by local and regional representatives of the Church. This is also the case with notions of masculinity and femininity. The parallel between the holy and the secular family is drawn by the *gringos*. The ideal family is talked about as the one where 'the husband is the head of his family, as God is the head of the Church'. When they are asked to specify what this means, terms such as authority, security, protection, advice and maintenance are used. Even though informants rarely refer directly to the Virgin when they are talking about the ideal woman, the qualities emphasized – such as dedication to the family, love, care and mildness, sacrifice and mediation between children and father – are closely convergent with those associated with her. In general terms, both men and women take it for granted that these particular gender differences exist and, to a large extent, are biologically determined and part of the celestial order, even though they recognize the importance of proper upbringing. This does not mean that there is total congruence between the ideal and the real. Certainly, *gringo* women manoeuvre in that they manipulate and negotiate with their husbands, and gender relations have changed over time. However, because these negotiations and manipulations – and changes – have hitherto taken place within the constraints set by the dominant gender ideology, they do not threaten the dominant 'gender order'.[11]

Because the Church is also, to some extent, a political institution, its dictates change over time, and there are internal contradictions and frictions that allow the faithful a certain flexibility and room for manoeuvre. Regarding gender issues, however, adaptations and changes in Santa Cecilia generally take place within frameworks that do not challenge the core of the doctrines, or cause a rupture with those doctrines that assign a domestic and subordinate position to women. I believe that liberal priests, with their more flexible approach, even help to prevent a deeper questioning of the Church's position on gender.

The *criollos* also define themselves as Catholics. They believe in God and the saints, in heaven and hell. They often express a special devotion for the black madonna, the Virgin of Itatí, whose image they have on the wall or in a small shrine. However, their religious beliefs and practices have little to do with the official Church. They seldom attend Mass, and pay little attention to the sacraments and the Church's moral commandments. According to them, the church building, as well as the institution and its rituals, belong to the *gringos*. This is an opinion which is to a large extent shared by the *gringos* themselves, even though they officially emphasize that the church is for everybody. The *gringos* – historically and at present – have a very close relationship with the church; they *are* the church in this community.

The theology of liberation which gained momentum in the 1960s in Latin America, and also in my area of study, did not bring about major lasting changes in the relationship between the Church and the two ethnic groups. To understand why, it is necessary to look more carefully at the role of the Catholic Church in a wider perspective. Different from the Brazilian Church – which, according to Levine and Mainwaring, advanced from being comparatively weak to become 'the most visible, intellectually forceful and progressive Catholic Church in the world' – the Argentine Catholic Church is defined as the most conservative in Latin America, both theologically and politically.[12] Historically, there has been a close relationship between state and Church in Argentina. The Church has always supported conservative governments and military regimes. The Argentine 'tercermundista' priests, who were the most radical in Latin America in the 1960s and 1970s, managed to bring about only very limited internal reforms. Most of them left the priesthood, were expelled, or even killed during the 'dirty war'.[13]

In my area of study, radical priests motivated by liberation theology's message of social justice and equality tried to mobilize the poor to become involved with the church. In Santa Cecilia this happened through the so-called 'rural groups', part of the Rural Movement of Catholic Action. Due to the class and ethnic polarities within the rural communities of this region, the priests could not address the poor population directly to the same extent as they did in other areas which were more ethnically homogeneous. The mobilization of the *criollos* would have been interpreted as a betrayal by the *colonos*. The strategy of the Rural Movement, therefore, was to involve the *gringo* population, especially the youth, in a process of increasing awareness of the poverty problems in their communities. Young men and women were trained to take the lead in the creation of 'el hombre nuevo' (the new man) and 'un campo más sano y cristiano' (a more sound and Christian countryside), which were central slogans of the Rural Movement in this region.

In other words, the radical priests tried – through the Rural Movement – to improve the situation of the *criollos* by motivating the *gringos* to become better patrons and better Christians. Since the problems of the *criollos* tended to be attributed primarily to an individual lifestyle, the result of uncontrolled sexuality and promiscuity – in short, lack of responsibility – a major effort was made to try to change their way of life. The *gringos* should be the motivating force in this process. They should help the *criollos* to overcome their vices, and thus to improve their economic situation. This meant, for example, that the *gringos* actively invited them to participate in the different religious groups. They also tried to convince the unwed couples among their workers to marry by helping them with 'los trámites' (the paperwork), which is expensive and time-consuming, and they would contribute to the arrangement of the wedding party. A day of baptism was arranged during the harvest months, to get the *criollos* to baptize their children. Members of the *gringo* families committed themselves as godparents, and the *gringo* community, together with the priests, arranged a big fiesta on that occasion. In short, the project was to transmit to the *criollos* the values associated with being a 'good Catholic': hard work, a regulated family life, and controlled sexuality. The project was aborted when the Rural Movement started to collaborate with the Agrarian Leagues, a farmer organization which became a political force in Argentina in the early 1970s. The Argentine bishops decided to stop the Action part of the Rural Movement, which was associated with the theology of liberation.[14] This implied a shift of emphasis for the Church – away from social and temporal problems towards spiritual ones and the life to come, much in the same way as before 1960. It also implied the disappearance of most radical priests from the area. This change coincided with an increasing repression of all types of social movement in the region and in the country. When the military regime took power in 1976, it was with the blessing of the Church hierarchy. In Santa Cecilia, the Church and its values and practices are now – as they have always been – associated with the patrons.

Conclusion

The case of Santa Cecilia illustrates the power of gender discourses in the legitimation and perpetuation of inequality between men and women, as well as between members of different social classes and ethnic groups. The dominant gender discourses are associated with social and economic dominance. They depict men and women as different sorts of individuals embodying different and mutually exclusive abilities and vocations, thereby contributing to 'naturalize' the sexual division of roles in the *gringo* family and in the community in a way that maintains *gringo* men's control over material and organizational resources and, through that, the control of their women.

The dominant gender discourses are particularly powerful,

since they are rooted in Catholic beliefs and practices in a context where the Catholic Church is the most important producer and transmitter of gender ideology – not only through the Church itself, but also through other institutions of civil society. This implies that gender values and practices at the level of face-to-face interaction reflect and find support in a wider ordering of notions of femininity and masculinity.

The farmers conceive of themselves as existing within the ideological universe of Catholicism. In this universe they are the models for 'la vida sana y cristiana' (the sound and Christian life) and the moral superiors of the *criollos*, who are often referred to as 'gente sin moral' (people without morality) and 'bad Catholics'. As I have already indicated, this sense of superiority is associated with hard work and the observance of Catholic family and gender values. Sexual behaviour – particularly female sexual behaviour – is an important distinguishing factor and a key metaphor in defining ethnic and class differences. Moreover, we have seen that prosperity and 'progreso' are associated with the image of the 'good Catholic', while poverty and lack of prosperity are associated with the opposite. Consequently, the *criollos* who are defined as 'bad Catholics' have got what they deserve.

The processes of legitimation and perpetuation of inequality within and between the ethnic groups are quite different. Men's control over women is based on values that are shared by the farmers and their wives. These values are not shared by the *criollos*, who advocate contrasting discourses on gender and do not accept the dominant view of their moral inferiority. Drawing on central concepts in recent discussions on the place of the individual within structures of power and domination, I suggest that gender relations within the group of farmers are character-ized by complicity, while resistance is what characterizes the relationship between the two ethnic groups.[15]

The complicity in male–female relations is achieved through hegemony.[16] This concept refers to dominance based on common values or shared meaning rather than on coercion, and implies a large measure of consent. This consent is achieved by the transmission of values through the institutions of civil society, such as the family, the Church, the education and legal systems, and the mass media. When I claim that male farmers' dominant position in Santa Cecilia is not challenged by their women, it is because they actively support the dominant notions of gender difference and hierarchy transmitted through the local institutions, and make choices that are compatible with its maintenance. The women are aware of the existence of different gender discourses and practices. They are exposed to alternatives – not only those in their own surroundings, which they deprecate, but also through the media, especially television. However, there is still no acceptance of alternative ways of being men and women in this community.

The dominant discourses on gender are not challenged by the *criollos* either, despite the fact that they question their validity and do not aspire to live in accordance with the values they convey. The *criollos* are proud of their *sangre caliente*, contrasting it with the *sangre fría* of the *gringos*, and of their freedom from conventions and their ability to enjoy life. However, being a marginal group in society, poor, uneducated and 'immoral', their oppositional values and practices, rather than challenging the dominant values, contribute to confirming them. These values and practices also prove their moral inferiority in the eyes of their patrons and of society at large, and may be used to explain their 'falta de progreso'.

Notes

This essay is based on anthropological research in Santa Cecilia, where I spent eighteen months in 1973–74 and eight months in 1988 with financial support from The Norwegian Research Council. I am grateful to Marit Melhuus and Eduardo Archetti for constructive criticism and helpful suggestions on earlier versions.

1. H. Moore, *A Passion for Difference*, Cambridge 1994; A. Cornwall and N. Lindisfarne, *Dislocating Masculinities: Comparative Ethnographies*, London 1994; N.B. Dirks *et al.*, eds, *Culture, Power and History: A Reader in Contemporary Social Theory*, Princeton, NJ 1994.
2. Moore, p. 59.

3.   S.B. Ortner and H. Whitehead, 'Introduction: Accounting for Sexual Meaning', in Ortner and Whitehead, eds, *Sexual Meanings: The Cultural Construction of Gender and Sexuality*, Cambridge 1981.

4.   For a more thorough picture of the history of agricultural colonization in Argentina, see R. Schopflocher, *Historia de la Colonización Agrícola en Argentina*, Buenos Aires 1955. On Friulian colonization in Northern Santa Fe province, see M.I. Cracogna, *La Colonia Nacional Pte. Avellaneda y Su Tiempo*, Avellaneda 1988.

5.   Cracogna 1988.

6.   'Calle' literally means street, and contains a connotation with the urban. People in Santa Cecilia, however, use the term in referring to spaces outside the farm. 'Casa' literally means house or home, but in the local use it may also include the immediate surroundings of the house. If, for example, a woman washes clothes in the patio, or weeds her tomato plants in the vegetable garden, she is considered to be 'en casa' (at home). The fields constitute a separate category. If a man is weeding his cotton field, he is said to be 'en el campo' (in the fields). Thus, in the local categorization, *calle/casa* is analogous to the public/private dichotomy, while the fields are in between.

7.   Catalina Weinermann has carried out a study of ideas and values regarding women and work in what she defines as the five most important domains of production and transmission of gender ideology in Argentina: the Catholic Church, the legal system, the education system, the social sciences, and the media. She demonstrates that there is an 'ideological core' common to all the discourses analysed, which is rooted in the gender doctrines transmitted by the Argentine Catholic Church and highly congruent with the doctrines conveyed by the Holy See in Rome: 'El mundo de las ideas y los valores: mujer y trabajo', in C. Weinermann *et al.*, eds, *Del Deber Ser y el Hacer de las Mujeres*, Mexico 1983. I reached a similar conclusion, based, among other things, on a revision of schoolbooks and participant observation at the local school, and on revision of TV programmes and magazines consumed by my informants. The result is presented in K.A. Stølen, *The Decency of Inequality: Gender, Power and Social Change on the Argentine Prairie*, Oslo 1996, pp. 262–4.

8.   In an earlier publication I have treated more extensively the influence of Catholic gender doctrines in the relationship between men and women in Santa Cecilia, taking into account the discrepancies between the theology and values held by the Church hierarchy and the values and practices of individual priests or among the faithful: 'The Gentle Exercise of Male Power in Rural Argentina', in *Identities: Global Studies in Culture and Power*, vol. 2, no. 1, 1996.

9.   The examples are representative of much broader material based on public orations given by the local priests and lay leaders on occasions such as Mass, the celebration of the Word and religious festivals, as well as on

more private and focused conversations. I also reviewed written publications and recorded what informants (both priests and parishioners) told me about face-to-face situations such as confessions and more informal conversations. The translations of the texts are mine.

10. W. Christian, *Person and God in a Spanish Valley*, London 1972; K. Harris, *Sex, Ideology and Religion: The Representation of Women in the Bible*, New Jersey 1984; S.L. Skar, 'Christian and Quechua Beliefs Contrasted: Towards the Ideal Content in Man/Woman Relationship', in F. Bowie and S. Ardener, eds, *The Past and Present Impact of Missionary Activities on Women*, Oxford 1993.

11. The tensions between continuity and change in gender relations in Santa Cecilia are dealt with in more detail in *The Decency of Inequality: Gender, Power and Social Change on the Argentine Prairie*.

12. D. Levine and S. Mainwaring, 'Religion and Popular Protest in Latin America: Contrasting Examples', in S. Eckstein, ed., *Power and Popular Protest: Latin American Social Movements*, Berkeley, CA 1987.

13. D. Lehmann, *Democracy and Development in Latin America: Economics, Politics and Religion in the Postwar Period*, Cambridge 1990.

14. E.P. Archetti, 'Ideología y organización sindical: Las ligas agrarias del Norte de Santa Fe', *Desarollo Económico*, vol. 28, no. 111, 1988.

15. L. Abu-Lughod, 'The Romance of Resistance: Tracing Transformations of Power through Bedouin Women', *American Ethnologist*, vol. 17, no. 1, 1990; A. Ong, *Spirits of Resistance and Capitalist Discipline: Factory Woman in Malaysia*, New York 1987; I. Halsema, *Housewives in the Field: Power, Culture and Gender in a South Brazilian Village*, Amsterdam 1991; Stølen 1996.

16. A. Gramsci, *Selections from the Prison Notebooks*, New York 1971; R. Williams, *Marxism and Literature*, Oxford 1977; R.W. Connell, *Gender and Power: Society, the Person and Sexual Politics*, Stanford, CA 1987.

8

Power and Self-Identity:

The Beekeepers of Ayuquila

Magdalena Villarreal

> *'These idle and irresponsible women don't have husbands to control them: their old men are* mandilones *[men who wear aprons, who let their wives boss them around], and cannot provide for them, so they send them to work, that is why these women go around as' [The end of the sentence was often left to the listener's imagination.]*

Such was village gossip concerning the members of a women's beekeeping group in Ayuquila, a rural community of Western Mexico. Who exactly said what was not clear, but the words were constantly repeated by different people as having been said by someone else.

Talk like this is not uncommon in rural Mexico. The imagery it calls forth quickly invites us to draw conclusions concerning the performance of a dominant discourse which frames the behaviour of women, and restricts their actions to the sphere of the household and to their roles as housewives and mothers, setting the scene for male authority and control.

However, such hasty inferences tend to petrify the circumstances and obscure the workings of power, of those precise social relations that make for the reproduction of what one might want to label a 'dominant' gender discourse. The concept of 'dominant discourse' conveys the notion of a fixed frame of ideas, images, labels, performances and ways of addressing social situations and actors which govern the endeavours of those under its subjugation. It generally refers to the imposition of ideas and categorizations by those in positions of hierarchy or authority, and to their widespread acceptance and legitimation. In overemphasizing 'dominant' imagery, researchers tend to assume that ideas pertaining to those in hierarchical positions are oppressing passive victims. This can lead to black-and-white pictures which portray the notion of a discourse which is almost solely responsible for the exercise of power and subordination.

Although one might very quickly identify those images and frames of ideas which serve to delimit the space for women and subjugate their actions to particular relations *vis-à-vis* men, the question of how they are generated and reproduced remains; we are left with a very limited understanding of the actions of those in subordinate positions, thereby eclipsing the space for 'alternative' discourses and the degree to which processes of resistance take place. Our challenge, I believe, is to come to grips with the processes whereby particular notions are produced, accepted, internalized or rejected and transformed. My aim, then, is to show how images and labels are generated, modified, negotiated, sanctioned and re-enacted with the effects of restricting the projects of others, channelling them into more 'controllable' domains, or reinforcing, expanding or changing their meanings.

I ground my analysis in a study of interface situations wherein a women's group – the focus of the gossip quoted above – are exposed to encounters with people from 'the outside' and to different definitions, ideas, representations and interpretations of their reality. I describe the struggles the women had to undergo in defence of their own space in interacting with the *ejido*[1] – commonly labelled a 'men's world' in the village – but also with representatives of the state, who appear to push forward an 'alternative' discourse. Through the description of different interface situations I hope to show how diverse discursive elements were mobilized within concrete circumstances and reinterpreted to form part of other discourses. Power was implied in the exercise, but one cannot speak of a totalizing discourse in the hands of a master, of unclouded, 'alternative' discourses, or of clear-cut, articulate processes of resistance. As Foucault suggests:

> Indeed, it is in discourse that power and knowledge are joined together. And for this very reason, we must conceive discourse as a series of

discontinuous segments whose tactical function is neither uniform nor stable. To be more precise, we must not imagine a world of discourse divided between accepted discourse and excluded discourse, or between the dominant discourse and the dominated one; but as a multiplicity of discursive elements that can come into play in various strategies.[2]

Actually, in the case I am about to describe, the projects of state officials, of women beekeepers and of other villagers were interlocked, associated or played against each other, in combinations or in apparent agreement, and one can see how power was dealt with at different levels, from different perspectives. The analysis of moments of interaction in the forging of the beekeeping project provides the grounding for an exploration of the intricate workings of power relations between women and men in the village, and how these are intertwined with power relations between the women and the state as well as among the women themselves. It also exposes the crucial association of power with the reconceptualization, negotiation and sanctioning of gender images.

Here constraints on action and difficulties of access are significant, but the issue is much more complex. It involves the unpredictability of emergent situations; it is interwoven with interpretations, with loyalties and emotions, with life histories and particular perceptions of the future. Hence one needs to look closely into the ways in which discursive elements are drawn together in an effort to negotiate the appropriateness of specific gender images and labels, to adjudicate status or authority, and to define values. This also entails focusing on mechanisms of exclusion, of rating and ranking, which can lead to practices of gender subordination and provide grounds for power relations.

A Strategic Conception of Identity as Rural Women: Government Rhetoric

The group was created in 1980 in the small community of Ayuquila, a *mestizo* town of 174 households located within an important irrigation district along the main road linking the municipal capital, El Grullo, to the state capital, Guadalajara, in Jalisco, Western Mexico. It was organized as a UAIM [*Unidad*

Agricola e Industrial de la Mujer Campesina: Agrarian and Industrial Unit of Peasant Women], a government programme backed by the Federal Law of Agrarian Reform. The programme stipulated that groups of women should be encouraged to participate in economic activities by being allotted plots of agricultural land and supported with credit from official institutions to set up small enterprises. The UAIMs were established by state decree in 1971 during the presidency of Luis Echeverría, a period of intense peasant organization and mobilization. It was during this time that the World Conference of International Women's Year (1975) took place in Mexico. Government programmes involving women were centred mostly on family planning, but state rhetoric strongly emphasized the need to 'integrate women into development'.[3] This might not have had anything to do with the intention of questioning patriarchal gender relations in rural areas, or changing the economic situation of rural women, but it certainly became important in the context of state legitimation towards specific national and international audiences, in terms of directing discontent away from unwanted peasant unions and co-opting large sectors of the population into its institutions. Hence, although in some ways the programme can be seen as providing a 'liberating' discourse for women, the 'alternative' imagery pushed forward by officers was instrumental in the state's wielding of power.

The head of the programme of UAIMs in the State of Jalisco – Silvia, a female lawyer from BANRURAL (the Government Rural Bank) – when the present study took place claims:

'The programme is part of the women's struggle for their integration into the world of production, while at the same time recognizing them as liable to receive credit. It is a consequence of the struggle of peasant women, fruit of a social movement.'

The social movement to which Silvia is referring here is the Mexican Revolution which took place in 1910, after which the PRI [*Partido Revolucionario Institucional*] – the ruling party, to which she must adhere as a civil servant – took over. While she is describing the women as yearning to incorporate themselves into what has become known as the 'men's world', she is also defining the nature of the state. She is eager to portray an image of the state bank, for which she works, as an institution sensitive and responsive to social problems.

Silvia's interpretation of the programme and its prospects is more or less shared by other government officials who, in one way or another, have influence over the women's groups. But while government rhetoric concerning women's programmes called for radical change, the creation of UAIMs was not intended to threaten local authorities, or land tenure patterns; neither was the intention to change the terms of gender organization in the household or in the fields.

State officers were required to enlist peasant women in rural policies. By 1985, it was reported that 6,461 units of organized women (UAIMs) had been created in the country.[4] Not all have been successful, according to official expectations: some disappeared soon after their creation, others were taken over by a few women or controlled by male authorities, and most faced severe economic setbacks.

The different actors within the state portrayed diverse and very specific interests and motivations in initiating and promoting the programme. Each defined characteristics for their own and others' identities, building upon shared values and points of consensus. To begin with, it is impossible to produce a precise state image of rural women, as the state itself is not a consistent entity which acts according to uniform interpretations. Meanings change from one actor to the other and from one situation to the other. But most state officers expressed the aim of the national programme in terms of stimulating the organization of women in such a way that they would be incorporated into the 'production process', which would eventually lead to lessening gender inequalities. The 'world of production' is depicted as a world of progress, of development, of free enterprise that will provide a way out of poverty, and a world which, of course, is the domain of the 'experts' – naturally, from outside the rural scenario.

A male officer from the Ministry of Agriculture and Water Resources (SARH) in El Grullo (the municipality to which Ayuquila belongs in politico-geographical terms) gave us his view of the beekeepers. According to him, the women should:

'develop and integrate themselves, so that they do not see their actions as merely subsistence and hobby, but in terms of a managerial mentality; it is important that they [the women] understand that they can grow with the products they have. The group can export their products, and become a source of development for all the beekeepers in the region. Of course, they would first need an intensive technical training, in order that they are more prepared.'

He envisaged 'entrepreneurial roles' for the women beekeepers, but he did not seem to be aware of the fact that this had implications for their roles within their households and vis-à-vis their different networks in the village. He stressed that the women would become models for other peasant women, and even for other men.

The state representatives were building upon an interpretation of what their crucial audiences (such as international funding agencies, feminist groups, critical academics and trade unions) considered to be the nature of women's problems and the ways to solve them, but they were also pushing forward new connotations which had to be 'sold' back to these and other audiences, to the women, to the *ejidatarios* and local officials. The women were expected to acquire a 'strategic conception' of their own development as peasant women – that is, they should see themselves as an important social force, and disregard small, trivial interests which might hinder their progress. To initiate UAIMs, to get women to accept the institution as theirs, these women must see themselves as lacking participation in the production process, as not being fully developed in their potential as women. To keep the UAIM going, the women must perceive themselves as entrepreneurs. To overcome obstacles such as cultural beliefs and male demands, they must understand that these belong to the past, to backward traditions that must be eliminated. Here, processes of exclusion acquired crucial relevance. It was important to plant 'new' ideas and images in rural women's conceptions of themselves, their projects and their expectations, so it became necessary to exclude 'old' images and frames of reference. From Silvia's point of view this was not easy, and some obstacles had to be overcome:

'There is *atavismo* [ties to old, backward ideas], and *machismo* as well as inferiority complexes in the women, and they come out with things like "My husband doesn't allow me", "My brother does not want me to join the group". The problem is the different interests that exist between them, the different conceptions of life and development which do not allow people to see further. We are facing social atavisms, and it is a matter of fighting them with appropriate education. If you manage to get two or three women together, you sing victory, because they can become small poles of development.'

But let us start exploring these issues in the context in which the project was initiated from the point of view of Victoria, a 'progressive' woman who used to be a member of the group.

Victoria: The Genesis of the Group and the Accepted Norms for Village Women

I had heard a lot about Victoria before I met her. From what villagers told of her, she was a strong, wilful, interesting woman. Socorro, her mother, pretended to disagree with the way Victoria sat down to eat with the men at the table,[5] waiting to be served instead of serving them herself, but she could not disguise a proud smile. Her father respected her: 'She is like a man,' he said.

Victoria was then already a successful schoolteacher with a stable position in Michoacán, a neighbouring state. In the afternoons, she held another post as director of a primary school. Her husband shared – to some extent – household chores and the care of their two children, although he worked all day teaching himself. Before she left Ayuquila with her family to occupy her post in Michoacán, Victoria had been an enthusiastic member of the beekeeping group. She spent most of her holidays visiting her parents, and was considered a citizen of Ayuquila. In my conversations with her, Victoria provided what seemed to me a clear picture of the genesis of the group, which had been a difficult theme to draw out from most of the beekeepers.

She considers that Ayuquila has progressed a great deal, owing to the fact that many of its citizens – like herself and her brothers, but unlike her sisters – have pursued further education outside the village. She says that about 2 per cent of Ayuquila's inhabitants have some academic title or another, but complains strongly about social prejudices and how they have constituted an obstacle to women's progress:

'It was hardly tolerated that we women go out and study or work at the time. The idea prevailed that whoever went out was *libertina* [loose, licentious]. And that idea still predominates. I can count only about three or four men from this last generation who have changed their ways of thinking. Before, a woman could not go to El Grullo alone. . . . My mother says these prejudices were justified because one saw "many things" happening by the canals and the river when women went to wash their clothes or when they went to the fields to pick up leftovers of beans or maize. Some women became pregnant, and as a consequence of the bad reputation of two or three, the rest were not trusted. New generations are leaving that behind, but the prejudices and ignorance of men still hinder many women from studying. . . . Before, *qué esperanzas* [no chance] they did not let you go to Autlán [a nearby town], much less Guadalajara [the state capital] alone. It was always associated with *libertinaje* [looseness, too much licence]. Then, if the woman *fracasaba* [blundered, meaning became pregnant], she had to leave the village [*el rancho*]. That was what Josefina and Margarita had to do. But this does not apply to those who are *preparadas* [prepared, those who have studied]. They stay at home and have their babies as if nothing has happened.'

In Ayuquila, an image of vulgarity and low status was implied in the label *libertina*. A *libertina* was a woman who would not comply with the social restrictions attributed to her gender, particularly with respect to the possibility of sexual relations with men. Speaking to men (generally applied to men who are not kin) in overfamiliar terms, drinking with them or providing space for gossip by travelling outside the village without a very good excuse, could be interpreted as *libertinaje*. Women should see themselves under the guidance, protection and authority of fathers, uncles, brothers and husbands. A *libertina* did not behave according to accepted norms and was seen as irresponsible, uncaring towards kin and family. She was considered indecent and low.

A *fracasada*, on the other hand, is a woman who has failed to establish a decent life for herself by getting pregnant out of wedlock or without having a permanent male partner. As Marit Melhuus[6] puts it: 'morally she has fallen from grace . . . she has come to grief'. She thus has to 'reinstate her chastity'. This points to the ways in which women were expected to confine their movements to certain social and physical spaces, and to the interpretations other men and women could legitimately attribute to their actions.

Victoria reacts strongly to what she describes as the idea that women *son las que tienen que fregarse más* (are the ones who have to work the most, who carry the heaviest burden). She exclaims that it is important for her to be seen as equal to men. The women discussed these things with each other, but they had some conflicts at home. She explains that she could count on the support of her mother, who was convinced of the validity of her work, but her brothers and father did not like it. (At this point her brother, who overheard our conversation, interrupted, claiming that they only tried to avoid her being gossiped about.) Victoria, however, makes her points strongly:

> 'I do not like to be dependent, and although sometimes I have to conform, I perform with another idea. I remember very well what motivated me to change. When I was thirteen or fourteen years old, I decided I did not want to live like other women in Ayuquila, who do not have their own pocket money. I wanted better conditions.'

She had, in fact, managed to establish a somewhat independent image of herself, building in part upon her status as an 'educated woman'. The label of 'being like a man' referred to Victoria's command over situations, to not subordinating herself to others. But however independent she wanted to appear, Victoria herself did not want to be labelled a *libertina*, accepting that 'a few guilty women were the cause for others to be accused', and that women 'instigate' the situation: 'they start it and are not capable of stopping before it's too late'.

Victoria was home on vacation from school in 1980, when the beekeeping group was formally started. She accepted the invitation to attend the meeting, encouraging her sister and her mother to come as well. A number of women were present. Several had come out of sheer curiosity; others attended because the invitation came from the head of the *ejido* and they felt it was impolite to turn him down. Some of them – including Victoria, her mother and her sister – signed the documents, agreeing to become members. Others waited to consult their spouses and family or simply dismissed the possibility, claiming that they did not have time. In this way a group was formed, and they were recognized as fit to receive aid under the government scheme.

Two years passed after the Ayuquila group was formally initiated under the guidance of a social worker from the Ministry of Agrarian Reform (during which time the women never met as a group) until another social worker, this time from BANRURAL, came to offer them credit to raise goats, pigs, or chickens, produce honey, or start whatever economic activity they wanted, as long as it fitted into the formal requirements. The group now had twenty-two members. In the intervening period some of the women had dropped out, including Victoria, who – as we have seen – was already working as a school-teacher. Some had married, and their husbands would not allow them to continue; others had gone out to work or study. The group finally chose beekeeping, as it did not involve a daily commitment.

The project was granted a loan of 775,000 Mexican pesos (approximately 1550 US dollars) from the Government Rural Bank for the purchase of the beehives and basic equipment. They started with fifty beehives, which they bought in a nearby village with the aid of the social worker, who helped them choose the new equipment and explained how they should keep their accounts and minute books. In addition, the beekeepers received some formal training from a bank extension worker, although the women claimed that it was too theoretical and of little value. Although financially the members never managed to earn significant profits, they worked hard to pay back the loan and managed to consolidate themselves as a group. In 1988 local officers considered them one of the 'successful' UAIMs in Western Mexico.

Self-Identity and Boundaries

This did not imply that the group members simply internalized and took over 'alternative' discourses and ideas pushed forward by state officers. But becoming part of a state-sponsored project had many implications for the women beekeepers, not the least of which concerned alterations in their views about who they were, what they could do, and who they could or could not be. New patterns of organization which affected their lifestyles were introduced, as were discourses concerning their own identity, and different perceptions entailing a reconsideration of the future before them. Yet to say that such patterns were introduced is to put it too strongly, as the women reinterpreted the project and its spirit in diverse ways at different moments. They generated links to other people in and outside the village, disowned roles attributed to them, and forged a project of their own, despite the fact that the project was shaped by multiple interests. Victoria argues:

> 'We started to participate because we were looking for entertainment, for a way out, something that would take us out of the routine of everyday housework, which was really tough and tedious. The group gave us the opportunity to think about different things, in addition to obtaining some cash without having to leave our housework. I became interested in the group when they assured us that one day we would earn money. I was also interested in obtaining rights to possess *ejido* land.'

It was clear that all the group members were hoping to receive economic benefit from their work, but the beekeepers had different interpretations of the scope and possibilities of such a project. They conceived its prospects within the boundaries of what they considered their roles, and orientated their activities to suit their own aspirations and immediate needs.

In my talks with them they often declared that their priorities were in the household, and that earning a few coins was a complementary activity. *Ama de casa* (housewife) was a term they often used to describe themselves. In striving to fulfil their roles as mothers and wives, the women engaged in specific activities such as getting their children through school and teaching them proper values, keeping their husbands 'in line' by not allowing them to drink too often, making their lives as comfortable as possible by providing clean clothes and nice meals, as well as keeping out of village gossip. This entailed constraining their actions within established boundaries: they should not be seen as too 'loose' in their interaction with men, for example; and, generally speaking, they should not impinge on the frontiers of the men's world.

None claimed explicitly to be a model housewife, but Petra, the president of the group, often boasted about her cooking skills and was proud of the way she had reared her children, despite problems with her husband, who wanted her to spend more time in the house. Sara (another member of the group) spoke with satisfaction about how good her sons were, the way they went to church on Sundays, but also about her kind and faithful husband, and how she walked kilometres across the fields to take him a hot lunch, then stayed a bit to help out with his chores. She proudly showed her sewing and embroidery to her visitors. Socorro bragged quietly about how she cooked for her family, which was now composed only of boys, since the girls had married out. The idea of keeping their household in 'good order' was often conveyed.

Moreover, the beekeepers described themselves many times as *mujeres pata rajada* (women with cracked feet). *Pata rajada* is commonly used in this region to describe a hard-working, un-cultured but tough person who can work in the fields barefoot, thereby getting cracked soles. Fissures on the soles are the result of walking barefoot on the hot earth, or wearing typical *huaraches* (cheap sandals). The term is used locally to refer to a trait or characteristic of a lower category of people, in contrast to *la gente refinada* (refined people), who wear shoes and there-fore do not suffer from cracked soles. Sometimes, however, the word was used by the beekeepers with a mocking connotation, a way of 'putting themselves down' strategically. They were, as Victoria phrases it, 'performing under another idea'.

The label *mujeres empresarias* (women entrepreneurs) pushed forward by state officers was seldom used among the women themselves in serious conversation. Becoming entrepreneurs entailed, first of all, neglecting their families, leaving small children behind when they were working with the bees, and not being at home when their husbands came in from work. In all probability they would have to travel outside the village often – frequently alone with lorry drivers. It also meant negotiating with men in the market. Although there were a few women in the village who undertook such activities without being stigmatized as *libertinas*, this generally meant trespassing the boundaries of their roles as housewives. Some toyed with the idea of becoming real entrepreneurs, but for others it was a step out of line. Sometimes they would employ the label when they were having fun, satirizing it, and expressing it as something remote and impossible. But much was at stake, as became evident in their conflicts with the *ejido*.

Mandilones and *Abejeras*:
Conflicts with Men in the Village

Most of Ayuquila's residents rely on small-scale agriculture, trade and transport, as well as remittances from family members in the United States. A vast portion of the land is *ejido* property. The majority of forty-seven officially registered *ejidatarios* are male; there are only five women, two of whom are widows – and have inherited the title from their husbands. At least half the women in Ayuquila combine household work with other family-based economic activities such as running small shops, selling milk, or making and selling *tortillas* (a maize-based staple of the Mexican diet). Some sell clothes, shoes, perfumery and prepared foods; others are dressmakers. Many regularly assist their husbands with agricultural tasks such as planting, weeding and hoeing, or taking the cows home and cutting grass for the horses. Most of the women keep chickens, and a few have some goats or pigs. A few women in Ayuquila work as teachers or secretaries, and a dozen or so work as day labourers for the tomato companies.

There is a shortage of land in the *ejido*, with some *ejidatarios* having less than one hectare of arable land. In comparison with neighbouring *ejidos*, Ayuquila had been slow to gain access to land after the expropriation following the revolution. Different versions of the story of how they finally acquired it are told and retold by the members of the *ejido* and the oldest people in the village, stressing the struggles they underwent, how much suffering it entailed for their families, and how a few trailblazers risked their lives for the sake of others. Land had acquired multiple meanings. It was not only a resource in terms of the agricultural produce that could be obtained from it, it was also a compensation for those who struggled and suffered for it.

In accordance with the law, the *ejido* was compelled to give up a piece of land for the new UAIM initiative. A number of *ejidatarios* were reluctant to comply with such stipulations. Some wanted to use the land themselves, some did not think the women deserved to be allotted land: they had not struggled for it and wouldn't even know how to use it properly. But the situation also provided the chance for a small but combative group of *ejidatarios* who were in conflict with the head of the *ejido* to seize the opportunity of subverting his decisions.

It was at this point that gossip about the beekeepers began. They were accused of not knowing anything about agriculture and enterprises, of neglecting their households, and of being idle and irresponsible. The image of *libertina* was implied, but worst of all, their husbands were labelled *mandilones*. The words stung. By accusing their husbands the gossipmongers were accusing them; they did not want to be described as lousy mothers or wives. As a group they had not intended to take sides in the village gossip circles, but now they appeared to be in the midst of it all.

The label *mandilones* is a strong one. The accused is likened to a weak, impotent male who has no voice *vis-à-vis* his wife. Implicit reference is made to feeble male sexuality, giving the epithet a forceful character. An analogy between a man who cannot control his wife and one who cannot make proper decisions was stressed. However, the villagers who resorted to the images of *mandilones*, *libertinas*, and irresponsible women were not necessarily aiming at restricting the space of the beekeepers or thwarting processes of change concerning the dominance of males over females in the village. Basically, they were defending their interests with respect to access to land, and seizing the opportunity to subvert the authority of the head of the *ejido*. In so doing, they drew upon commonly held views which accentuated the exclusion of women from what were considered 'male roles'. Gender imagery was thus used as a powerful instrument in their struggle, and wives' dependence on and subservience to their spouses was reappraised as 'respectable' behaviour to be used as an argument in the context of a dispute which only partly concerned the women.

To clear their husbands' and their own names, the beekeepers were obliged to defend themselves from village gossip. They were placed in a position that required them to stress their spouses' authority. This implied emphasizing their image as good housewives and mothers. By disowning the notion of *libertinas* and struggling to disclaim the label of *mandilones* for their husbands, they were in some ways legitimizing their respectability while simultaneously reproducing the very gender imagery used to undermine them.

Local state officers sometimes endorsed images of *libertinas* and *mandilones* in their everyday discourse. A female social worker from the state bank complained that her male colleagues never understood the aims of the programme concerning the improvement of women's status, and that they often took advantage of their position to harass different UAIM members sexually, claiming that women who were willing to engage in economic groups were actually looking for fun. I observed how a state agronomist who came to instruct the beekeepers on the prevention of bee diseases tried to flirt with them, suggesting to one of them that they could meet later in town.

However, the state officials had been assigned to promote the project; it was in their interest to argue in favour of the women. In so doing, they resorted to the 'alternative' views advanced by the programme rhetoric. Such 'alternative' images were used as powerful instruments in their endeavours (note here the use of a mirror-strategy to that of the *ejidatarios*, who resort to 'traditional' images in an attempt to wield power). Hence they often spoke of the need to change 'traditional' views concerning women's roles. They stressed that women were crucial on the road to progress, and should no longer be perceived only as housewives. They insisted that the law should be obeyed, and that the beekeepers should be granted a plot by the *ejido*. In the end this was accomplished, and the UAIM was allotted a hillside plot.

Plots on the hillside were used either for grazing cattle or for producing fodder for sale. The women's group adopted the same strategy of selling fodder. With the money they earned, as well as that received from the sale of their honey, they decided to build a small store.

The decision to construct a store was unanimous, given the need for a physical space in which to work, to store their things and to hold meetings. An *ejidatario* sold them a small piece of his urban plot, and they contracted a local bricklayer. This entailed an investment of 1,113,000 Mexican pesos (approximately 1,113 US dollars at the time). Although the store was small, it satisfied the requirements of their enterprise. They needed only sufficient space for the extractor and the decanter, a space for capping the combs, and a place to keep the boxes and frames. The space was also big enough for the sixteen members to meet. Benita, one of the beekeepers, caressed the walls fondly: 'This' – she said – 'this is ours'.

The construction of the store had implications in terms of the women's conception of themselves as part of a project. It sealed an unwritten pact to proceed as a group, and revealed ambitions to continue the enterprise, however small. The beekeepers would carry on despite criticisms from some of their neighbours, who had scornfully labelled them *abejeras*.[7]

However, they took it lightheartedly, and half-mockingly assumed the term themselves, giving it a different connotation altogether. *Abejeras*, pronounced by the members of the group, implied a *pata rajada* who worked in the sun, covered from head to foot in dirty, smelly clothes (they explained that bees do not like the smell of perfume and attack more readily when they use this or certain soaps), but at the same time it denoted 'progressive' women who defied criticisms and dared to shoulder a responsibility such as the beekeeping enterprise.

Changing Boundaries

To what extent the women's self-identities and the boundaries they set on their expectations and activities changed with the beekeeping project is subject to debate, but perhaps this is less relevant than the ways in which images and self-identity were used in the negotiations for power and the creation of space for manoeuvre.[8]

In acting out roles in the village in order to avoid social problems, while attending meetings, when interacting with government officers, and in committing themselves to beekeeping activities and following the rules set out by the state for the project, the beekeepers did seem to have changed many of their views about their identity as women and as beekeepers. However, the women presented themselves differently according to the audience and circumstance. Asked directly, the beekeepers might spontaneously address themselves as housewives. But when they were accused of being only housewives who knew nothing about production, they defended themselves and the project by identifying themselves as 'entrepreneurs'.

Crucial situations involving change in the beekeepers' margins for action originated with the visit of officials from another Ministry, the SARH (Ministry of Agriculture and Water Resources). The regional office of the Ministry fostered a development programme orientated to peasant organization. They were having problems finding groups willing to collaborate in their programme because of its orientation to collective work. The UAIM of Ayuquila was interesting to them for several reasons: it already had a legal status, they were backed by an *ejido* institution, they were women and they were working collectively. These arguments could be used to attract financial resources and political prestige to their own government agency.

Thus, they offered to create a 'real' agro-industry, which implied a larger storehouse, more modern implements – including an electric extractor and perhaps even a vehicle – and more beehives. Embodied in the new enterprise was the notion that women should view their activities with a managerial attitude, that they should think of honey as a commercial product which could be exported. Of course, they would first need intensive technical training.

Once again a 'new' discourse was thrust upon the beekeepers, whereby they were exhorted to take on different roles as 'entrepreneurs'. They were asked to engage in the beekeeping enterprise as a full-time job, and to think big. This obviously had implications for their roles within their households and in the village, further reinforced by the suggestion that the beekeepers could become a model for other peasant women, and even for other men who were reluctant to organize and 'develop' themselves further.

Petra, the president, was quite enthusiastic about the promise of a new store. She saw her dreams of a productive and efficient enterprise reflected in this project. Since she was a Jehovah's Witness, and eagerly embraced commercial activities, the project fitted in nicely with her own personal aims.

Petra wielded a degree of power within the group. She was president, and her views were not dissimilar to those promoted by the project. But she was also supported by a network of close ties, centred around the current office-holders and women in her kin grouping, although they, like the rest of the group, had some reservations. They feared that they would run out of money halfway through the project and not be able to fulfil their commitments. Some felt that the present store was enough for their needs, that it was near and convenient for everyone. Dora, one of the young beekeepers, for example, could leave her newborn baby with her mother, who lived close by, and could then easily go to meetings and still be within calling distance. Benita had quite severe problems with varicose veins, and when she could not work because of this, she could at least get to the meetings. These individual problems had collective under-pinnings: the perception of themselves as housewives more than entrepreneurs led them to desire a small, centrally located meeting-place, which would allow them to combine beekeeping with home responsibilities.

Furthermore, the idea of a new store implied looking for a new plot. They wanted a centrally situated place where they could be observed by neighbours and kin, in order to avoid gossip. This would be hard to obtain. The new plot would also involve more problems with the *ejidatarios*, who were in fact short of land and had been quite reluctant to donate the first one. An additional problem was that they would have to accept a new loan from the bank for the agro-industry. They were relieved that they had almost finished paying the original loan, and were therefore reluctant to take out a new one.

On the other hand, most of the members agreed that it was an opportunity they could not easily turn down. Although they had already declined the offer of the new store, an imposing visit from the mayor – considered an important local authority – made them reverse their decision. He was invited by the Ministry to help convince the beekeepers. He offered the women help if they ran out of money, but most significantly, he stressed their importance in the region as a group – how they were now becoming 'relevant to our village and our country'. The bee-keepers often told the story of his visit, emphasizing his remarks about the enterprise being different from crude business, because it could provide jobs and bring fame to the village. Furthermore, the women's personal projects within their village networks and kin loyalties were at stake. The head of the village exerted pressure on them, as he had special interests in the new enterprise. His own relations with the mayor and the Ministry could be jeopardized if the women did not accept the new store. He was a respected person in the village and had helped them on many occasions, which made it even more difficult to refuse. As women in close relation to an institution such as the *ejido*, they had commitments: they should listen to the authorities, understand that what they said was best for them. Hence, defining their position towards the new store also implied defining their identity as 'peasant' women, 'respectable' women and *abejeras*. These images also served as points of consensus influencing their decision.

In the end, the women decided to accept. The agreement was that the bank would provide credit for the necessary implements, plus – and here lay an important problem – the purchase of at least 400 more beehives. The officers alleged that to justify the investment they had to think big, to think of a 'real enterprise'. A hundred hives was not enough.

As a consequence, the women now needed an urban plot for the group. This plot should be a flat accessible piece of land, not far from the urban area. This involved a series of new negotiations and confrontations with the *ejidatarios*, who controlled the distribution of *ejido* land. (It would be unthinkable to buy a plot from private landowners, as such a plot was not available and they would not have the money to do so even if it were.) They were supported – or, rather, pushed – by government officials who also put pressure on the *ejidatarios* to accept.

In the negotiations two important processes took place. One process was that in the practicalities of asking for a new plot of land, the women had to accommodate themselves to the *ejidatarios*' established procedures, as well as to their own commitments within their networks. They had to act within particular discourses, which implied the need to measure their steps carefully and make sure they did not transgress any social norms, consulting prominent male members of their kin networks. Hence they had to manoeuvre to maintain an acceptable position as 'the wife of' or 'the niece of' particular people. This brought into the group some of the power struggles going on between family groupings within the village, since the request would affect the personal interests of whichever *ejidatario* had claims over the selected plot, or hoped to use it in the future.

The other process was that the women were obliged to defend themselves as entrepreneurs, and in so doing they used the very notions they had been questioning earlier. Hence they resorted to words and labels used by state officers to back their arguments. While defending the project, they were also coming to terms with its importance. In the end, the plot was grudgingly granted, and the store was built.

Gender Imagery and the Issue of Power

If one is to identify the impact certain images have on gender relations, one cannot avoid looking closely into the meanings attributed to them and, further, into the processes by which such meanings are negotiated, reproduced and transformed. Exploring the social construction of meaning, however, reveals the ambiguities of power processes: the predominance of 'official' interpretations is not to be taken for granted. Even high-ranking officers cannot change the agendas entirely or avoid them completely. They can manoeuvre and manipulate particular discourses to influence understandings, but power relations are re-created in the interaction, not totally imposed. Power is not inherent in a position, a space or a person; it is not possessed by any of the actors and it is not a zero-sum process whereby its exercise by one of the actors leaves the others lacking.[9]

It is clear that in the forging of the project, different actors negotiated relative positions of power resorting to specific gender imagery. The *ejidatarios*, for example, recalled traditional notions of women as housewives and mothers to make their points; they wounded male (and female) pride by labelling the beekeepers' husbands *mandilones* and accusing them of not acting out their roles as authorities within their households. The attack was not directly intended to constrain the women, it was aimed at the head of the *ejido* in order to thwart the decision of allotting the beekeepers a plot of agricultural land, and the *ejidatarios* themselves did not necessarily hold such traditional views to their full extent (we have seen how some ended up accepting and even admiring Victoria's lifestyle, for example). A certain conflation occurred, whereby a particular rhetoric – entailing reified gender images – was used to feed into another in order to legitimate specific claims and win a dispute.

But the use of labels such as *libertinas* and *mandilones* did serve to monitor the behaviour of both men and women, and confine the scope of their activities to what was considered respectable conduct. The boundaries they set on their projects and activities were thus constrained by others' perceptions of their gender roles and of how they stood *vis-à-vis* other people. Many village women – including most of the beekeepers – did not disclaim the gender imagery used by the *ejidatarios*. They were always mindful of village values concerning gender, and particular discursive practices seemed to frame their behaviour at all times. They did not want to jeopardize other personal projects with their kin and village networks. Again a conflation of discourses took place, whereby the women accepted existing views to defend other spaces.

The fact that power processes are ambiguous, however, does not minimize their impact. On the contrary, it is such ambiguity that allows them to be accepted, reproduced and even encouraged by their 'victims'. It is not that the beekeepers had all the choices in the world to overcome, resist or counteract the images imposed on them, but the complex webs of constraints they faced were tied up with loyalties, with spaces they wanted to retain or create, with emotions, compensations and rewards.

Here the state representatives could be seen as providing an alternative discourse, one that offered a degree of space for women and in many ways subverted local 'dominant' discursive practices. In fact, a conflation of discourses was taking place here as well, since the officers were also resorting to reified images of women entrepreneurs and progressive women – which they did not always believe themselves to their full extent – in order to defend the aims of the project. Although such discourse actually contradicted traditional views of women's roles and capacities, it was instrumental in negotiating a better position of power. Did they not in the end manage to direct the women into an entrepreneurial furrow? Did they not use the group for political purposes?

On the other hand, the women managed to subvert some of the meanings entailed in the gender imagery imposed on them, as when they were labelled *abejeras*. They changed the connotation of the label and gave it a different meaning. A similar process took place with the notion of entrepreneurs, the implications of which they never fully accepted if we consider state officers' conception of it.

Thus, morally correct behaviour, accepted roles or 'proper' identities cannot have an impact unless they are internalized and reworked by the actors. Discourses are not coherent units of speech, behaviour or norms; they cross each other, containing incongruities and discrepancies. Discourse is constituted through processes of interlocking and segregation of voices, where meanings and interpretations are attributed and disowned, infractions are defined and negotiated, and standards are reconciled. Discourses were drawn upon in the forging of the project to encourage or block certain modes of women's action, but the beekeepers amended and rectified labels, and struggled to protect and sustain their own definitions of the 'reality' of their interests and their moral standards. Notions such as *libertina* and *abejera* were reconceptualized and shaped through social relations. Indeed, the validity of such categories and classifications was itself constantly negotiated. And the possibility of using the very same images to different aims – be it maintaining power relations or transforming them – stimulated their reproduction.

Notes

1. The *ejido* is a socio-legal entity concerned with the administration, defence and distribution of communal land. Legally, all the members of the

206   MACHOS, MISTRESSES, MADONNAS

ejido, the *ejidatarios*, have rights to land and a say in decisions pertaining to it.

2. M. Foucault, *The History of Sexuality, An Introduction*, New York 1980, p. 100.

3. See Velázquez Gutiérrez, *Políticas Sociales, Transformación Agraria y Participación de las Mujeres en el Campo: 1920–1988*, Cuernavaca, Morelos 1992.

4. See L. Mantilla, *La Unidad Agricola Industrial para la Mujer Campesina (UAIM)*, Cuadernos de Difusión Científica 12, Centro de Investigación Educativa, Guadalajara 1989, p. 12.

5. Sitting at the table with men is not uncommon for women in Ayuquila, although it is expected that they first serve the rest, and see that everything is ready. However, *tortillas* have to be heated or made just before they are consumed, otherwise they get cold. Generally a woman is expected to be heating *tortillas* and replenishing food while the rest eat. When there are several women in the household, only one of them carries out this task while the others sit at the table. Often daughters or daughters-in-law wait for 'the second table' and eat with their mothers. Victoria's attitude is notorious because she has several brothers and often expects them to get up themselves for warm *tortillas* or more food.

6. M. Melhuus, '*Todos tenemos madre. Díos también*': Morality, Meaning and Change in a Mexican Context, unpublished PhD thesis, University of Oslo, 1992, p. 172.

7. There is no direct translation of this word, as it is not a proper word in Spanish. *Abejeras* is used instead of *apicultoras*, which is the technical word for beekeepers. One can draw a parallel between this labelling and the commonly used *zapatero remendón* – instead of the normal *zapatero*, which literally differentiates actual shoemakers from shoe 'patchers', thus stressing the differences between 'experts' and laymen within this trade.

8. See N. Long, *Creating Space for Change: A Perspective on the Sociology of Development*, Wageningen 1984.

9. See also M. Villarreal, *Wielding and Yielding; Power, Subordination and Gender Identity in the Context of a Mexican Development Project*, PhD thesis, Wageningen Agricultural University 1994.

9

The Production of Gendered

Imagery:

The Concheros of Mexico

Susanna Rostas

Introduction

Miguel is sitting on the ground, slowly and carefully inserting ostrich feathers, dyed in bright greens, reds and blues, into a headdress which he wears to dance as a Conchero. The rest of his clothing consists of a loincloth fashioned from brightly coloured materials and decorated with Aztec symbols made from gold and silver plastic appliqué. Round his neck he will place a collar even more elaborately embellished, while round his ankles he will tie leg rattles made from large dried seeds. Propped against a wall is his feathered shield on which is depicted Huizilopochtli, the supreme Aztec deity. His companion, Maria, is already dressed. Her costume is less sumptuous, for she is clothed in a cotton shift decorated with similar symbols and wears undyed pheasant feathers in her headdress, but she has more highly elaborated leg rattles.

Miguel and Maria are from the outskirts of Mexico City, and have come into the centre as have the rest of their group of Concheros to attend one of the big events of the year, the dance at La Villa in honour of the Virgin of Guadalupe.[1] Maria has an important role in the group – she is the *saumadora*, the tender of the incense burner. For the dance she thus takes up a position in the centre of the circle beside the General, who is the group's leader. Maria and Miguel describe themselves as warriors who have come to join the battle – that is, the dance. Their fight is for indigenous autonomy, their motto 'Union, Conformity and Conquest'. Miguel also has a particular role: he is one of the sergeants. Predominantly, he thus dances holding up a banner, insignia of the group, on which the Virgin of Guadalupe is depicted flanked by the figures of various saints. At other times he joins the circle of the dance and plays his *concha* as he performs. The *concha* is the stringed instrument that is special to the Concheros. Fashioned from an armadillo shell and played by many of the dancers as they dance, it gives them their name and is seen as their principal 'weapon'.

In this essay I look at the dance of the Concheros as a producer of gendered imagery, for the dance as a whole projects a powerful and varied visual, verbal and bodily imagery that has cohered from various sources. Much of the religious symbolism is Roman Catholic; some comes from literary sources, while the military nomenclature is Spanish, despite the Concheros' claims that the dance is about the reconquest of Mexico for the Mexicans. Increasingly today the imagery also comes from pre-Hispanic sources such as the codices made both before and after the conquest, and from the writings of such early Spanish chroniclers as Sahagun or his latter-day interpreters. The visual imagery is also based on photographs of various present-day indigenous groups and their artifacts, while some of the ideological imagery has come from indigenous people who are known to the Concheros (or ethnographies they have read). But it is also compounded of the many ideas the dancers have, not so much about the indigenous cultures of Mexico *per se*, but, rather, about 'Indianity'. By 'Indianity' I mean their ideas about Indianness, which have been culled from both popular movements and popular culture – for example, films, posters, songs, newspapers and magazines.

Miguel and Maria come from a quite 'traditional' group of Concheros. Other groups, such as those who call themselves the Mexica, have rather different representations. The gendered imagery the dancers display is manifested not just in the kinds of clothing they wear but also by their body movements, by the various kinds of decoration exhibited, by the words of the prayers, those of the songs, the nomenclature of the dance personnel, and the ideology behind the dance. I shall therefore look not at the gendered imagery of everyday life but, rather, at that produced for or under ritual .conditions – that is, as evidenced during performance. I shall offer a general description of the origins of this imagery which is in part historical, based on how 'Mexicanness' has been characterized since the Spanish conquest, but more specifically of what the representations displayed have to do with the way the dancers 'imagine' Mexico. In Anderson's terms the Concheros are very much an imagined or 'imaged' community drawing on the cultural capital available to them of 'Mexicanness', which is historical, political, mythological, artistic and literary.[2] I also aim to show that those who dance as Concheros, although they are mostly from backgrounds where the male is apparently valued above the female, according to literary stereotypes as well as ethnographies, are – by means of the dance and its complex of imageries, both visual and verbal – seeking, consciously or otherwise, a way in which this gender imbalance can be rectified: if only, in the first instance, for the duration of the dance. For the Concheros are using powerful imagery to gain, among other things, a way of defining gender which is much closer to that found in indigenous communities than to that in the wider context of *mestizo* society, and by this means, and the dance in general, to seek both external and internal empowerment. The recent emergence of the Mexica, however, is tending to reverse this trend, but I shall return to this theme later.

The need to assert or create 'Mexicanity', to search for a Mexican identity, is not new. It has developed over time in terms of an archetypal and/or stereotypical imagery which is reflected in writing produced during the course of the twentieth century. I look briefly at this literature, before relating it to movements concerned with 'Mexicanity', which it undoubtedly influenced and which were significant in the formation of the Concheros. I then discuss the most recent writings on the latest movement, *Mexicanidad*, and the emergence of the Mexica. Overall, I thus concentrate as much on the influences of the literary side of Mexican culture as on those of the popular. But I want to begin with some background information about the Concheros before moving on to look at how the dancers fit into the wider context of Mexicanness.

The Concheros

The Concheros meet to perform a circle dance, and hold all-night vigils throughout the year. The major dances are held in places that are both Catholic religious sites and locations of pre-Hispanic significance, such as La Villa, where all the groups from the various Associations perform together: these dances are held on three significant dates in the Catholic calendar.[3] But each group also holds smaller dances, sometimes as frequently as every other week, for some important event in its own tradition, to honour a local saint's fiesta or, by invitation, to perform on a cultural occasion. A vigil is usually a more private, internal and informal affair than a dance, which it frequently precedes. During a vigil, flower forms are created which are later refashioned and used to ceremoniously cleanse those present. On the following day, at the dance, men and women perform together, placed alternately in the circle. The dance steps and sequences are identical for both men and women. During a dance, the leader of the group positions himself in the centre, with his *saumadora*. All groups sing the same songs and perform the same dances, some of which are named after pre-Hispanic deities such as Tlaloc or Quetzalcoatl. There is, however, great divergence in the clothing worn, which is indicative of the various groups' differing ideologies as to what the dance signifies.

The Concheros come from all walks of life. They range from rural *campesinos* and urban workers to a large urban contingent, consisting of lower-, middle- and upper-middle-class dancers. Rural dancers can often offer little explanation as to why they dance; it is part of the Catholic tradition that runs in their family. Among the less educated in Mexico City the dance is still predominantly religious, but it is also more clearly about indigenous identity. For the large group in the middle, ranging from non-manual workers, to professionals, to those involved in the arts – dancers, painters, potters, actors – to academics, the dance is seen as part of a search for personal fulfilment through the experience it provides. There are also upper-middle-class housewives with time on their hands or the more numerous young people interested in the esoteric, for whom the dance is a more self-conscious search, often linked to that of other spiritual paths, such as Sufism or the Way of Gurdjieff.

In addition, there are the 'New Age' dancers, whose main concern is with ecology and attaining a balance with nature by means of a certain lifestyle, a stance more akin to the indigenous view of the world. There are also those who reject the Catholic Church completely and are establishing a pre-Hispanic autochthonous form of religiosity incorporating elements from the Aztec past. Such dancers call themselves the Mexica, and for them the dance involves a more clearly invented ethnicity.

The dancers not only come from a wide range of social levels but also have diverse levels of education – from no schooling at all for some of the rural dancers and *gente humilde* in the City to a sophisticated knowledge of Mexican culture among the intelligentsia. The discourse on the dance is thus multiform; it is many different things to its various practitioners, although overall it seems to be about identity.

I now want to discuss how the production of gendered imagery varies from group to group, and the significance of this. To return to Miguel and Maria: the source of the imagery for their costumes is Aztec; the designs are loosely based on depictions in the codices, although the clothing itself is fabricated from modern materials. If asked, the couple would claim that they are Concheros primarily for religious reasons, and certainly a vigil is predominantly a religious affair – a dance perhaps a little less so. What they wear indicates, however, that the group has definite ideas about 'Mexicanity'.

The style of costume that Miguel and Maria wear is one that has been around for some time and has superseded little by little that which is generally known as 'Chichimeca'. Today predominantly only country people wear 'Chichimeca'-style clothing, which covers the entire body; both males and females wear tunic, chasuble and cloak, fashioned from brocaded materials with fur trimmings. According to myth, the dance of the Concheros is said to have begun among the Chichimeca at the time of the conquest. They were subsequently forced out of their rich farmlands into the arid regions further north, where they would have needed little clothing.[4] This style of vestment, and the materials used to make it, could not thus be less Chichimeca, as we now understand the term. It is still, however, worn today in those previously indigenous communities which were drawn into the nation-state and the Catholic Church well over a century ago. These are the communities where the dance first established itself as a separate association distinct from the Catholic Church, although such dancers are often still involved in Catholic *cofradia* (brotherhood) activities within the community itself. The origins of this style of clothing for the dance are unknown. It seems probable, however, that it developed under the influence of the Catholic Church, and reflects European rather than indigenous ideas about decency and the need to cover the body. The other representations of such groups are clearly Catholic. They dance under banners portraying images of the Virgin of Guadalupe, or other well-known saints in the Catholic pantheon, and their beliefs are predominantly Roman Catholic: they are practitioners and usually attend Mass.

Miguel and Maria belong to a group [*mesa*] of which there are an increasing number, both small-town and more particularly urban, which have begun to question the role of the Church. As they see it, the Catholic Church, because of its European origins, should not have hegemony in a country which is ever more conscious of its autochthonism. The 'Aztec' dancers evince a Mexicanness which is not highly verbalized, although many know that some of their songs and prayers have been translated from Nahuatl, the language of the Aztecs, into Spanish, and are thus indicative of pre-Catholic origins. While they still claim to be believers [*creyentes*] of the Catholic Church, they attend Mass only rarely and are (vaguely) aware that the Aztecs had a distinct religion of their own. But the dominant verbal discourse of such groups still centres around Christian imagery, that of Jesus Christ, the Virgin Mary as the Virgin of Guadalupe, and various other saints. Although such dancers signal an interest in a more indigenous past by means of their dress, they are still religiously conservative.

Recently this position has been taken much further by the Mexica, who have adopted a much more rigid aesthetic. The Mexica, as groups of dancers, are a recent phenomenon. They aim to use only Aztec representations, and consciously reject any aspect of the tradition which is Spanish: they thus make music only on instruments of pre-Hispanic origin: various flutes and drums such as the *huehue* and *teponaztli* (slit drum). They completely reject the *concha*, which, they claim, is Hispanic, as also is the name 'Conchero'. They too dress in Aztec-style costumes, but based more closely on the codices and fabricated only from natural materials that would have been available before the Spanish conquest, such as skins for the men's loincloths. If they have banners – which many groups do not, as they also are Hispanic in origin – they depict not Catholic saints but symbols from pre-Columbian iconography – abstract designs signifying Aztec concepts or the forms of their deities. The Mexica are learning Nahuatl, and they aim to use it as their ceremonial language. Many have adopted Nahuatl names, and their groups have such designations as 'Huehueteotl'. The Mexica advocate a return to the Aztec past; they claim that they are taking the dance and its associated practices back to their pre-Hispanic form. They espouse *Mexicanidad*, a more clearly conceptualized ideology than the milder Mexicanity of the Aztec Conchero dancers, and they are part of a much larger movement which began to grow rapidly in the late 1980s, to which I return below.

Thus the Concheros, and more especially the Mexica, are in the position of wanting to fabricate a Mexicanness, of donning a mask or putting on a costume which in the first instance has little to do with their everyday lives but which, bit by bit, becomes an increasingly important part of them. I do not want to imply that they create a new persona – that is, that they change personality – nor that they are enacting a psychological type other than the one they have developed through their lived experience. But I do want to emphasize that for many, once they have become Concheros (or Mexica), the dance dominates their lives. They begin to talk predominantly about the dance, dream the dance, think the dance, increasingly to spend time with other dancers and, when they socialize, to socialize with them. Some become quite obsessed with 'Concherria' in all its aspects (while the Mexica, in their turn, bring *Mexicanidad* into everything with which they are involved).

But although apparently a recent phenomenon, the interest in 'Mexicanity' has a long history. There is not only a literature that has helped to foster and form archetypes and/or stereotypes of Mexicanness for the Mexicans, there have also been various movements that have actively developed 'Mexicanity', sparked off by a desire that Mexico should be a nation with a distinct identity; all these have fed either directly or indirectly into the Concheros' imagery of themselves.

The Literature on Mexicanity

Nations as they emerge and begin to assert themselves, tend to be self-conscious. Not only do they have to establish a nationalist constitution or manifesto – that is, find their own 'style' and justify it (by myth or some other means) – but this often brings in its wake a corpus of written or visual self-examination by intellectuals on how well the clothes of the nation fit the inhabitants who have to wear them.[5] Mexico has been no exception. The literature on Mexicanity has until recently been perpetrated largely by the elite, for the elite and a somewhat wider but educated audience. It consists predominantly of stereotypes, drawn from an imagined lifestyle, which do not necessarily feed back into the lives of those who provided the inspiration; for those who acted as the 'imagined' models for such stereotypes were often not familiar with this literature when it was first published, because they were themselves largely illiterate. It must, however, have had, and still be having, a recursive effect on them in the sense that it will to some extent shape the way the wider public see and/or conceptualize people like themselves.

The literary works on this theme burgeoned in the 1950s, and again in the 1980s, but had begun much earlier. Mexico gained its status as a nation after the Revolution of 1910. The new epoch was ushered in with the academic writings of Caso and Vasconcelos, the chief proponents of *indigenismo*; they aimed to show how Mexico as a nation had to be fashioned to include the many elements of indigenous culture. The philosopher Samuel Ramos attempted to define the Mexican character and its traits by means of various characterizations or stereotypes.[6] The later work of the so-called *pensadorees* was more literary; the best exemplar and the most widely read by outsiders, as well as by Mexicans themselves, is still Octavio Paz's *The Labyrinth of Solitude*.[7]

The discourse of these early writers develops the theme of the 'Mexican' transported from his rural roots to a state of urban anomie. The 'stooping' Indian is characterized as melancholy – that is, as passive and indifferent to change, as pessimistic, resigned and timorous, and without consciousness but independent. He has been depicted by Diego Rivera in his murals as a man in a sarape wearing an enormous sombrero who squats as he waits patiently (for whatever awful event is to befall him next). His urban counterpart, known as the *pelado*, suffered the tragedy of human solitude. For Ramos he constituted the 'most elemental and well-portrayed expression of the national character'. The *pelado* is typified as coarse and uneducated, the user of uncouth language, someone who retains some of his rural primitivism but has in reality lost his roots, and who, according to Ramos, has burned his boats:

> He is a man who has forgotten his rural cradle . . . a man who must face a situation that is alien to him because it is not yet his own. He is trapped and, therefore, potentially violent and dangerous. His traditional spirit has been ruined, and in his heart modern cadences are not yet heard. The modern age has only ripped his flesh, leaving him subject to the pincers of industry and the dangers of the street; his spirit is in a state of disorder, if not rebellion. Hence the violent energy he generates, which must be harnessed to create the cosmic race, to fortify the impoverished nation, to destroy the colonialist, to mould the revolutionary proletariat.[8]

He is thus an outsider living in an unfamiliar context, the City, where he manifests aggressive behaviour because he is dominated by feelings of inferiority.

Much play is made of this notion of inferiority by both Ramos and Paz. The idea of the Mexican nation put forward during the Revolution was based on a reappraisal of Indian cultures and the identification of the 'Mexican' with 'the *mestizo*', thus valorizing a racial mix or type that had not been acceptable before. The Revolution reconstructed an ideology of hierarchy under the aegis of a protectionist state. The state was thus built up by a white elite and was an organization to which the masses had no entry or access, despite the fact that the Revolution was to have been theirs; hence the sense of inferiority.

Just as the image of 'the Indian' developed by Gamio as a

prototype of what traditional Mexico had been or still was in the countryside was necessary 'to forge an "indigenous spirit"', if only temporarily, so a stereotype of the urban Mexican, the *macho*, began to harden.[9] According to Gamio, he was even more nebulous and mysterious than the figure of the *pelado*, but his formulation was necessary for the fashioning of the new state. The *mestizo* is a 'contradictory, hybrid figure in whom two conflicting currents collide'; he has a double ancestry, both indigenous and *mestizo*.[10]

As many later analysts have pointed out,[11] the problem with these outpourings on Mexicanness is that they are not based on actual people; these are not ethnographic vignettes of the real but stereotypes constructed from a position of hegemony. They are the product predominantly of male literary writers or intellectuals and are usually of men, portrayed in the first instance in verbal imagery. The traits condense into characters such as the Indian Pedro Paramo in the novel of that name,[12] or are popularly invested in actual heroes such as Emiliano Zapata, who gained what might be called identity notoriety.[13] They were also given visual substance by various mural painters, particularly Rivera, but also by Orozco and Leal.[14] Predominantly, however, the *mestizo* and the Indian were imaged stereotypically, both verbally and visually, and this has been carried into the present via films, *telenovelas* (soaps) and photographic strip cartoons.

But how much did this body of writing influence the Concheros? I suspect initially only indirectly, as such stereotypes were more about the type of people who became Concheros than the Concheros themselves. The stereotypes go some way in helping to explain why being a Conchero was an attractive proposition, as it provided a way of finding indigenous rural-style roots in an otherwise alienating environment. More importantly, however, the writings give a sense of the backdrop against, or the way in which, the dancers would have been judged or seen, as they became more apparent to a middle-class public who knew – and still know – little at first hand, about indigenous Mexico or the urban dispossessed.

The Concheros themselves were probably more influenced in the formation of their present imagery by an organization known as the Confederated Movement for the Restoration of Anahuac, founded in the late 1950s by Rudolfo Nieva. Its membership, which was totally middle-class and white, aimed to restore a mythical pre-Hispanic culture by means of *Mexicayotl*, a doctrine propounded in a book of that name written by the founder. The movement also published a monthly bulletin, *Izkalotl*, containing ideas about how an autochthonous Mexico might be reconstructed. Members enacted ceremonies to honour Aztec heroes, and Nahuatl lessons were offered.[15]

The male stereotypes, however, gain more significance when they are seen in relation to the female. Paz describes women 'as silent and idol-like fetishes' that 'fuse into the night, the earth, the stone'.[16] Images of the female generally got short shrift from the earlier male writers. This is probably because the fashioning of the nation-state was seen by the men involved as an activity that predominantly involved the male sex; indeed, in 'modelling' the nation-state, emphasis tended to be placed on the masculine. That the national identity of Mexico is a masculine one is shown not only by male writers but also by more recent female writers such as Rosario Castellanos and Elena Garro.[17]

Where the male mythology is bipartite and political, the stooping indigenous Adam of 'paradise subverted'[18] versus the *pelado/macho/mestizo* of the Revolutionary but hegemonically dominated and controlled City, the polarity of the female is different. Rather than traits that are located in types or historical characters or stereotypical heroes, for the female there are two contrasted mythologies: the sacred and the profane. The imagery is thus more archetypal than for the male: the Virgin of Guadalupe, Mexico's most powerful saint, virtually a goddess, vies for attention with La Malinche, the exchanged indigenous woman who acted as intermediary between Hernan Cortés and the indigenes.

For centuries, for the indigenes, La Malinche was identified with the magical power of the Spanish; she was 'the medium for conquest'.[19] But the role of La Malinche has altered through time as ideas about Mexican history have changed. From being seen as the enabler of the Spaniards, when she was known as Doña Marina, she has come to be seen as the betrayer of the Aztecs. Her previously honoured characteristics of beauty, intelligence and motherhood, as the first mother of the Mexican nation, have been replaced by a series of negative images of a selfish, rejecting and evil woman, likened to the biblical image of the serpent in the Garden of Eden, a Mexican Eve, both traitor and temptress.[20] La Malinche, or Malintzin (her Nahuatl name), thus provides an image neither of femininity nor of motherhood but of betrayal; she 'translated' for the Spaniards – that is, literally committed 'treachery'.[21] Although this is currently the received interpretation, it is one that has gradually increased in strength, as Cypess points out, since the period of transition in the early 1800s from colonialism to nationhood.

According to some writers, the dominant male gender myth is that the trait of male chauvinism is attributable to the perfidity of La Malinche. The *mestizo* male – who, because of his mixed blood, is one of her many sons – is still shamed by her rape (the conquest), and thus seeks to deny the feminine side of himself. He sees this, according to Paz, as devalued, passive, mauled and battered, and what he has of La Malinche in himself as *la chingada*: the female part of himself that has been violated, screwed over, fucked, and yet is . . . [itself] a betrayer'.[22]

The *mestizo* man is typically *macho* – that is, tough: he mixes only with the boys, and sees women as disposable.[23] Yet he can – and does – cry, and has been – or still is – dominated by his mother, the linchpin of the family, who is identified with the other dominant female image, that of the Virgin of Guadalupe. The *macho* image of masculinity is thus constructed in the first place through negativity and the female figure of La Malinche, but also through the Virgin of Guadalupe.

The Virgin of Guadalupe did not change her persona as Mexico became a nation-state. The Virgin of Guadalupe is everything that the reinterpreted La Malinche is not – forgiving, pious, virginal, nurturing and good.[24] The Virgin represents saintly submissiveness, a dominant subservience – everything the *macho* man needs in a mother/woman. She is also indigenous (at least in part), as she has brown skin and is said to have first appeared to a Christianized Indian, Juan Diego, at Tepeyac, where today the church of La Villa stands. According to the conventional interpretation of the imagery with which she is usually portrayed, – crushing a serpent and in possession of the heavens from which she protects her chosen people – she is usually seen more as the woman of the Apocalypse than the Mother of Christ. Another interpretation of that imagery enables her to be seen rather as both worldly, to do with the 'Mexican nation', in that she is standing on the snake, the symbol of the founding of Tenochtitlan (Mexico City) by conquest, and also goddess-like, spiritual, in her celestial connections. In this guise she is, rather, Tonantzin, the collective name given by the Mexica/Aztecs to the range of goddesses who represented the power of the earth and its fecundity. As such she was an indissoluble part of the duality of Ometeotl, the supreme deity who incorporated both masculine and feminine elements and earthly and heavenly aspects.[25] It is no coincidence that Tepeyac is the site where Tonantzin formerly had a shrine, and where the Concheros now dance! The Virgin of Guadalupe thus encompasses in her imagery, very effectively, both the Virgin and the mother.

We thus have two female figures or images that predominate over all others, while for the masculine we have a plethora of lesser ones, none of which has that archetypal force; no one dominates. On the other hand, there are some historical women who are part of mainstream Mexican imagery, about whom Franco has recently written, but they are more peripheral and have had less effect in forging the imagery of Mexican woman than the many men who have held positions of power.[26] Thus for the masculine we have not only a range of stereotypes to be found now in both popular thought and literature and the writings of the *pensadorees*, but images based on historical figures such as Zapata or, going further back, Moctezuma, supreme ruler of the Aztecs when they were defeated by the Spaniards, or pre-Aztec deities such as Quetzalcoatl, all of which feed into the imagery of the male. But although, as I have already indicated, Mexico as a nation has an apparently masculine valency, the iconicity of the female is the more powerful: the Virgin of Guadalupe is *the* national symbol shared by *mestizo* Mexicans.

For most people the past has never been seen as a closed system but, rather, as part of a wider field of representations that undergo a constant process of reinterpretation and reinvention. The Virgin of Guadalupe or La Malinche has iconic value as a sign, but as signifiers their meanings frequently change, as we

have already seen for La Malinche. Similarly, the Virgin of
Guadalupe has a different significance for 'an atheistic politician
than for a proclerical one, for an Indian than for a worker, for a
shantytown dweller than a university professor'.[27] So what, if
anything, do these further representations of the male and the
female mean to the Concheros?

The Concheros' Imagery

First, the feminine. Predominantly those who dance as
Concheros are people who were born into the Catholic Church
and have been religiously educated in the complete panoply
of Catholic imagery, which is dominated by the Virgin of
Guadalupe. Images of the Virgin are ubiquitous in *mestizo*
Mexico. They are to be found in all churches, in most homes,
and in countless locations such as shops, public spaces, and on
calendars! There is no one single male image as powerful as that
of the Virgin, not even that of Jesus Christ; probably because
of the lack of indigenous identification with him. For the
Concheros, as we have already seen, the Virgin appears in
various guises on many of the banners carried by the groups.
She is central to their prayers; their most sacred song is the
'*Guadalupana*'; while their most important dance is held on the
anniversary of her appearance. She is always a sign, however, a
representation, never a person.

On the other hand, La Malinche appears, or is said to be
represented, in the figure of the *saumadora*, the female dancer
responsible for the incense burner in the centre of the circle. Here
she does not have the negative connotations of the nineteenth-
century translator-seen-as-betrayer; rather, she personifies the
idea of translator, the one who can resolve differences between
self and other; for the *saumadora* is responsible for ensuring that
the energies of the group are well balanced. If two dancers have
quarrelled, they can discuss it with La Malinche and attempt to
resolve it. If she cannot do anything, she will place the dancers
in such a position in the circle that they cannot affect each other
and hence everyone else. Her role is thus to sense the energies of
the group, to aim to improve the balance between the sexes, and

ultimately to help the group to transcend. La Malinche, as 'the medium of conquest', now transposed from betrayer of the Aztecs to enabler of Mexicanity, is an important part of the fight for 'reconquest'. For as indicated above, the Concheros see their dance as a 'battle' for indigenous autonomy. The *concha* is their principal weapon; the others are the drums, especially if they are pre-Hispanic, the seeds tied round their ankles and the rattles they hold in their hands as they dance. Thus in the first instance the nomenclature or verbal imagery of the dance appears to be masculine, because it is so obviously military but also, surprisingly, literally Spanish. It is in essence a metaphorical language which they use to talk about empowerment; they are all soldiers, and to vanquish is to be empowered. A dance is considered to have been successful if it has been either well balanced and/or well received in a new location, and is talked about as a 'conquest'. The figure of La Malinche is thus of great significance to the Concheros, and it might be thought that her representation would also be of importance, to the Mexica. But among them, La Malinche has reverted once again to the status of traitor. Their version of the dance does not lay emphasis on the feminine; they pay little tribute to the Virgin of Guadalupe even though she is brown-skinned and transposes nicely into the Aztec deity Tonantzin.

At this point it is clear, I hope, that the two female archetypes are utilized fully by the Concheros; the Virgin of Guadalupe is, after all, part of mainstream Catholic iconography in Mexico, while La Malinche is a mythological figure who has long since entered the discourse of everyday life. The available male imagery, on the other hand, although it is more historical, more plentiful and more dominant, seems not only to be more diffuse or piecemeal but also not to have the same iconicity, the same power.

For the Concheros no one male image dominates, and this could perhaps be why the gender imbalance of everyday life can be rectified in the dance. As we have seen, when the Concheros dance they form a circle, men placed alternately with women. The dancers never touch but aim to move in harmony, attaining as the day advances a state of *communitas*, which is more easily gained if the group has held a vigil the night before. By placing man next to woman, by ensuring that both sexes hold responsibility within the circle, gender balance is attained. Thus for the duration of the dance, as a transcendent state is slowly reached, the gender inequalities or differences of everyday life are erased. The dance as a ritual thus has similarities to ceremonies in indigenous communities. For if *mestizo* Mexico is *macho*, indigenous Mexico retains, rather, something of the duality of the pre-Columbian deities. Men and women are different rather than unequal and, like the Aztec deities, together make up a whole. In most indigenous communities, masculine imagery does not dominate the feminine. The public sphere may exclude women, but in the spiritual sphere men and women perform ritual together. There are both male and female deities, the male having only a slightly greater significance than the female. Furthermore, in the more indigenous areas – in Chiapas, for example – the Virgin of Guadalupe is virtually unknown and La Malinche definitely so, as she belongs to another mythology;[28] she is part of national, not indigenous popular, culture. In the *rus*, Spanish popular saints who have been superimposed on indigenous deities predominate, but closer to the Valley of Mexico, and to the *urbs*, the more Catholic Mexican representations dominate (although these again have been superimposed on indigenous Aztec/Mexica deities).

The Imagery of the Mexica

The gender balance achieved by the Concheros, however, is lost on the Mexica. The Mexica's dance is more aggressive. They dance the same dances, but much faster, more competitively, and espouse a chauvinism based, they claim, on Aztec models. Little attention is given to their female dancers, in the sense that no attempt is made to dance at a speed with which they can keep up; harmony between the sexes is not attained during the dance. Nor has any effort been put into developing an imagery based on pre-conquest models of the Aztec woman or female deities. The Mexica give less attention to the feminine and have a more *macho* stance than any other group of dancers. The Mexica dancers have thus moved from a position of projecting an imagery of 'different but equal' to one of inequality, which may seem surprising at first in the present climate of a global interest in feminism. Why should this be the case?

To attempt to answer this question, I want first to look at the context in which *Mexicanidad* has emerged, then at what the Mexica are trying to do. During the late 1980s a new phase of Mexican nationalism could be said to have begun in which the Indian soul, one of the foundations on which the Mexican Revolution had been based, was beginning to be forgotten as *mestizo* Mexico moved closer to the USA and became more and more '*gringo*ized'. Roger Bartra's *The Cage of Melancholy* is a plea for democracy, for allowing the Mexican to emerge as a fully developed man instead of encaged by a paternalistic authoritarian government. For many see the political structures of the Revolution enshrined in the PRI (Institutionalized Revolutionary Party) as no longer sufficiently democratic for a country that is tiring of its current uniform and wants – or needs – to try on new clothes.

Of even more significance is Guillermo Bonfil's *Mexico profundo*, which immediately became a bestseller; for Bonfil is read widely, not just by intellectuals.[29] The book's popularity seems to stem from the fact that it calls for a rethinking of the place of the so-called 'profound' indigenous Mexico in the Mexico of the PRI which privileges the white, 'wields the power and . . . presumes itself to be the bearer of the only valid national project'.[30] Bonfil suggests that Mexico needs to face not outwards but inwards, towards its indigenous and civilizational roots.

Mexicanidad is clearly a similar project, but at a more popular level still. It took off at about the same time as Bonfil's book was being written, and has without doubt drawn from his ideas after its publication. But the strongest 'literary' influence has probably been the popular novels of Antonio Velasco Piña. Piña's aim is to represent life in the Aztec world in a manner easily accessible to a wide audience, as he does in *Tlacaelel*.[31] He is thus into the familiar business of constructing stereotypes, but stereotypes that can be acted out. The Mexica can read his books, then enact their lives in an Aztec fashion. His novels are also esoteric: he claims that the present age is an important one cosmically for Mexico, for she is to become the spiritual centre of the world, as this moves away from Tibet; for this, collective 'sacrifice' will be necessary, the theme he develops in *Regina*.[32]

Mexicanidad appears to exert a powerful influence on its followers. For many of those involved it is becoming even more of a way of life than being a Conchero. Some Concheros are followers of *Mexicanidad* but would not dance as Mexica, and although not all the followers of *Mexicanidad* dance, many do. The Mexica, apart from going to the same dances as the Concheros, often attend demonstrations in *chitontiquiza* (the dance), held twice weekly outside the Cathedral in the central square of Mexico City, or go to Nahuatl lessons given by more or less qualified teachers in various parts of the City.[33] The Mexica, as a subgroup of *Mexicanidad*, are predominantly young, male, *mestizo* and urban, or from communities that have strong links with urban culture.

The Mexica are representative of Mexico's urban under-privileged, who feel belittled, marginalized and discriminated against. They are the 'angry' young men of the moment who, on the whole, reveal themselves as fanatical and intolerant not only of each other but also of other groups of dancers. Like Ramos's concept of the *pelado*, the Mexica appear to feel trapped; 'the modern age has . . . ripped [their] flesh, leaving [them] subject to the pincers of industry . . . and [they generate a] violent energy (see p. 215).

The Mexica, when they dance, are not looking for gender balance and harmony but are assertive and aggressive. Thus groups of Mexica present a very different ethos from that of the Concheros. There appears also to be an incipient class or ethnic 'battle' between on the one hand the middle- and upper-middle-class Conchero dancers, who are sometimes also Tibetan Buddhists or followers of Gurdjieff, and thus in a sense clearly not fully dedicated to Mexicanness, and the Mexica, who are usually struggling to survive in an economic and political climate that has little concern for the well-being of the less well educated but self-determined person. Essentially, the Mexica are those who feel disempowered, and hence inadequate. They also suffer from the not-so-hidden racism that still exists between those who can have more easily (because they are clearly whiter and more Hispanic, or perhaps I should say more *gringo*) and those who have not (because of clear indigenous descent). *Mexicanidad* is probably the first popular cultural-political movement.

Mexicanidad is thus an ideology which privileges the masculine over the feminine, and appears to continue to perpetrate the worst aspects of *machismo*. But perhaps this is not a moment for gentleness and balance, where male and female share the same imagery or can wear the same costumes.[34] Perhaps it is a moment when Mexico has to do battle for its place in the postmodern world as a nation in its own right – not one forged by the Spaniards but one that existed prior to that connection, nor one to be dictated to by its more economically powerful neighbour to the north, the United States, which it has largely managed to keep out of its hair since the Revolution of 1910. The gendered imagery of the Mexica – a return to Aztec models in many aspects of the dance, including their costumes – may appear retrogressive, but it is perhaps a response to an increasing uncertainty as to what Mexico is in the present, and hence a desire to put on the clothing of a mythical past once again, and so to become the 'warriors' for an uncharted future.

Mexico is going through not only a political crisis but also a crisis of representation. As Bartra puts it, Mexican national conscience is 'little more than a bunch of rags from the scrapheap of the nineteenth century, a costume patched together by the intellectuals of the first half of the twentieth century so that . . . [the Mexicans] would not show up naked at the nationalist carnival'.[35] The Concheros have worn one sort of costume, and now the Mexica are sporting another which indicates a strong desire to return to Bonfil's *Mexico profundo*, as does their support of indigenous political movements.[36] Thus the present 'battle', rather than being one for gender balance and internal development or consciousness-raising, has become, rather, an external one, a fight for survival and, almost coincidentally, one for political consciousness-raising about the plight of Mexico's indigenous people.

The Mexica have produced a gendered imagery that is more male than female, and possibly more powerful than that of previous scenarios or stage settings because it does not compromise. It is not *mestizo*, it does not attempt to accommodate Catholicism or the multi-iconicity of the Virgin[f] of Guadalupe. Where in the past her image dominated Mexican popular culture with its inbuilt Catholicism, now is the moment of the 'Aztec', bedecked in huge feather headdress. Images of him (and much less frequently of her) are becoming increasingly common on postcards, in publications and on calendars. The Mexica are playing their part to ensure that Mexico does not turn up naked at the carnival.

Notes

I would like to thank the British Academy not only for making two short periods of fieldwork for this project possible, but also for funding my journey to the International Congress of Americanists in Uppsala, Sweden (1994), where the paper that constituted the original version of this essay was given.

1. La Villa is the site of the church dedicated to the Virgin of Guadalupe. The Concheros hold their dance here on 12 December each year, the day dedicated to the Virgin in the Catholic calendar. The other major dances are at Chalma and Los Remedios.

2. Benedict Anderson, *Imagined Communities*, London 1983.

3. As already indicated, 12 December is the day dedicated to the Virgin of Guadalupe. 1 September is the day of the Virgin of Los Remedios, while 8 September is the birthday of the 'Santissima' Virgin; the dance at Los Remedios is thus held over the two adjacent weekends. The dance at Chalma is held some seven weeks after Easter during Whitsun, in late May or early June.

4. 'Chichimeca' also became a pejorative term, referring colloquially to Indians more as dogs than as people.

5. The idea for the clothing metaphor was suggested by Diane M. Nelson in 'Gendering the Ethnic-National Question: Rigoberta Menchú Jokes and the Out-Skirts of Fashioning Identity', *Anthropology Today*, vol. 10, no. 4, 1994, p. 5; and by Jane Gaines and Charlotte Herzog, eds, *Fabrications*, London 1990.

6. Samuel Ramos, *El perfil del hombre y la cultura en Mexico*, Mexico 1934 (7th edn 1977).

7. Octavio Paz, *The Labyrinth of Solitude*, London 1950. Claudio Lomnitz-Adler (in *Exits from the Labyrinth: Culture and Ideology in the*

Mexican National Space, Berkeley, CA 1992) discusses what books he might suggest for vistors coming to Mexico to read to give them a flavour of what Mexico is like. He notes, slightly regretfully, that rather than offering them the works of social scientists such as Oscar Lewis on Tepoztlan or Mexico City (*Life in a Mexican Village*, Urbana, IL 1963; *The Children of Sanchez*, London 1964) he often suggests literary works, but in particular *The Labyrinth of Solitude*. For a discussion of the role and relevance of texts such as that of Paz to the anthropological endeavour, see Marit Melhuus, 'The Authority of a Text: Mexico Through the Words of Others', in Eduardo Archetti, ed., *Exploring the Written: Anthropology and the Multiplicity of Writing*, Oslo 1994.

8. Roger Bartra, *The Cage of Melancholy*, New Jersey 1992, p. 91, discussing Ramos's ideas.

9. Manuel Gamio was one of the leading indigenists; his *Forjando Patria* was first published in 1916 (Mexico, see p. 25). For a succinct summary, see David Brading's 'Manuel Gamio and Official Indigenismo in Mexico', *Bulletin for Latin American Research*, vol. 7, no. 1, 1988.

10. Quoted by Bartra, p. 92 from Gamio, p. 25.

11. For example, Bartra, Lomnitz-Adler and Limon. Roger Bartra's *The Cage of Melancholy* is part of the most recent efflorescence of writing that looks at Mexicanness to have emerged in the 1980s. Bartra's book aims to go beyond the stereotypes of the earlier, more literary writers. Lomnitz-Adler's *Exits from the Labyrinth* is also a plea for an escape from the entrapment of the labyrinth set up by the establishment of the PRI, the Institutionalized Revolutionary Party, which has held power continuously since its establishment after the Revolution. See also José Limón, 'Carnes, Carnales and the Carnivalesque: Bakhtinian *batos*, Disorder and Narrative Discourses', *American Anthropologist*, vol. 16, no. 3, 1989, pp. 471–86.

12. Juan Rulfo, *Pedro Paramo*, Madrid 1985.

13. He is being used by the guerrillas in Chiapas, the so-called Zapatistas, as a gendered political image.

14. In 1921 Leal, in fact, painted a mural of the Dancers of Chalma which depicts Indians seated on the ground, the men in sarapes, the women with their heads covered. The dancers' headdresses are remarkably like those seen today, while the rest of their costumes are considerably more theatrical.

15. For more details of the movement, see Susanna Rostas, 'The "Mexica": The Appearance of the Re-Vindicating Indian', in John Rogister, ed., Cambridge, forthcoming. For a full analysis, see Lina Odena Guemas, *Movimiento confederato restaurador de la cultura de Anahuac*, Mexico DF 1984. See also Maria del Carmen Nieva, *Mexicayotl*, Mexico DF 1969; and *Izkalotl*, the newspaper of the movement, published since 1960 but now produced only very irregularly.

16. Quoted by Lomnitz-Adler, p. 312.

17. See Jean Franco, *Plotting Women: Gender and Representation in Mexico*, New York 1989, p. xxi.

18. Bartra, p. 137.

19. Franco, p. xix.

20. Sandra Messinger Cypess, *La Malinche in Mexican Literature: from History to Myth*, 1991, p. 9. Cypess discusses the novel *Xicontencatl*, published anonymously in Philadelphia, probably in 1826, and thought initially to be by a Mexican. Luis Leal considers it one of the first texts to present a negative view of La Malinche; see his 'Female Archetypes in Mexican Literature', in Beth Miller, ed., *Women in Hispanic Literature: Icons and Fallen Idols*, Berkeley, CA 1983, pp. 227–42.

21. Franco, p. 131.

22. Quoted by Franco, p. xix, from Paz, *The Labyrinth of Solitude*.

23. Cypess, p. 8.

24. Ibid., p. 6; and A. Mirande and E. Enriquez, *La Chicana: The Mexican American Woman*, Chicago 1979, p. 28.

25. In Aztec cosmology, the feminine side of the essential duality of earlier androgynous representations was played down as the Aztecs asserted their chauvinist and expansionist ideology; see Susanna Rostas, 'Divine Androgyny but "His" Story: The Female in Aztec Mythology', in Carolyne Larrington, ed., *The Feminist Companion to Mythology*, London 1992.

26. In *Plotting Women*, Franco is more concerned with the contexts in which women struggled to gain a voice, and concentrates on women such as Sor Juana Inez de la Cruz, about whom a feature-length film was recently made; on the painter Frida Kahlo, increasingly an icon of the feminine in Latin America and throughout the world; and on present-day writers such as Elena Poniatowska.

27. Lomnitz-Adler, p. 312.

28. See Susanna Rostas, *From Ethos to Identity: Religious Practice as Resistance to Change in a Tzeltal Community, Tenejapa, Chiapas, Mexico*, unpublished D Phil thesis, Sussex University, 1987.

29. Guillermo Bonfil Batalla, *Mexico profundo*, Mexico 1990. My copy, the second (or third) edition, claims a print run of 44,000.

30. Bonfil, p. 244, trans. Lomnitz-Adler, p. 248.

31. Antonio Velasco Piña, *Tlacaelel*, Mexico 1979.

32. Antonio Velasco Piña, *Regina*, Mexico 1987.

33. For details of the other kinds of activities generated by *Mexicanidad*, see Rostas, 'The "Mexica"'.

34. The Chichimeca-style apparel gave by far the most equality visually, for men and women were dressed almost identically, the style being rather similar to priestly garments. Interestingly, some groups, such as the well-established 'Corporación de Concheros', are currently revitalizing the Chichimeca style.

35. Bartra, p. 4.

36. The Concheros, with the Mexica, have given symbolico-religious support to many growing indigenous political movements such as the FIPI (Frente Independiente de Pueblos Indios).

10

Power, Value and the Ambiguous

Meanings of Gender

Marit Melhuus

Introduction

In this essay I would like to address particular aspects of Mexican *mestizo*[1] gender imagery. More specifically, I am interested in eliciting some implicit links that may be inferred from the way gender is represented at a more general level – what could perhaps be called a hegemonic discourse[2] – and the way gender is enacted and reflected in a specific local discourse. I hope thereby to throw light on what I consider the enigma of Mexican *mestizo* gender imagery: a male-dominant society which nevertheless places its highest value on the feminine, indicating a split between power and value. In other words, contrary to Octavio Paz, who states that woman is the enigma,[3] I suggest that the way the categories of gender are represented ultimately reflects an enigma which is intrinsic to the relation, not to the separate categories. My argument is *not* grounded in an assumption that local discourses are mere reflections of dominant representations, but neither are they dislocations or subordinate variants of the dominant representations. Rather, I argue that there is an inherent ambiguity to the configurations of gender[4] and, moreover, that this ambiguity prevails at different levels – or circuits – of discourses evoking gender. Hence, representations of gender can meaningfully be grasped only within the terms set by this very ambiguity. I intend to illustrate the work of this ambiguity and its implications for the representations of gender and the meanings of gender relations.

A central contributing factor to this ambiguity is the difference in the forms of evaluation of men and of women. Whereas women appear to be classified discretely, as either decent or not decent, men are classified along a continuum, in positions relative to each other, as either more or less a man. Hence masculinity can be – and is – continually contested. Femininity (in women) seems to be a non-issue: it is, rather, the moral character of each woman which is at stake.[5] I suggest that this quality of the gender relation imbues gender with a certain elusiveness which contributes to make gender a rich discursive field.

As for the interlocking issue of gender imagery and power, I am interested in two dimensions of this power: the perceptions of power as they are articulated within gender relations and the power with which gender relations are imbued, through the imagery they evoke, to 'speak to' broader issues, that is, their power to create meaning not only *in* the world but also *of* the world. In order to develop my argument, I will draw on very different sources, in a perhaps somewhat unorthodox way. I will juxtapose three quite disparate fields of Mexican reality which separately and together bear on the issues I have set out to explore. These three fields are the literature on 'lo mexicano' – Mexican intellectuals' own exegesis about what it means to be Mexican; the myths of the Virgin of Guadalupe and La Malinche;[6] and local perceptions of gender and the gender relation as gleaned from my own fieldwork among villagers of a Spanish-speaking Catholic village in the state of Mexico.

By expanding my ethnographic 'field' to include both myths and literary sources I am not only acknowledging the importance of confronting different forms of cultural representations of gender but also admitting the possibility of establishing a circuit of meaning which somehow underpins the various expressive forms. This tack permits me to trace the contours of various discourses on gender and elicit their points of convergence, as well as those of discrepancy. Both the myth of La Malinche and that of the Virgin of Guadalupe reflect the ambiguity attached to defining females and, by implication, males. Moreover, the literature which feeds into the ongoing discourse about 'lo mexicano' represents fertile ground for eliciting representations of gender – so much so that the force of gender imagery is such that it is also invoked in discourses on the nation.

It is important to keep in mind that Mexico is a multi-ethnic, markedly stratified society, encompassing vast differences in sociocultural and economic conditions. Mexico is a modern, industrializing nation, a secular state the majority of whose population are Catholic. There are competing political discourses as there are competing moral discourses, grounded in different world-views. These differences will necessarily impinge on the discourses about gender, and hence on the construction of gender relations, the salience of the representations and their wider significance. Nevertheless, my aim is not to elaborate the multiplicities of gendered discourse but, rather, to identify different instances of the workings of gender in order to discern the contours of a configuration.

My point of departure, then – which is grounded in my fieldwork – is the contrasting but mutually constitutive imagery of male and female. Whereas the former is inscribed in notions of power – *el poder* – and *machismo*, the latter is mediated through the veneration of the Virgin of Guadalupe as the Virgin Mother, and the local meanings of virginity which are reflected in a particular perception of the ideal of suffering, which in turn is linked to motherhood. These representations of gender are articulated through a local moral discourse based on the notions of honour and shame.

Beginning a Dialogue

I will enter the literature on 'lo mexicano' by way of Roger Bartra and his critical reflections on studies about the Mexican national character – not merely as literary and mythological phenomena but, rather, as the way these stereotypes become 'part of the cultural and social structure of Mexico'.[7] There are several reasons for my interests in Bartra's work. On the one hand, he approaches the literature on 'lo mexicano' as empirical material; thus his book addresses the debates on Mexicanness as cultural phenomena in their own right. On the other hand he is a native, an anthropologist and a male, addressing, among other things, the myths of La Malinche and Guadalupe. And lastly, the construction of the book itself offers interesting evidence of the hold gender has on invoking particular meanings of social relations – and, moreover, how difficult it is to escape that very grasp.

Bartra's reflections on 'lo mexicano' – or what constitutes Mexicanness – places itself in the ongoing discourse of nation and nationhood and the creation of a modern Mexico that followed in the wake of the Mexican Revolution. Mexican intellectuals have battled with this project for years, but it is perhaps Octavio Paz, with his book *El laberinto de la soledad*,[8] who has been most influential. This book summarized ideas circulating at the time, and has served as a sounding board for many subsequent approaches to the issue of Mexican identity.[9] As I have extensively elaborated on Paz elsewhere – as have many others – I will briefly summarize a few central points.[10] In his discussion on what constitutes Mexican identity, Paz is very much concerned with gender – so much so that gendered attributes are the metaphors through which he constructs his Mexican. He describes masculine and feminine in terms of closed and open respectively, where being closed is the desirable state because it serves as a protection against the world, a defence of one's own intimacy as well as that of others. The notion of closed, then, is associated with that of being invulnerable – that is, impenetrable. Conversely, opening up is seen as a weakness, a disgrace – ultimately signified by the notion of *la chingada*, a core symbol of Mexicanness, according to Paz. In the chapter 'The Sons of Malinche'[11], Paz invokes both Guadalupe and Malinche in order to elaborate the significance of *la chingada*. This term is derived from the verb *chingar* which, although it has various meanings, denotes above all violence, a penetration of another by force. *La chingada* is 'the Mother . . . [she] is one of the Mexican representations of maternity . . . or "the long-suffering Mexican mother". . . . *La chingada* is the mother who has suffered – metaphorically or actually – the corrosive and defaming action implicit in the verb that gives her her name'.[12] Where the *chingon* is the one who opens, *la chingada* is the opposite: the inert, passive one who is open and opened. '*La chingada* is the Mother forcibly opened, violated or deceived. The *hijo de la chingada* is the offspring of violation, abduction or deceit.'[13] Yet Paz extends this qualification: 'every woman – even when she gives herself willingly – is torn open by the man, is the *chingada*. In a certain sense all of us . . . are *hijos de la chingada*.'[14]

In this sexual imagery it is neither rape nor the fact of being the result of an illicit relationship which is the issue, but the meaning of penetration. To be penetrated implies laying oneself bare to the power or force of another. The result of being penetrated (both the offspring and the person penetrated) carries negative connotations. Moreover, Paz carries the metaphor of the *hijos de la chingada* to mean 'the others': 'strangers, bad Mexicans, our enemies, our rivals . . . that is, all those who are not as we are'.[15] He leaves no doubt as to who Malinche is – she is *la chingada par excellence*, opening Mexico to the others. Thus Paz draws attention to origins, sets the image of Malinche as the betrayer, and thereby inscribes her in one of the continent's dominant master narratives.[16] Although the Virgin does not fall into the category of *chingada*, she nevertheless also represents a passive state.[17]

In contrast to Arizpe[18] – who, in her study of Mexican beliefs, feels compelled to abandon the myths created by the intellectual elite in order to find out what people of 'flesh and bones' (as she says) think – Bartra takes precisely the opposite tack. He sees these myths as important in the legitimizing process of the modern Mexican state, a process which has functioned, he claims, in order to hinder the development of modern democracy.[19] Thus, Bartra has a special interest in analysing these myths. The studies on the shape of the Mexican character interest him 'because their *object* of reflection (the so-called national character) is an imaginary construct that they [the studies] themselves have formulated'.[20] For Bartra, these images of Mexicanness are not a reflection of popular consciousness but are, rather, 'codified by intellectuals, the traces of which are, however, reproduced in society, creating an illusion of mass culture'.[21] He sees them as myths produced by the hegemonic culture, which 'end up constituting a sort of meta-discourse . . . to which many Mexicans (and some non-Mexicans) turn in order to explain the national identity'.[22] He explains the lack of development of modern democracy in Mexico (despite the political stability which Mexico has enjoyed) by the enormous weight of the nationalist myth.

Bartra presents the dominating representations of what is perceived as Mexican, and looks at their implications for the continuity of the structures of power. For him, these myths are not a reflection of the reality in which the masses of peasants and workers are immersed. Neither are they false, in the sense of 'false consciousness'. The myths are part of the Mexican culture, a prolongation of social conflicts by other means. They are not, therefore, reality, nor are they a lie. They are a mimesis, an imitation which corresponds to the national structures of power, and Bartra's interest lies in isolating those elements which help us to understand the mechanisms for the production and reproduction of power.

The final chapter of his analysis is significantly entitled 'A la chingada', and represents the culmination of his interpretations. Bartra's last lap in his tour through Mexican identity plays with the idea of 'a return to the original unity, the mother'.[23] It is perhaps worthwhile, therefore, to note that the very first entry – the prologue – is entitled 'Penetration'. In order to discuss further the points Bartra raises in relation to gender imagery and power, I now turn to the myths of Guadalupe and Malinche as they have been handed down. Salient aspects of these two myths capture the ambiguous images of gender in a significant way, and serve to highlight the enigma I have drawn from my own empirical material. I then go on to a short discussion of my major findings as they relate to the implications concerning the understandings of power and value. In conclusion, I will return to my dialogue with Bartra and the force of the gender imagery.

A Master Narrative? Looking to the Past

Both La Malinche and the Virgin of Guadalupe belong to the realm of myths. They are lodged in the Mexican consciousness of Mexico, and embody some vital meaning which can be created and re-created in attempts to come to terms with the past and the future. The myths are instructive, imparting knowledge about origins, sexuality, loyalty and betrayal. They are therefore significant vehicles of representation, conveying meaningful, albeit multivocal, messages. What makes them particularly significant is not only that they are evoked and inscribed in a discourse on nationalism or national identity, but also the way this is done.

The figures of Guadalupe and Malinche coincide in historical time in so far as they are both a product of the conquest. The Virgin of Guadalupe appeared to Juan Diego (a converted Indian) in 1531. La Malinche was the Indian woman who was given to Hernán Cortés in tribute after he had defeated the Indians on the coast of Tabasco in 1519. She was his interpreter and 'mistress'. The Virgin of Guadalupe is not only seen as unique to Mexico, a singular creation, but as a national symbol she is extremely powerful, supercharged, embodying various meanings. Moreover, she is sacred, pertaining to the realm of the divine. Her shrine – a colossal monument on the outskirts of Mexico City – is the focal point of pilgrimages and penances all year round, from all over the country and even beyond, culminating on 12 December, when thousands upon thousands gather to celebrate in her honour. She moves – and has moved – people in very visible ways, and is very much part of everyday life.[24]

Not so with La Malinche. She has no cult, no shrine, no followers or devotees, no sway or place in daily consciousness. She does not have the power with which Guadalupe is endowed. At most, she is 'known' through her representations in museums and in art, and her story is relayed in history books, her image displayed in records of the conquest.[25] Yet Malinche has come to symbolize the conquest and the form of the 'encounter' between the Spanish invaders and the subjugated native populations. Hers is one of the compelling myths used to evoke not only the origin of the *mestizo* – this half-breed of Spanish and Indian descent – but also modern Mexicans' predicament in coming to terms with their identity.[26] Thus, the myth of La Malinche represents not only the creation of a people but the birth of a nation. Whereas Guadalupe is invoked by every man and woman, Malinche has been appropriated by intellectuals, those modern 'elders' who debate the state of affairs, or – to paraphrase Bartra – those scholars, poets, philosophers who are prepared to play midwives to the new worlds that are born every day. Malinche has literally been written into the nationalist epic, the elements of her story providing the fodder on which the nation feeds.

Although Malinche is 'Mexican' (and I choose to place the adjective in quotation marks, as no Mexicans existed at the time of the conquest and her 'nationality' is obviously an invention), her story has come to represent the quintessence of Latin American *mestizo* origins. Couched in terms of violence, rape, suffering and deception, this origin is expressed through gender and race, articulating specific relations of power and dominance. It is the Spanish male – the pale-faced conquistador – who overpowers the foreign land and its people. He is the victor. His victim is the Indian woman, native of the land, who is raped by a stranger and subsequently gives birth to illegitimate children. Thus the territorial conquest is rephrased in terms of a sexual conquest. The rape of the woman is metaphorically equated with the rape of the land.

The persuasiveness of this image of the Conquest – which Malinche incarnates – has the semblance of being paradigmatic, and has prompted Gerald Martin to call it the 'grand historical narrative' of Latin America, 'which is effectively the continent's own dominant self-interpretation and which . . . can safely be said to have the relative stability of a great cultural myth'.[27] He finds its theme echoed throughout Latin American literature. The pervasiveness of the myth can also be deduced from the scholarly works that have been directed at its reinterpretation and deconstruction (not least by feminists) in order to restore the image of Malinche to a historical reality or render it meaningful in other terms.[28] However – and this is an important point – although the myth may carry weight in *mestizo* or *ladino* 'reality', it may not (and most probably will not) convey the same meaning for Indians. In fact, the very myth itself is built around a particular perception of Indianness where Indian becomes synonymous with feminine and feminine, in turn, with treachery. Precisely because the myth serves to invent the nation – a nation from which the indigenous populations have been excluded, and in part exclude themselves – it will speak very differently to those who consider themselves as belonging to that nation, or are striving to create a nation to which they belong, and those who do not. By the same token, the myth will necessarily imply different things for women and for men, as they are also variously implicated in the construction of nationhood. The way the myth inscribes the female in her role as 'founding mother' is undoubtedly an ambiguous one.[29] Coupled with the contrasting imagery of Guadalupe, this ambiguity is only underscored. Thus the very elements of which both the myths are made – Indian and women – are also the elements which appear to create confusion in their wake. Paradoxically, the notion of Mexican nationhood is simultaneously a glorification of the pre-Columbian past and the supremacy of the 'white man', where the problematic reconciliation of these images is passed over.[30]

The significance of the myth of Malinche as it has come to be portrayed lies on the one hand in the dominating representation of her role as collaborator, not only acting as Cortés's interpreter but also informing him of his enemies' movements, thus securing his victory. (Today the term *malinchista* is used of someone who sells out to foreigners.) On the other, it is brought out through the emphasis placed on her role as Cortés's mistress, and the birth of their son – hence the deduction that the first *mestizo* is the product of an illicit relationship. In this way, the imagery of Malinche conjoins the power of the word with the power of the womb.

In fact, it has been suggested that had it not been for Malinche the conquest would not have been possible, or would have taken a different turn.[31] Moreover, Palma,[32] in her effort to understand the condition of the *mestizo*, suggests that if Malinche had not existed, it would have been necessary to invent her in order to justify his (i.e. the *mestizo*'s) disgrace. Significantly, Malinche is not portrayed as the raped Indian woman, innocent victim of (foreign) male aggression. Rather, she assumes the part of an active accomplice – wilfully deceiving, wilfully conceiving.

The Virgin of Guadalupe and Malinche share a number of traits. They are both Indian, although their Indianness takes on different connotations: one of divinity and grace; the other of humility and shame. They are both mediators between powerful men and subject peoples, playing the role of intermediary, passing on vital information. Malinche delivers her people into the hands of the enemy; Guadalupe leads her people to victory. Malinche's words become poison and assume the guise of gossip; Guadalupe, accepting the prayers of her supplicants, intercedes on their behalf in the face of the wrath of God. Malinche's act is one of betrayal; Guadalupe's one of suffering and sacrifice. Malinche is the traitor; Guadalupe the saviour. Both are also mothers. However, Malinche is sexually violated and gives birth to an illegitimate son. The first *mestizo* is tainted from the start. Guadalupe, as the Virgin, conceives without sex and gives birth to the son of God, the Almighty Father. However, she is also the Mother of God and thus, by extension, of all humanity. In both cases the father is absent, though symbolically omnipresent. Moreover, procreation is conveyed as the imposition of men, the status of its 'product' depending on the virtue of women. Sexuality is portrayed as both flagrantly open and totally denied. Finally, Malinche is seen as acting on her own behalf, while Guadalupe acts on behalf of others. Centred as they are around two women, these myths have no heroes – no knight in shining armour who rescues a damsel in distress. This is surprising, perhaps, in a society that is so predominantly *macho*. What distinguishes these two women is their power to influence the outcome of the world. The myths tell us that nations owe their fall – and rise – to women; men owe their lives – and deaths – to women. What distinguishes the dominant representations of the myths is precisely the obfuscation of this power.

Both these myths are seen to originate in a critical transitional period, lodged as they are in the traumatic experience of the conquest. Hence they are about particular painful and ambivalent origins. They speak to the present through a specific conception of the past. Both pertain to the nation, albeit in very different ways. As with all mythical realities, the symbolic knowledge that resides in the myths is multiple, and refers to different experiential dimensions. Some of that knowledge may speak to us directly – it is easily accessible and recognizable. However, other aspects of this knowledge – the *gnosis* – are more opaque. In the case of the myths of Guadalupe and La Malinche, one salient aspect is the implicit and explicit knowledge they impart with respect to the perceptions of power. This knowledge is conveyed through the ambivalent construction of the nature of womanhood and hence, by implication, manhood. The myths reveal not only something about the perceptions of relations that obtain between men and women, but also something about the power of these relations as vehicles to speak about the world – to create meaning in the world.

Machismo: a Locus of Power

In Mexico, as elsewhere in Latin America, notions of power – *el poder* – are part of the male discourse. Power is usually assumed to be a male prerogative. It glosses all those attributes denoted as masculine, and represents a contested space for the articulation of masculine identity. It belongs to the penetrating realm of *machismo* and is associated with violence and aggressiveness, a particular form of self-assertion which more than anything implies being in control, being in command, having authority not only – or primarily – over women, but also over other men.

Machismo, derived from the generic term *macho*, meaning male, is used synonymously with masculinity; it implies, above all, the ability to penetrate, and is associated with being active, closed, unyielding.[33] Or, as Lomnitz-Adler says (with reference to Octavio Paz and Mexico): 'The value or aesthetics of "closedness" is a kind of idiom of power where "penetration" stands for domination and "impenetrability" stands for power.'[34] The male (body) literally and symbolically embodies salient aspects of power and power relations. This imagery spills over into perceptions of homosexual relations, where it is the act of penetrating as opposed to being penetrated which distinguishes the true man from the 'homosexual'.[35] Discourses of power are inherently male, explicitly sexual, and often conveyed in an idiom of violence.[36] They are framed in terms of being active, not passive. Conversely, the powerless are those who are penetrable, passive – in a word, feminine.

The stereotype of the *macho* is the violent, often drunk, unfaithful husband, or the hard-drinking, aggressive, sexually assertive young man. Concomitantly, the stereotype of the female counterpart is the self-effacing, suffering and enduring mother and the demure, withholding young lady. However, as much research indicates, these stereotypes – although they are vivid in people's minds – are no more than stereotypes. Obviously, the actual picture is much more complex. Nevertheless, it might be argued that 'el *machismo*' as essentially reflecting male dominance can be perceived as one of the fundamental myths in the construction of Mexican masculine identity.[37]

Precisely because the ideology of *machismo* – as a gloss for male dominance – is so often evoked to explain male behaviour (and, by implication, the situation of women), it is important to give a brief recapitulation of references to this term. There are several points:

1. *Machismo* underpins the continuous evaluation of men, and rests on the discrete categorization of women.
2. *Machismo* has men as its reference group: it is in the eyes of other men that a man's manhood is confirmed, but it is through women that it is reflected and enacted. Thus men are socially and emotionally vulnerable to other men, through the behaviour and moral evaluation of women.
3. The very articulation of *machismo* not only points to the precariousness of being a man but also underscores the ambiguity of being a woman, showing how women's sexuality is an ambivalent source of virtue.

Finally, it is important to bear in mind that the meanings of *machismo* are many and, in the case I am about to describe, can best be grasped with reference to the local morality of honour and shame. This local morality is mirrored in a specific sexual division of labour, which in turn is reflected in specific notions of male and female virtue.

Most anthropological studies of Mexico will have some reference to *machismo*, if only in passing.[38] The records at least indicate the salience of this term and some reflections on its implications for gender relations. In the village where I worked, the terms *macho* and *machista* are used to characterize a true man and real male behaviour. These terms are generally recognized and used, their meaning conveying an aura of being, in a sense, self-evident: everyone knows what a *macho* is and what *machismo* is all about. A man who is 'bien macho' is one who has to show he is in command ('tiene que monstrar quien manda'), with all that this implies. Both men and women would blame *machismo* for incidences of excessive drunkenness or unwarranted violence in men, as well as for the maltreatment of women. Women would use *machismo* as a general explanation for all their woes. In this sense, *machismo* was seen as detrimental to women. Nevertheless, women do not want a soft husband. They want a hard-working, responsible and respected husband – a true man, and this would imply one who is a *macho* in some sense of the word. Moreover, for a man there is an element of pride attached to being called a *macho*, the converse being that he is not deemed manly at all.

Ascriptions of feminine attributes are often used to denote the unmanly male. These may either have direct homosexual connotations, alluding to a man letting himself be penetrated, or may throw doubt on a man's virility by insinuating that he is not the father of his own children, or pointing to his impotence (if he has no children). Attacks on a man's masculinity may also be conveyed by throwing doubt on the virtue of his female kin (in particular his mother) or pointing to his inability to provide. All such insinuations subtract from a man's manliness and can be apprehended as a challenge to his respect, and ultimately his honour.

Aspects of virility and women's virtue are not the only attributes of maleness which are important for a man's respect. Values such as generosity, not being an egoist, being responsible *vis-à-vis* wife and children in the sense of providing for them, all constitute part of the masculine make-up and influence a man's reputation, as do his political connections, being honest, the number of godchildren he has, and his general character. Together these aspects connote what it means locally to be a *macho* in the positive sense of the word. It is precisely the notions of a hard-working, respected and responsible man which contradict the stereotypical perceptions of a *macho*. Both men and women would agree that a man's first responsiblility is to maintain his family – so much so that a husband/father who is unable to provide for his family, or is dependent on his wife for an income, is called a 'mantenido', literally a maintained man, which is regarded as very unmanly. A wife who is contributing to the household would go to great extremes to conceal her activities from her husband, as it would be considered a shaming of his honour publicly to display that he is not man enough to keep his family. In fact, a woman would put up with both infidelity and maltreatment as long as she received money for the upkeep of herself and her children – *para el gasto*, as they say.

There is also stress on a man's independence, and especially on his being in control. The importance of these attributes is underscored by the use of the term *lambiscon* to denote the man who is a political client, dependent on other men, an opportunist. *Lambiscon* derives from the verb *lamer*, to lick, or *lambisconear*, to lick or suck up to. Translated as 'greedy' and 'gluttonous' (*Collins Spanish Dictionary*), the local meaning conveys a man without integrity, and again alludes to sexuality.[39] *Machismo*, then, has both negative and positive connotations. It is ambiguous, multivocal, depending on the context, the situation and the man to be described as well as the person using the term. Thus the attributes of *machismo* which are ascribed to a young unmarried man will be different from those ascribed to a married, established man.

Machismo can be seen to represent a contested space for the acquisition of manhood structuring the relative position between men. Contributing to this evaluation, however, are men's relations to women. A man's manhood is enhanced not only by the number of women he conquers but also by the virtue of the women who 'belong' to him (mother, sister, wife, daughter) and to whom he must fulfil certain obligations in order to be considered a respected man. In fact, notions of female virtue are intrinsic to the construction of masculinity. However, the fact that the virtue of specific women is important for a man implies that women may impair their (i.e. men's) virtue by impairing their own (usually through illicit contact, actually or assumed, with other men). The very possibility of this represents a threat to men. In other words, women's actions may impinge on men's reputations, on their honour, revealing the precariousness of masculinity. A man may even have recourse to violence if his honour has been threatened through the behaviour of a woman.

In order to confirm his manhood, a man needs both the virtuous woman and the *fracasada* (literally a 'failed woman') a local term used to describe the woman who has fallen from grace – that is, one who has had sexual intercourse before marriage or a child out of wedlock. This discrete categorization of women, classifying them into two kinds, is a prerequisite for this construction of masculinity. However, it is also central to the construction of female identity, but with differing connotations: whereas men need 'bad' women if they are to remain men, women need indecent women if they are to remain good. Thus female virtue is an issue which serves to underscore the differing grounds of evaluation for men and for women. Aspects of both men's and women's sexuality come into play, stressing virility for men and chastity for women. Where sexual prowess is important for men – so much so that it is considered 'falta de hombría' (lack of manhood) not to recognize illegitimate children – the converse holds true for women. Yet women do not abstain from sexual relations before marriage, even though this is the ideal. Nevertheless, the fact that sexual purity is not an issue for men, but is so for women, obviously places the woman in a more precarious position than the man.

Women's Sexuality: an Ambivalent Source of Virtue

Women's sexuality, then, represents a problem not only for men, but also for women, albeit in a different form. Where men 'solve' their problem by controlling their women, women find grace in the Virgin. For a woman, her sexuality is an ambivalent source of virtue. On the one hand, the ideal of her moral rectitude is stressed and expressed through the symbolic value of virginity, which carries particular significance in relationships between men, grounding the discrete classification of women. On the other hand, motherhood is the epitome of womanhood – so much so that if a mother's children do not come to her aid in her old age, this is interpreted as a sign that she has been a poor mother, and within the terms of this discourse, to be a poor mother is to be a poor woman. Girls are not only brought up to be mothers; in a sense they are also brought up to be virgins.[40] In all important ceremonies where girls are involved, the allusion to virginity as an expression of purity or chastity is overtly demonstrated. Moreover, parents are careful with their daughters, chaperoning them whenever possible. It is important to point out, however, that in this local context it is not so much virginity *per se* that is stressed as the connotations of virginity: being a respected, decent woman.

The various aspects of respect and decency are signalled in different ways. They are expressed through a woman's daily conduct, in particular in what she refrains from doing – casual visiting, loitering and gossiping [*andar de metiche*] are all considered negative – and through what she is expected to do: preparing meals, doing housework, and taking care of the children. Moreover, married women are not expected to work, in the sense of being employed outside the home. Not only does a working woman show visibly that her husband is not man enough to be able to provide for her (and their children); a working wife also brings to the fore a husband's jealousy. In fact 'los celos' (jealousies) was the reason most often given, especially by young married women, for why they stopped working once they were married. Thus a married woman's paid work has a double implication: it detracts from her husband's honour and is associated with her being public, potentially making herself available to other men. That 'public' is associated with sexual availability is also conveyed through the local saying 'A house that lacks a man lacks respect'.

Women are by definition 'of the house' (as men are 'of the streets'), and a house is not a respected one if it is not headed by a suitable male. Ideally, then, a woman should not live alone – without a suitable man as guardian of her virtue – as that would be tantamount to being publicly available, that is, a prostitute. A single woman living on her own could modify her position by, for example, 'adopting' the children of relatives. Ideas of virtue are also expressed through notions of not being an egoist, which in local terms would imply putting herself before the children. Women are extremely mindful of their reputations, and gossip is an effective sanction, as they are sensitive to what people say ('el que dirán'). Significantly, men also find women's gossip threatening, and the threat of gossip was given as one of the main reasons for husbands not wanting their wives to visit, and hence controlling their movements. According to the women, men assume that women will pass on knowledge about men's meanderings. This knowledge should ideally circulate between men, as it is potentially disruptive to families.[41]

As we have already seen, within the terms set by the local morality women are categorized into two kinds: 'la mujer decente' (the decent woman), 'que no le falta el respeto' (who does not lack respect), 'que tiene vergüenza' (who has shame), and the woman who lacks these qualities. Varying terms are used to describe such a woman. The most common are that she has no shame; that she is open; that she does not keep her distance. All these expressions have sexual connotations, alluding to the availability or accessibility of the woman's favours. They are all definitely negative and imply a voluntary aspect – that these indecent women are exposing their sexuality and 'asking for it', as we would say. That women are thus dichotomized is intrinsic to the local morality, and springs directly from the emphasis placed on female virtue. Nevertheless, which women fall into which category is contextually determined, not given a priori. Thus, a single mother abandoned by her husband, who lives alone and is working in order to maintain her children and herself, will not automatically gain respect. Her status will first and foremost depend on whether she knows how to treat people ('saber tratar la gente'). And to know how to treat people is first and foremost presented in terms of not being presumptuous, not putting on airs, being polite and keeping her distance.

The elements which serve to coalesce the notions of female virtue and motherhood can best be grasped by turning to the images evoked by the Virgin, as virgin-mother.[42] The virgin represents the primordial symbol of femininity, the complete state to which women should aspire. Yet this state – one of impenetrability – is mediated through a denial of sexuality. The symbolism of the Virgin makes visible the ambivalence embedded in female sexuality as a source of virtue. In order that motherhood can be equated with virtue, the tension between virgin and mother must be overcome. It is the imagery related to the suffering mother which serves to resolve this tension. In the local interpretation of the Passion of Christ and the crucifixion, what is stressed is the suffering the son bestows upon his mother, the suffering Mary underwent in witnessing the death of her son. His suffering becomes her suffering. She suffers for him, not vice versa. Thus the link which works to bridge this ambivalence of pure and impure (decent and indecent), and also represents the shared experience between women and the Virgin, is suffering or, more precisely, the suffering inherent in motherhood. In a metaphorical transformation, 'virginity' comes to be 'like the Virgin' by virtue of the suffering they have in common. The notion of suffering, then, operates on different levels. On one level, and more implicitly, it serves to cancel out sexuality; yet on another, more explicit, level aspects of sexuality appear to be equated with suffering.

It is through the particular suffering evoked by the Virgin that the basis for women's chastity is generated.[43] It is suffering, explicitly expressed in a form of self-sacrifice, which serves to transcend sexuality and becomes the mark of motherhood. Thus suffering becomes a virtue, and women are its victims. In this transformation the children are crucial, as they create the mother, as it were, in bestowing upon her her motherhood, and hence her legitimate grounds for suffering. She will suffer for them, as through her suffering she can enhance her virtue and make it visible to herself and to others. Women share this ideal of martyrdom, and recognize it when they see it. They are the ones who first and foremost evaluate and condone the degree and kind of suffering to be acknowledged. The discourse on suffering, then, is one that circulates among women, but 'needs' men in order to be set in motion. Men are excluded from this moral community of suffering and self-sacrifice, but they are necessary and conducive to its maintenance.[44]

Suffering is perceived as a female virtue, and forms part of a moral discourse which is exclusive to women and serves to enhance their self-esteem. The gist of the logic is: the more you suffer, the better you are – albeit within the limits of what is perceived as the morally correct source of suffering. Not all suffering qualifies as virtuous. The suffering involved in being abandoned by her children does not enhance a woman's esteem, neither does rape. Whereas the former is interpreted as a sign that one has been a poor mother, rape is framed in terms of being a loose woman, that is, being where you are not supposed to be or doing what you are not supposed to be doing. However, to be abandoned by a man (which is not uncommon) does qualify as suffering, as does maltreatment (which is common). Such events were also commented upon in terms of suffering. A wife will rarely leave her husband, despite continued maltreatment, because of the children. She knows she will receive no support for them. Moreover, it is very rare that women (whether abandoned or widowed) will remarry, as it is assumed that men will not be responsible for another man's progeny. A wife/mother who abandons her husband or considers remarrying (in cases of being abandoned, widowed or divorced) would be considered egotistical, a selfish woman. She would be regarded as putting herself before her children, an act which is unacceptable.

There is an intrinsic link between womanhood – motherhood – and suffering. In fact, my data suggest that in the last instance, to be a mother – to have children, whatever the circumstances – is in itself a value. At a conceptual level, all mothers suffer, and by implication, motherhood, if not an actual mother, is in itself virtuous. Thus to impair one's virtue by, for example, becoming pregnant outside marriage is not necessarily a failure. When I discussed the implications of being a *fracasada* with Doña Clara, she said: 'How can we say that it is a failure to have children? To be a mother can never be a failure!' Her statement highlights, perhaps, the most important aspect of the uneasy relationship between virgin and mother: if to be a woman is to suffer and to suffer is to be a mother, to be a mother cannot be a failure. This is reinforced by Doña Tella's remark: 'Una sola no sufre – con los hijos, si, se sufre' ('Alone a woman does not suffer – with the children, then one suffers'). In many respects, it seems that motherhood overrides any other categorization of a woman, and to be a mother is good enough.

Parallel to a male discourse of dominance and power, then, there is a female discourse of suffering and motherhood. In both discourses women's virtue is at stake, but with differing implications. In the former, notions of the virtuous woman underpin the dual categorization of women and are used as schemata for evaluating both men and women. They nevertheless serve primarily to uphold men's honour. In the latter the distinction between the decent woman and the indecent woman is reduced to the very ambiguity women embody. By making a virtue of suffering and motherhood its ultimate expression, women's sexuality is transformed, and comes to represent an empower-ment.[45] Thus it seems that the very notion of female virtue works to encompass different meanings of woman's sexuality – so much so that women accept the loss of virtue in the first sense, which is so precious to men, only to regain it in the second. In other words, the evaluation of women along the dimension of suffering is not necessarily coterminous with the distinction between moral and immoral women.

The configuration which emerges is most aptly conveyed in a statement made by one of the women in the village: 'Everyone has a mother, and God does too'. If male authority is recognized as supreme – as in God the Father Almighty – nevertheless, this authority is undermined, albeit subtly, by elevating the mother to a superior position, and thereby subordinating the father. One way of grasping this gender configuration is to picture it as two hierarchies, or symbolic orders, one which establishes the masculine as encompassing and subordinating the feminine; one which does exactly the opposite: the feminine is seen as containing the masculine. Dominance is expressed through the discourse on *machismo*, through men's overt control over women and contested control over other men. It is also expressed through the idea that women are the keepers of men's honour while men are the guardians of women's virtue. Although this reflects a mutual complementarity between the sexes, it is never-theless framed in a male idiom. However, it is also possible to isolate a symbolic ordering where the Virgin (Mother of God) eclipses the image of the dominant father, where the female is singular and separate. The non-sexual-woman-represented-as-mother is an all-embracing value, ultimately placing femininity simultaneously within and without the confines of the male. In other words, there is a double structuring permitting both dominance and complementarity for both male and female – but where the female seems to escape the male in a way that the male cannot escape the female.

'Lo mexicano': Man or Woman?

All the arguments above serve as a backdrop for my concluding reflections as I now return to Bartra, and more specifically to his last chapter, entitled 'A *la chingada*'. Bartra opens this chapter by referring to the fascination generated by the peculiar combination of exaggerated *machismo* and fanatical love for the mother in the figure of the Virgin of Guadalupe. He hails Guadalupe as the mother of all Mexicans, but quickly establishes the shadow of La Malinche as belonging to the same figure. The thrust of his argument is precisely to demonstrate that the two female images are interlinked: 'two incarnations of the same original myth'. In order to do this, he evokes the imagery of the 'Virgin-for-maidens' exchange.[46] This exchange took place when the Indians offered Cortés twenty maidens – Malinche among them – in a plea for peace. In return, Cortés offered the Indians the Virgin, Mother of God. However, whereas the maidens submitted to the Spanish, the Virgin was transformed by the Indians. She became the reincarnation of Tonantzin, the ancient goddess of the Aztecs.[47] In Bartra's view, it is

> these primordial images of the woman who is capable of penetrating, or being penetrated by, another world – the dominator or dominated, virgin or whore, queen or slave [which] were set to be the raw materials with which in time the essential image of the modern Mexican woman would be formed.[48]

Significantly, he not only reconfirms the discrete categories of women, he does so by introducing his series of dichotomies with an unusual opposition: the woman who is capable of penetrating versus the woman who is penetrated. Granted that we understand penetrating (in this context) as a representation of power, Bartra (perhaps inadvertently) is, by ascribing to women an attribute normally associated with masculinity, creating a powerful woman. Moreover, this representation of female imagery finds an echo in the myths of La Malinche and Guadalupe: Malinche is capable of penetrating another world (by first having been penetrated by one of its powerful members); she is open, yet actively dominating. The Virgin is by definition impenetrable (yet she has penetrated people's moral imagination); she is closed, yet passively powerful. This imagery also finds an echo in my interpretations of local gender representations and the ambiguity attached to female virtue and male power. However, Bartra's main concern is to demonstrate how 'Mexicans' (and of course, granted the nature of the Spanish language it will remain unclear if by 'los mexicanos' he is referring to Mexican men and women, or just Mexican men) have shaped the image of the Mexican woman, tracing the various images to their origins while at the same time illustrating their modern articulations.

On the one hand, he evokes the image of a woman who is both penetrating and penetrable (whose implications, mythical or otherwise, he does not pursue). On the other, he sees the images of women not only as the creation or invention of men, but also as no more than what these men deserve. What Bartra in fact says is that Guadalupe and La Malinche – the Chingalupe – 'is the woman *deserved by the Mexican* whom the national culture has devised; she is created for him so that he will have a partner in his expulsion from Eden'.[49] His conclusion echoes the view of man-made woman, but also the impotence of the Mexican male: 'The Mexican Adam does not want women as he has made them, nor is he capable of making them how he wants them.'[50] Thus Bartra posits (yet again) the image of women as being created and men as the creators, obscuring women's power to create men. The original unity of the Mother, which he invokes – sentimentally? – ironically? – at the outset, is superseded by the creative powers of the male, yet this power is in some way limited: men make women, do not like what they make, but cannot make them otherwise!

Somehow, Bartra falls prey to the very myths he is seeking to deconstruct, inscribing himself in the hegemonic discourse of the national myths and reproducing the power relations he wishes to disclose. Power, as the reader may recall, was one of my initial interests in writing this essay – not only the power articulated in gender relations but also the constituting power of gender to 'speak to' the world. More than anything, perhaps, the mere fact that Bartra addresses the myths of La Malinche and Guadalupe indicates their hold on contemporary minds. But this is an obvious point to make, and does not necessarily support my contention that gender is a powerful signifier. Bartra discusses many other 'myths' as well (although it is questionable whether they are all on the same level or all of a piece). However, it is perhaps his very handling of the myths of Guadalupe and La Malinche which is interesting, because his analysis suggests that there is a certain elusiveness to gender, despite the seemingly clear-cut imagery.

My reasoning is as follows: by conjoining Guadalupe and La Malinche to become one and the same, Bartra is creating a Mexican woman. Yet the only 'space' he can give this woman is one that conforms to an image of her held by the Mexican male. Thus the woman somehow 'speaks to' the Mexican male, but yet again ambiguously: she is not what he wants, but there is nothing he can do about it. Thus, the woman is a male invention yet outside man, beyond his reach. It seems to me that Bartra's representations only reflect the double hierarchy or symbolic orders that I have outlined above: he creates (or re-creates) a woman who is placed simultaneously both within and without the confines of the male; while he gives men creative abilities, he also imbues them with a certain impotence, limiting their domain of dominance (at least implicitly) to concern primarily that of their own sex. In fact, the very inconsistencies in Bartra's argument may perhaps be explained by the inconsistencies in the imagery, whether this is portrayed by myths, people's own perceptions, or the literature. In other words, if my interpretation and construction of this gender configuration have some validity, he only confirms it. The power of the gender imagery, then, would seem to lie in its very potential to contain alternative and even contradicting perceptions: at a certain level, there seems to be no way of escaping the restrictions of the gender relation as it is perceived. This is best drawn out by Bartra's own suggestion of the Manichaean vision of both men and women. Yet it is my contention that it is precisely the power of this image – which seemingly denies any other perceptions of either men or women: you are either *macho* or *maricon*, you are either virgin or whore – that provides the space for creating ambiguous meanings with respect to power and value. Finally – and this is an implication of Bartra's analysis, not a theme which he addresses – he does not draw the very obvious conclusion that it is not possible to change woman, or perceptions of her, without changing man, or perceptions of him. You cannot refigure the feminine without refiguring the masculine.

The Word and the Womb

Many aspects of the representations of La Malinche and Guadalupe reflect the Christian notion of woman's double nature. It would therefore be tempting – and many have been tempted – to interpret the myths of Malinche and the Virgin of Guadalupe as New World representations of the Old World's Eve and Mary (Bartra partly follows this tack). This would be all the more compelling taking into consideration the zeal of the missionaries who followed in the wake of the Conquest and the subsequent impact of the Catholic Church on the whole continent. However, although such an interpretation may also be valid and meaningful, in my opinion the power of these myths and the imagery they relay lies in the way they have been – and still are – inscribed in the creation of modern Mexico. They are significant because they yield not only the very language through which power is perceived, but also the symbolic imagery through which the nation is constructed.

Perhaps it is not hard to understand why the myths of Guadalupe and La Malinche are so compelling, and feed neatly into a discourse on nationalism. Explaining the conquest in terms of a woman's treachery is one way of exonerating the lack of male valour. It also points to women's potentially threatening nature. The fact that the innocent Virgin attains a position of glory and triumph as protector of all men [sic] not only elevates female asexuality as a public value (thus not threatening men) but also elevates the mother to a paramount position. The sexual woman is thus definitively, if only symbolically, excluded from public male enterprise. Nevertheless, there is a catch here. Whereas the asexual woman is public, belonging to no one, the public sexual woman (read prostitute) belongs to all men. However, the real sexual woman belongs to one man and is by definition private, of the house. And being of the house implies, among other things, not meddling in the affairs of men. The significance of Malinche is not that she is a mistress and a mother, consorting with the enemy, as it were, but, rather, that she transgresses the boundaries between private and public, putting herself at the service of one man, and thereby betraying other men. Had she not spoken the word, her womb might not have been questioned.

Notes

The fieldwork on which this essay is based was carried out in 1983–84 and 1989. It was financed by the the Norwegian Research Council and the Department and Museum of Anthropology, University of Oslo. Earlier versions were presented as papers at the Department of Anthropology, University of Cambridge, and at the symposium on the Power of Latin American Gender Imagery, Uppsala. Both presentations prompted lively and fruitful discussions, provoking me to rethink some of my assumptions. In preparing the final version, I have benefited from helpful comments from Eduardo Archetti, Signe Howell and Kristi Anne Stølen.

1. I use the term *mestizo* warily. Although it is commonly used in the literature to refer to those peoples who are not indigenous and not Spanish, but somehow seen as representing people of mixed Indian and Spanish descent, *mestizo* is not a term people themselves would use to refer to themselves – at least, not where I did my fieldwork. In their minds, they are definitely not 'indigenas', but they are Mexican. For a discussion of the meanings of *mestizo*, see Guillermo Bonfil Batalla, 'Sobre la ideología del mestizaje (o cómo Gacilaso anunció, sin saberlo, muchas de nuestras desgracias)', in José Manuel Valenzuela Arce, ed., *Decadencia y auge de las identidades*, Mexico 1992.

2. See Andrea Cornwall and Nancy Lindisfarne, 'Dislocating masculinity: gender, power and anthropology', in Andrea Cornwall and Nancy Lindisfarne, eds, *Dislocating Masculinity: Comparative Ethnographies*, London 1994, pp. 11–47.

3. Paz says: 'la mujer . . . también es figura enigmática. Mejor dicho, es el Enigma'. Octavio Paz, *El laberinto de la soledad*, Mexico 1988 [1950], pp. 59–60. All further reference to this book will be made to the English edition, *The Labyrinth of Solitude: Life and Thought in Mexico*, New York 1961, trans. Lysander Kemp.

4. I use the term configuration to evoke a notion of a cluster or set of cultural elements which pertain to the realm of gender.

5. Femininity in men is absolutely an issue. For a further elaboration of this argument, see Marit Melhuus, 'The Troubles of Virtue: The Values of Violence and Suffering in a Mexican Context', forthcoming, in Signe Howell, ed., *The Ethnography of Moralities*, London.

6. The Virgin of Guadalupe appeared to a converted Indian in 1531; Malinche was the Indian woman given in tribute to Hernán Cortés.

7. Roger Bartra, English trans. Christopher J. Hall, *The Cage of Melancholy: Identity and Metamorphosis in the Mexican Character*, New Brunswick 1992, p. 3. For all further references I use the English version; the original version is *La jaula de la melancolía. Identidad y metamorfosis del mexicano*, Mexico 1987.

8. Paz 1988 [1950].

9. Early forerunners in this debate are Manuel Gamio and Samuel Ramos; more contemporary are Carlos Monsiváis and Leopoldo Zea.

10. See, for example, Marit Melhuus, '*Todos tenemos madre. Díos también*': Morality, Meaning and Change in a Mexican Context, unpublished PhD thesis, University of Oslo, 1992, esp. pp. 120–49; Marit Melhuus, 'The Authority of a Text: Mexico through the Words of Others', in Eduardo Archetti, ed., *Exploring the Written: Anthropology and the Multiplicity of Writing*, Oslo 1994. See also Lourdes Arizpe, *Cultura y Desarrollo. Una etnografía de las creencias de una comunidad mexicana*, Mexico 1989; Bartra 1987; and José Limón, 'Carne, Carnales, and the Carnivalesque: Bakhtinian *batos*, Disorder, and Narrative Discourses', *American Ethnologist*, vol. 16, 1989, pp. 471–86.

11. Paz, pp. 65–88.

12. Ibid., p. 75.

13. Ibid., p. 79. Paz contrasts the Mexican expression 'hijo de *la chingada*' with the Spanish expression 'hijo de puta' (son of a whore), and says: 'the difference is immediately obvious. To the Spaniard, dishonor consists in being the son of a woman who voluntarily surrenders herself: a prostitute. To the Mexican it consists in being the fruit of violation.'

14. Ibid., p. 80.

15. Ibid., p. 75.

16. See, for example, Milagros Palma, 'Malinche. El malinchismo o el lado feminino de la sociedad mestiza', in Milagros Palma, ed., *Simbolica de la femininidad. La mujer en el imaginario mítico-religioso de las sociedades indias y mestizas*, Quito 1990; Gerald Martin, *Journeys Through the Labyrinth: Latin American Fiction in the Twentieth Century*, London 1989.

17. Here we can already discern ambiguities with respect to the dual imagery of women. The Virgin is by definition passive – and within the terms set by this imagery, this is negative. Yet she is perceived as never having been penetrated; she is closed – thus making her and her offspring singular. La Malinche is seen as *la chingada* – open and opened – yet she is

also a betrayer – a role which presupposes action, and is hence positive. Not only do these women embody contradictory meanings within the terms set by Paz; the meaning of children is also equivocal. For a critical reading, see Melhuus 1992; Joann Martin, 'Motherhood and Power: The Production of a Women's Culture of Politics in a Mexican Community', *American Ethnologist*, vol. 17, no. 3, pp. 470–90; Sandra Messinger Cypess, *La Malinche in Mexican Literature: From History to Myth*, Austin, TX 1991. Cypess says: 'Paz brings to surface the root paradigm for Mexico when he equates la Chingada with the historical figure of La Malinche' (p. 95).

18. Arizpe 1989.

19. Bartra, p. 126. Bartra evokes various mythical images, among them the Mexican Revolution itself, the peasant hero, notions of time tied to a primordial hero; the Mexican notion of death; the Mexican inferiority complex; notion of progress and the 'new man'; the *mestizo* and *el pelado*.

20. Ibid., p.1.

21. Ibid., p. 2.

22. Ibid., pp. 2–3.

23. Ibid., p. 147.

24. Where I did my fieldwork, the Virgin is invoked in rituals to secure a good harvest; pilgrimages to her shrine are organized annually, as well as local processions. I was told that Protestant missionaries had literally been driven out of the village because they did not venerate the Virgin. Historically also her image has been important. The Virgin of Guadalupe was on the banners of the fighters for Mexican Independence. She was also invoked during the Mexican Revolution. For a detailed interpretation of the meaning of the Virgin of Guadalupe for the development of the Mexican notion of a nation, see Jacques Lafaye, *Quetzalcóatl and Guadalupe: The Formation of Mexican National Consciousness 1531–1813*, Chicago 1976, trans. Benjamin Keen. Lafaye (p. 3) states that 1531 is a 'false' date, as 'this date does not correspond to any established fact in objective chronology; it appears for the first time in a work published in Spanish in 1648', and this work in turn draws on a Nahuatl manuscript of dubious authenticity. For a further reading on the signifi- cance of this symbol, see Octavio Paz, 'Foreword', in Lafaye 1976; F. de la Maza, *El Guadalupanismo mexicano*, Mexico 1981; Eric Wolf, 'The Virgin of Guadalupe: A Mexican National Symbol', in W.A. Lessa and E.Z. Vogt, eds, *Reader in Comparative Religion: An Anthropological Approach*, New York 1979; Melhuus 1992, pp. 150–90.

25. For details see Cypess 1991.

26. Paz 1988.

27. Gerald Martin, p. 8. It seems important to point out that for countries like Argentina and Uruguay, basically immigrant countries, this image of the conquest does not carry much meaning (Eduardo Archetti, personal

communication). Thus there is reason to modify Martin's statement.
28. Or, to quote Cypess:

> I consider La Malinche to be a root paradigm in the way Victor Turner uses the term. . . . a cultural root paradigm goes beyond the cognitive and the moral to the existential domain. . . . A root paradigm is a cultural model that is continually reinvested with vitality within the social drama. (p. 7)

See also Jean Franco, *Plotting Women: Gender and Representation in Mexico*, New York 1989; J. Martin 1990; Palma 1990; Cypess 1991; Bartra 1987.
29. In his discussion of the problems of *mestizaje* and the symbolic meanings of the *mestizo*, Bonfil equates Indian with mother:

> constatamos que la ideología del mestizaje intenta armonizar la reivindicación de un ancestro indio (la madre), equiparable o aún superior en sus valores al otro ancestro europeo (el padre), con la negación del indio de hoy, que toda dé identidad al *mestizo*, no porque represente a su progenitor, sino porque es lo que el *mestizo* no es.

> we observe that the ideology of *mestisaje* attempts to harmonize the claim of an Indian ancestry (the mother), seen as equal or even superior in value to the other, European ancestry (the father), while at the same time negating the Indian of today. It is this Indian who gives the *mestizo* his identity, not because he represents his progenitor, but because he is what the *mestizo* is not. (Bonfil Batalla, 1992, p. 44)

It is worth pointing out that in Batalla's construction not only is the feminine (mother/Indian) ambiguous, being simultaneously superior and inferior, but all the other elements ('the Father', 'the European' and 'the Indian', and hence the *mestizo*) embody double meanings.
30. See also Tzevetan Todorov, trans. Arne Kjell Haugen, *Erobringen av Amerika. Forholdet til den andre*, Oslo 1992; David Brading, trans. Soledad Loaeza Grave, *Los orígenes del nacionalismo mexicano*, Mexico 1980.
31. See Franco 1989; Bartra 1992.
32. Palma 1990.
33. Paz 1988; Roger Lancaster, *Life is Hard: Machismo, Danger and the Intimacy of Power in Nicaragua*, Berkeley, CA 1992; Eduardo Archetti, 'Argentinian Football: A Ritual of Violence?', *The International Journal of the History of Sport*, vol. 9, no. 2, 1992.
34. Claudio Lomnitz-Adler, *Exits from the Labyrinth: Culture and Ideology in the Mexican National Space*, Berkeley, CA 1992, p. 259.
35. See Prieur, this volume, Chapter 4; also Annick Prieur, *Stealing Femininity. Male Homosexuality in Mexico*, Chicago (forthcoming).

36. See, for example, Paz 1988 for a discussion of the notion of '*la chingada*'; also Melhuus 1992; and Melhuus forthcoming.

37. The personality of the *macho* is then seen as representing the 'new man', creature of the Revolution, later disgraced and transformed, 'a deeply sentimental man despite his tough gestures' (Bartra, p. 114). See also Lomnitz-Adler 1992.

38. See, for example, George Foster, *Tzintzuntzan: Mexican Peasants in a Changing World*, Boston, MA 1967; Oscar Lewis, *The Children of Sanchéz*, Harmondsworth 1966; Erich Fromm and Michael Maccoby, *Social Character in a Mexican Village*, Englewood Cliffs, NJ 1970; Lola Romanucci-Ross, *Conflict, Violence, and Morality in a Mexican Village*, Palo Alto, CA 1973; Lomnitz-Adler 1992; and Sarah LeVine, *Dolor y Alegría: Women and Social Change in Urban Mexico*, Madison, WI 1993.

39. Similar derogatory terms for dependent men are used in Argentina: 'lameculos' – one who licks asses – and 'chupamedias' – one who sucks another's socks (Eduardo Archetti, personal communication).

40. See also LeVine *et al.*, 'The Marital Morality of Mexican Women: An Urban Study', *Journal of Anthropological Research*, vol. 42, no. 2, 1989, pp. 183–202; LeVine 1993.

41. It is obvious that there is a flaw in their logic, as this argument assumes that the same knowledge circulating among men would not disrupt families – that men are complicit about their doings. Yet a man who is having an affair with another man's wife would not let this be 'known' among men in general. Interestingly enough, I came across only one case locally of a married man being involved with another married woman, and the circumstances were very particular (see Melhuus forthcoming).

42. That the virgin is a motivated symbol for women will not be further argued (but see Melhuus 1992). For a further substantiation of her significance with reference to the Virgin of Guadalupe in Mexico, see Note 23 above; and also E. Campbell, 'The Virgin of Guadalupe and the Female Self-Image: A Mexican Case History', in James Preston, ed., *Mother Worship: Theme and Variations*, Chapel Hill, NC 1982.

43. For a much more detailed argument and concrete discourses on suffering, see Melhuus 1992, pp. 150 ff.

44. This is not to imply that men do not suffer, but as far as I was able to ascertain they do not have an explicit discourse on suffering, as do women.

45. See also J. Martin 1990.

46. Bartra, p. 148.

47. Ibid., p. 149:

So occurred the first carnal exchange, both symbolic and material, of virgins and mothers between the Spanish and the Indians. Both were protective and maternal symbols; both were seduced and raped. The Malinche betrayed her people just as the Virgin did, since both surrendered, and their purity was stained. The first began the lineage of the *mestizos*; the second was reborn as the dark-skinned Indian Virgin.

48. Ibid., p. 150.
49. Ibid., p. 158. Emphasis added.
50. Ibid., p. 162.

Notes on the Contributors

Eduardo Archetti is a professor of social anthropology at the University of Oslo. He has written extensively on society and culture in Ecuador and Argentina. His most recent book is *El mundo social y simbólico del cuy* (1992), and he is the editor of *Exploring the Written. Anthropology and the Multiplicity of Writing* (1994). Archetti is currently conducting research on the construction of national identity in Argentina through the study of tango, football and polo.

Mary Crain is a social anthropologist affiliated with the University of Barcelona. She has written extensively on rituals, politics and gender relations in both Spain and Latin America (Ecuador). She is the author of *Ritual, Memoria Popular y Proceso Político en la Sierra Ecuatoriana* (1989) and co-author of *España Oculta: Public Celebrations in Spain, 1974–1989* (1995). Crain is currently conducting research on identity construction and global ethnoscapes both in highland Ecuador and in Washington DC.

Christian Krohn-Hansen is a social anthropologist working as a researcher at the University of Oslo. He has conducted research on livelihood strategies among peasant tobacco-growers in Colombia, and on political culture in the Dominican Republic. He has written several papers based on his work, and is currently finishing a book: *From Violence to Boundaries: The Production of the Dominican Republic in the Dominican–Haitian Borderlands*.

Marit Melhuus is professor of social anthropology at the University of Oslo. She has conducted fieldwork in Argentina, Norway and Mexico. Her research interests cover a wide range, but she is particularly concerned with the comparative study of moralities, processes of social change and modernity. She has published extensively on gender, her most recent contribution being 'The Troubles of Virtue: The Values of Violence and Suffering in a Mexican Context' (1996). She has co-edited, with Signe Howell, a book on regional ethnography: *Fjern og nær. Sosialantropologiske perspektiver på verdens samfunn og kulturer* (1994), and is currently working on a book about gender and morality in Mexico.

Lorraine Nencel is working at CEDLA (Centrum voor Studie en Documentatie van Latijns Amerika [Center for Latin American Research and Documentation]), Amsterdam, where she is currently finishing her PhD thesis on the meaning of gender among female prostitutes in Lima. She has conducted research among female houseworkers in the same city. She is co-editor of *Constructing Knowledge: Authority and Critique in Social Science* (1991).

Annick Prieur is a sociologist and senior lecturer at the University of Oslo. She has carried out research on male homosexuals in Oslo, on the clients of prostitutes in the same city, and on homosexual transvestites in Mexico City. She is the author of *Stealing Femininity. Male Homosexuality in Mexico*, Chicago (forthcoming); *Kjærlighet mellom menn i Aidsens tid* (1988); and *Å sette pris på kvinner. Menn kjøper sex* (1989).

Susanna Rostas is a social anthropologist working at Goldsmith's College, University of London. She has conducted fieldwork in Chiapas and Mexico City. She is co-editor of *The Popular Use of Popular Religion in Latin America* (1993), and is currently finishing a book on the Concheros of Mexico.

Kristi Anne Stølen is a social anthropologist and professor in development studies at the University of Oslo. She has conducted research on gender, power and social change in Argentina, Ecuador and Zambia, and written extensively on gender topics. She is the author of *A media voz: Relaciones de Género en la Sierra Ecuatoriana* (1987) and *Gender, Power and Social Change in the Argentine Prairie* (1996); and co-editor of *Gender and Social Change in Developing Countries* (1991).

Magdalena Villarreal is a research fellow and lecturer at the Centro de Investigaciones y Estudios Superiores en Antropología Social, based in Guadalajara, Mexico. For twelve years she was a development worker in rural areas in western Mexico, before she decided to pursue an academic career and become a researcher. Her extensive field experience is reflected in several papers dealing with gender and power within contexts of development projects. She is the author of *Wielding and Yielding: Power, Subordination and Gender Identity in the Context of a Mexican Development Project* (1994).

Index

Critical Studies in Latin American and Iberian Cultures

Titles published by Verso

DRAWING THE LINE
Art and Cultural Identity in Contemporary Latin America
Oriana Baddeley and Valerie Fraser

THE MOTORCYCLE DIARIES
A Journey around South America
Ernesto Che Guevara

PLOTTING WOMEN
Gender and Representation in Mexico
Jean Franco

THE GATHERING OF VOICES
The Twentieth-Century Poetry of Latin America
Mike Gonzalez and David Treece

MAGICAL REELS
A History of Cinema in Latin America
John King

Translations from Verso

IN SEARCH OF WAGNER
T.W. Adorno
Translated by Rodney Livingstone

MINIMA MORALIA
T.W. Adorno
Translated by E.F.N. Jephcott

QUASI UNA FANTASIA
T.W. Adorno
Translated by Rodney Livingstone

INFANCY AND HISTORY
Giorgio Agamben
Translated by Liz Heron

FOR MARX
Louis Althusser
Translated by Ben Brewster

TRANSLATIONS FROM VERSO

CHARLES BAUDELAIRE
Walter Benjamin
Translated by Harry Zohn

ONE-WAY STREET
Walter Benjamin
Translated by Edmund Jephcott and Kingsley Shorter

UNDERSTANDING BRECHT
Walter Benjamin
Translated by Anna Bostock

THE ORIGINS OF GERMAN TRAGIC DRAMA
Walter Benjamin
Translated by John Osborne

LIBERALISM AND DEMOCRACY
Norberto Bobbio
Translated by Martin Ryle and Kate Soper

WALTER BENJAMIN
Momme Brodersen
Translated by Malcolm Green

COMMENTS ON THE SOCIETY OF THE SPECTACLE
Guy Debord
Translated by Malcolm Imrie

PANEGYRIC
Guy Debord
Translated by James Brook